Upanishads
in Daily Life

A *Vedanta Kesari* Presentation

Sri Ramakrishna Math
Mylapore, Chennai - 600 004

Published by
Adhyaksha
Sri Ramakrishna Math
Mylapore, Chennai-4

III-2M 3C-8-2011
ISBN 978-81-7823-493-9

Printed in India at
Sri Ramakrishna Math Printing Press
Mylapore, Chennai-600 004

Publisher's Note

'Upanishads are a mine of strength,' said Swami Vivekananda. But a mine has to be excavated in order to obtain its treasures and profit from it. That the Upanishads have a timeless treasure of wisdom and practical guidelines waiting to become a part of daily life became clear when *The Vedanta Kesari* (the English monthly of Ramakrishna Order published from this Math) brought out a special issue in December 2007 on this subject. The issue received a hearty welcome by all those who read it. 'Oh, this is what the Upanishads are calling upon us to do!' responded one of the readers. Numerous other communications, in various forms, followed—expressing happiness and appreciation of the whole approach to this serious theme.

We are happy to present that special issue in the form of this book with the same title with which it was brought out—*The Upanishads in Daily Life.*

Swami Ramakrishnananda Jayanti
30.07.2008

Contents

v

Chapter 1

Upanishads and We

SWAMI ATMASHRADDHANANDA

They and We

There is a sharp contrast in these two terms: Upanishads and we, the moderns.

Upanishads were composed (strictly speaking, 'revealed') at least 5000 years ago (though there are differences in opinion about this). 'We' live in twenty-first century.

The *rishis* or sages to whom these 'books' (as the Upanishads are sometimes referred to) were revealed lived in forests, ate simplest of food, meditated for long hours, and had no distractions such as Internet and multi-channel-television. We live in a modern setting, having a sophisticated life-style (despite a large number of people living in miserable conditions right under the nose of the more fortunate ones), eat varieties of instant delicious food, and have made Internet and TV viewing as part of our life.

They lived in hermitages or in small cottages, in tune with nature, with an abundance of trees, creepers, rivers, birds and even wild animals freely roaming around their place. We, on the other hand, live in an age of urbanization, deforestation, polluted rivers and a dwindling number of bird and animal species.

1

The rishis did not have any threats from terrorists or unscrupulous politicians or black-marketers. We, the member of modern society, have to be always on guard and have a large network of security and intelligence agencies to do it.

The rishis did not have to travel to participate in national or international conferences. They were mainly confined to their world of contemplation and quietitude. We, on the other hand, have plenty of opportunities to become busybodies. What to speak of professionals and officials, even high school students have many such events to attend to.

They and we, rishis and modern men, are therefore placed in radically different situations and contexts.

Should it mean, (oh, this childish suggestion!) that the rishis represented a primitive, yet-to-evolve human beings living at the dawn of the civilization? And we, the modern ones, represent progress and prosperity? This needs an objective and honest deliberation.

Though rishis and we differ much in our visible or palpable life-styles, there is much in common. Like the great rishis, we too seek the answer to ultimate questions of life; we too want to discover the ultimate purpose of life and unravel the mystery of creation. They longed to know what a human being is in his or her deepest core; why is a man born and why he suffers and where does he go after death. We, too, have been grappling with these issues in our own ways for centuries, our modernity notwithstanding. While we try to answer these questions by observing 'life' with our microscopes or telescopes, the rishis just closed their eyes, disconnected from the world of senses and entered into a world not seen by the senses. The rishis seemed to have succeeded and we are still struggling, rarely wanting to question our instruments and methods of investigation. All our 'answers' are temporary presumptions and the rishis throw quiet challenges to contradict their conclusions. So sure are they of what they have understood of life that the expression 'There is no other way' appears in many Upanishads.

Despite our 'progress and scientific advancements' we have not been able to solve the problems of life. Violence, in various forms, has not been rooted out. Nor has been cruelty, lust, jealousy and meaninglessness of life. Increase in the number of TV channels has in no way solved the problem of boredom. Nor have the signing of a number of treaties solved the problem of hunger, homelessness and poverty. We are in need of many moral and spiritual correctives while the rishis were the living embodiments of moral and spiritual perfection. We differ from the rishis on the surface; at the deeper level of seeking and wanting to solve the challenge of life and death, we share a common heritage. The only difference that is apparent is this: while they stand etched in our collective memory as the shining images of moral and spiritual perfection and lived exemplary lives, we, the modern men, are struggling and evolving to reach that state.

Another fact about rishis that we must not forget is that not all rishis were contemplatives living in forests. Upanishads harmonise all contradictions of life. This they do by making every act of life, apparently sacred or secular, as an act of worship of the Divine. We, thus, find among the Upanishadic rishis contemplatives, kings, housewives, and even a cart-puller. Says Swami Vivekananda:

'In various Upanishads we find that this Vedanta philosophy is not the outcome of meditation in the forests only, but that the very best parts of it were thought out and expressed by brains which were busiest in the everyday affairs of life. We cannot conceive any man busier than an absolute monarch, a man who is ruling over millions of people, and yet, some of these rulers were deep thinkers.'[1]

Now to sum up this pretended comparison between us and the givers of the Upanishads. There is much to learn from the sages of Upanishads. Despite the fact that we have come a long way from those wonderful times to the present state, we are yet to learn our lessons—many of them.

Discovering the Eternal Behind the Fleeting

Let us, however, be clear about one thing: the Upanishads are *not* old, in the conventional sense of the term. The word 'old' is associated with something outdated, worn-out, ineffective, and fit to be discarded. The Upanishads, however, are young with a timeless wisdom. How could something so old as the Upanishads be still effective and youthful, one might wonder? Suppose you go to a Himalayan river flowing for centuries. You stand on its banks, bend down and take a handful of its water. What have you done? You have touched an *ancient* river. The water of that river has been flowing like this for centuries. Though 'old', it is ever new. The river is always renewing itself. Though ancient, it is modern at the same time.

Nor does the term 'modern' have an absolute meaning. Its meaning keeps changing. A century ago also people called themselves modern just as we call ourselves modern today. What is modern today will become ancient or old tomorrow. The wisdom of Upanishads, however, is eternal. They are a body of 'eternal values for a changing society'.

Certain things, though they become old, never become outdated. Sun and moon are quite, quite old. Just because they are old, they do not stop dispelling darkness. The same can be said of the wisdom of the Upanishads. Though 'old', it is *ever* relevant. It is ageless. Its enduring value lies in the timeless message of the divinity and eternity of soul it preaches. The message of the Upanishads is long lasting because it deals with certain everlasting truths. They sing, as it were, the song of eternity.

The Upanishads are a book of discoveries—most of it about human personality, its structure and uniqueness, and also about the ultimate nature of Godhead and the universe we live in. One reads in the Upanishads, a sage lost in intense meditation, coming face to face with the Immortal Core of human beings, rising and addressing the whole creation, as it were,

'Hear, ye children of immortal bliss! Even ye that dwell in higher spheres! For I have found that Ancient One who is beyond all darkness, all delusion. And knowing Him, ye also shall be saved from death.'[2]

A Great Spiritual Event

This event, like the discovery of fire and then of wheel, must have happened *in* time though no records are available as to its date, place and the name of the person who first had it. (Countless men and women down the millennia have reaffirmed the validity of that experience.) What matters is not its historicity or how old it is but the genuineness and indisputable nature of this discovery. What the modern world needs is this Upanishadic idea of immortality of the soul and the oneness of existence.

How does this idea of immortality help us? The simplest value of this idea is that by thinking of this we get a great relief that we are not matter, we are not sinners or 'bad'. Essentially we are good, nay, divine. All that we call evil is not a part of our real Core whom the Upanishads call as *atman*. We are deathless and changeless and are children of immortality. Once we get convinced of this grand truth, our approach to life becomes positive and affirmative.

Besides this, the Upanishads also lay much emphasis on living a pure life as a natural corollary to realise this idea of atman. The Kathopanishad states:

'One who has not desisted from bad conduct, whose senses are not under control, whose mind is not concentrated, whose mind is not free from anxiety (about the result of concentration), cannot attain this Self.'[3]

In other words, the ideal of the immortality of the Self will take roots only if a person is morally strong and has disciplined his senses and mind. If this is not kept in mind, there is a possibility of mistaking the body or ego to be the Self and make us pleasure-seekers and arrogant.

The Upanishads illustrate this through the story of Prajapati's teachings to Indra, the representative of gods, and Virochana, the representative of demons. Both Indra and Virochana approached Prajapati requesting him to impart Self-knowledge to them. They were asked to undergo self-control for a set period and then both were given the same teaching: the image you see when you look into a mirror, you are That. While Virochana, not yet fully pure and hence less-qualified, got satisfied with it, Indra went deeper. He approached Prajapati, and after a prolonged period of self-discipline and self-purification, finally learnt the Truth his teacher had been trying to drive home.

Likewise, if we seek the truth of atman, we must be patient and persistent, and purify the mind in order to experience It.

The Challenge

The Upanishads are in no way afraid of the new frontiers of objective knowledge, which modern day science and technology are opening out. They never felt any contradiction between the two. Science of discovery of the Self (*atmavidya*) is not opposed to the knowledge of objective world. The knowledge of physics and chemistry and computers deals with the perceivable or palpable sensory data. The Upanishads deal with the *seer*, the Knower of all activities and objects. Physical Sciences are quite acceptable in their search for Truth and are welcome to come out with fresh technology and advancement. But to say that man's happiness or fulfilment will emerge out of it is underestimating man's hunger for happiness. 'Man wants the infinite', says the Chandogya Upanishad. The finite cannot satisfy him. And then comes a surprise. The Upanishads throw a challenge to the modern world:

'Only when men shall roll up the sky like a skin, will there be an end to misery for them *without* realizing God.'[4]

In other words, just as sky, which is formless and intangible, cannot be rolled up like a piece of paper or sheet of cloth (or animal skin), so also it is vain to claim that man can become happy and fulfilled without knowing God (or the Divine Self within us). Upanishads do not mince words in saying that only by Self-knowledge can a person become truly happy in life. No achievement, whether scientific or secular, can replace it.

Restating the Eternal Truths

Upanishads are a mine of Knowledge. But like many other important things in life, we tend to overlook them. One of the reasons for this is their language. There is always a need to restate and rephrase the eternal truths of the Upanishads. India has had a glorious history of many great spiritual giants like Sri Shankaracharya and the likes, who tried to draw our attention to the eternal relevance of the message of Upanishads. They had to *restate* the message in a language which the people could understand. In our own times, we have the similar effort being made in the life and teachings of Swami Vivekananda and Sri Ramakrishna. Swamiji said that he 'never quoted anything except the Upanishads'. All his teachings are a contemporary restatement of the eternal Upanishadic truths. Take for example Swamiji's well-known statement that each soul is potentially divine. Though a powerful statement, it is not new. In the Chandogya Upanishad, the rishi Uddalaka Aruni tells his son Shvetaketu, 'You are That.' By the word 'That', the sage Uddalaka meant Divinity or atman. So, the meaning is, 'You are atman.' Now look at Swamiji's words: 'Each soul is potentially divine'. They imply the same thing in a much more appealing way. Though atman, we are not aware of it. This ignorance makes the truth of atman unsure or 'potential'. This adds a whiff of freshness and originality to it.

Paying tributes to Swami Vivekananda's contribution to the restatement of the Upanishads in the modern idiom, Sister Nivedita says,

'The truths he [Swami Vivekananda] preaches would have been as true, had he never been born. Nay more, they would have been equally authentic. The difference would have lain in their difficulty of access, in their want of modern clearness and incisiveness of statement, and their loss of mutual coherence and unity.'[5]

Swamiji made Upanishads available to all. Before Swamiji came to the scene, the study of Upanishads was restricted and reserved to only a section of people. Not everyone was supposed to read them. But by restating them in modern idiom, Swamiji made them available to all. Not only that he restated them, he also gave, through reinterpreting them, befitting answers to numerous knotty problems modern man faces. He felt the problem of increasing violence and religious intolerance, for instance, can only be solved by adopting the Upanishadic view that all men and women are divine and each one is at one stage of evolution in perceiving this inherent divinity. He said,

'Man is not travelling from error to truth, but climbing up from truth to truth, from truth that is lower to truth that is higher.'[6]

This idea of solidarity of existence is also the real basis for love and service. To love others, in fact, is to love one-Self.

How to make the teachings of the Upanishads practical? Indeed Swamiji believed this to be the mission of his life. He said:

'The dry Advaita must become living—poetic—in everyday life; out of hopelessly intricate mythology must come concrete moral forms; and out of bewildering Yogi-ism must come the most scientific and practical psychology— and all this must be put in a form that a child may grasp it. That is my life's work.'[7]

In Conclusion

Strength and fearlessness is what the Upanishads preach. Strength comes from that which is enduring. And fearlessness comes from knowing our indestructible and immortal nature. When Janaka, the celebrated king mentioned in the Upanishads, 'realised' the truth of atman, it was said that he became fearless. Swamiji held the Upanishads as a treasure house of strength and fearlessness. Here, again, he restated the ancient truths in the modern idiom:

'This is the one question I put to every man. . . Are you strong? Do you feel strength?—for I know it is truth alone that gives strength.'[8]

Upanishads are the very basis of Indian culture and spiritual heritage. No one can ever understand or appreciate the essence of Indian culture without making a study of the Upanishads. They are like the forefathers of the Indian culture and civilisation. All Hindu beliefs, rituals and festivals, all systems of orthodox philosophical systems in India and also the lives and teachings of all the mystics and saints India has seen over the centuries are rooted in the mystic realisations of Upanishadic rishis.

This volume focuses on how and why the message of Upanishads is applicable to life in today's context. Various aspects of this subject have been explored. The approach is to relate the Upanishads to life and not just leave it to dry academic discussions. Eminent monastic and lay writers have contributed thoughtful articles. Our thanks to each one of them. We hope our readers will find this volume useful in their journey to appreciate the pressing need to make the message of the Upanishads practical. May this volume, in the language of the Upanishads, 'Godspeed you in your journey beyond the darkness of ignorance', (*svasti vah paraya tamasah parastat!*). □

References

1. *The Complete Works of Swami Vivekananda (Hereafter CW),*
     2: 293
2. *Shvetashvatra Upanishad,* 3.8
3. *Kathopanishad,* I.ii.24
4. *Shvetashvatara Upanishad,* 6.20
5. CW, 1: xiv
6. CW, 1:xii
7. CW, 5: 104-105
8. CW, 2:201

Chapter 2

'I Have Never Quoted Anything But the Upanishads'

SWAMI VIVEKANANDA

The Message of Strength

Strength, strength is what the Upanishads speak to me from every page. This is the one great thing to remember, it has been the one great lesson I have been taught in my life; strength, it says, strength, O man, be not weak. Are there no human weaknesses?—says man. There are, say the Upanishads, but will more weakness heal them, would you try to wash dirt with dirt? Will sin cure sin, weakness cure weakness? Strength, O man, strength, say the Upanishads, stand up and be strong. Ay, it is the only literature in the world where you find the word 'Abhih', 'fearless', used again and again; in no other

13

scripture in the world is this adjective applied either to
God or to man.[1]

And the more I read the Upanishads, my friends,
my countrymen, the more I weep for you, for therein
is the great practical application. Strength, strength for
us. What we need is strength, but who will give us
strength? There are thousands to weaken us, and of
stories we have had enough. Every one of our Puranas,
if you press it, gives out stories enough to fill three-
fourths of the libraries of the world. Everything that
can weaken us as a race we have had for the last
thousand years. It seems as if during that period the
national life had this one end in view, viz., how to
make us weaker and weaker till we have become real
earthworms, crawling at the feet of every one who
dares to put his foot on us. Therefore, my friends, as
one of your blood, as one that lives and dies with you,
let me tell you that we want strength, strength, and
every time strength. And the Upanishads are the great
mine of strength. Therein lies strength enough to invigorate the whole world; the whole world can
be vivified, made strong, energised through them. They
will call with trumpet voice upon the weak, the
miserable, and the downtrodden of all races, all creeds,
and all sects to stand on their feet and be free. Freedom,
physical freedom, mental freedom, and spiritual
freedom are the watchwords of the Upanishads.[2]

For centuries we have been stuffed with the
mysterious; the result is that our intellectual and
spiritual digestion is almost hopelessly impaired, and

the race has been dragged down to the depths of hopeless imbecility—never before or since experienced by any other civilised community. There must be freshness and vigour of thought behind to make a virile race. More than enough to strengthen the whole world exists in the Upanishads. The Advaita is the eternal mine of strength. But it requires to be applied.[3]

Ay, this is the one scripture in the world, of all others, that does not talk of salvation, but of freedom. Be free from the bonds of nature, be free from weakness! And it shows to you that you have this freedom already in you. . .[4]

What makes a man stand up and work? Strength. Strength is goodness, weakness is sin. If there is one word that you find coming out like a bomb from the Upanishads, bursting like a bomb-shell upon masses of ignorance, it is the word fearlessness. And the only religion that ought to be taught is the religion of fearlessness. Either in this world or in the world of religion, it is true that fear is the sure cause of degradation and sin. It is fear that brings misery, fear that brings death, fear that breeds evil.

And what causes fear? Ignorance of our own nature. Each of us is heir-apparent to the Emperor of emperors; we are of the substance of God Himself. Nay, according to the Advaita, we are God Himself though we have forgotten our own nature in thinking of ourselves as little men.[5]

We speak of many things parrot-like, but never do them; speaking and not doing has become a habit with us. What is the cause of that? Physical weakness. This sort of weak brain is not able to do anything; we must strengthen it. First of all, our young men must be strong. Religion will come afterwards. Be strong, my young friends; that is my advice to you. You will be nearer to Heaven through football than through the study of the Gita. . . You will understand the Upanishads better and the glory of the Atman when your body stands firm upon your feet, and you feel yourselves as men.[6]

The Ideal of Freedom

Whether you are an Advaitist or a dualist, whether you are a believer in the system of Yoga or a believer in Shankaracharya, whether you are a follower of Vyasa or Vishvamitra, it does not matter much. But the thing is that on this point Indian thought differs from that of all the rest of the world. Let us remember for a moment that, whereas in every other religion and in every other country, the power of the soul is entirely ignored—the soul is thought of as almost powerless, weak, and inert—we in India consider the soul to be eternal and hold that it will remain perfect through all eternity. We should always bear in mind the teachings of the Upanishads.[7]

It was given to me to live with a man [Sri Rama-krishna] who was as ardent a dualist, as ardent an Advaitist, as ardent a Bhakta, as a Jnani. And living with this man first put it into my head to understand the Upanishads and the texts of the scriptures from an independent and better basis than by blindly following the commentators; and in my opinion and in my researches, I came to the conclusion that these texts are not at all contradictory. So we need have no fear of text-torturing at all! . . . Therefore I now find in the light of this man's life that the dualist and the Advaitist need not fight each other. Each has a place, and a great place in the national life... Therefore any attempt to torture the texts of the Upanishads appears to me very ridiculous.[8]

Let me draw your attention to one thing which unfortunately we always forget: that is—'O man, have faith in yourself.' That is the way by which we can have faith in God.[9]

*1st must work on strength, then you
can have faith in yourself*

Learning to Solve the Mystery of Life

Our Upanishads say that the cause of all misery is ignorance; and that is perfectly true when applied to every state of life, either social or spiritual. It is ignorance that makes us hate each other, it is through ignorance that we do not know and do not love each other. As soon as we come to know each other, love comes, must come, for are we not one? Thus we find solidarity coming in spite of itself.

Even in politics and sociology, problems that were only national twenty years ago can no more be solved on national grounds only. They are assuming huge proportions, gigantic shapes. They can only be solved when looked at in the broader light of international grounds. International organisations, international combinations, international laws are the cry of the day. That shows the solidarity. In science, every day they are coming to a similar broad view of matter. You speak of matter, the whole universe as one mass, one ocean of matter, in which you and I, the sun and the moon, and everything else are but the names of different little whirlpools and nothing more. Mentally speaking, it is one universal ocean of thought in which you and I are similar little whirlpools; and as spirit it moveth not, it changeth not. It is the One Unchangeable, Unbroken, Homogeneous Atman. The cry for morality is coming also, and that is to be found in our books. The explanation of morality, the fountain of ethics, that also the world wants; and that it will get here.[10]

The Upanishads told 5,000 years ago that the realisation of God could never be had through the senses. So far, modern agnosticism agrees, but the Vedas go further than the negative side and assert in the plainest terms that man can and does transcend this sense-bound, frozen universe. He can, as it were, find a hole in the ice, through which he can pass and reach the whole ocean of life. Only by so transcending the world of sense, can he reach his true Self and realise what he really is.[11]

The Upanishads say, renounce. That is the test of everything. Renounce everything. It is the creative faculty that brings us into all this entanglement. The mind is in its own nature when it is calm. The moment you can calm it, that [very] moment you will know the truth. What is it that is whirling the mind? Imagination, creative activity. Stop creation and you know the truth. All power of creation must stop, and then you know the truth at once.[12]

Here I can only lay before you what the Vedanta seeks to teach, and that is the deification of the world. The Vedanta does not in reality denounce the world. The ideal of renunciation nowhere attains such a height as in the teachings of the Vedanta. But, at the same time, dry suicidal advice is not intended; it really means deification of the world — giving up the world as we think of it, as we know it, as it appears to us—and to know what it really is. Deify it; it is God alone. We read at the commencement of one of the oldest of the Upanishads, 'Whatever exists in this universe is to be covered with the Lord.'[13]

Ay, a glorious destiny, my brethren, for as far back as the days of the Upanishads we have thrown the challenge to the world: 'Not by progeny, not by wealth, but by renunciation alone immortality is reached.' Race after race has taken the challenge up and tried their utmost to solve the world-riddle on the plane of desires.[14]

The whole idea of ethics is that it does not depend on anything unknowable, it does not teach anything unknown, but in the language of the Upanishad, 'The God whom you worship as an unknown God, the same I preach unto thee.' It is through the Self that you know anything. I see the chair; but to see the chair, I have first to perceive myself and then the chair. It is in and through the Self that the chair is perceived. It is in

and through the Self that you are known to me, that
the whole world is known to me; and therefore to say
this Self is unknown is sheer nonsense. Take off the
Self and the whole universe vanishes. In and through
the Self all knowledge comes.[15]

Upanishads and Their Composers

There are [more than] a hundred books comprising
the Upanishads, some very small and some big, each a
separate treatise. The Upanishads do not reveal the life
of any teacher, but simply teach principles. They are
[as it were] shorthand notes taken down of discussion
in [learned assemblies], generally in the courts of kings.
The word Upanishad may mean 'sittings' [or 'sitting
near a teacher']. Those of you who may have studied
some of the Upanishads can understand how they are
condensed shorthand sketches. After long discussions
had been held, they were taken down, possibly from
memory. The difficulty is that you get very little of the
background. Only the luminous points are mentioned
there.[16]

The origin of ancient Sanskrit is 5000 B.C.; the
Upanishads [are at least] two thousand years before
that. Nobody knows [exactly] how old they are. The
Gita takes the ideas of the Upanishads and in [some]
cases the very words. They are strung together with
the idea of bringing out, in a compact, condensed, and
systematic form, the whole subject the Upanishads deal
with.[17]

Fanatics little understand the infinite power of
love in the hearts of these great sages who looked

upon the inhabitants of this world as their children. They were the real fathers, the real gods, filled with infinite sympathy and patience for everyone; they were ready to bear and forbear. They knew how human society should grow, and patiently, slowly, surely, went on applying their remedies, not by denouncing and frightening people, but by gently and kindly leading them upwards step by step.

Such were the writers of the Upanishads. They knew full well how the old ideas of God were not reconcilable with the advanced ethical ideas of the time; they knew full well that what the atheists were preaching contained a good deal of truth, nay, great nuggets of truth; but at the same time, they understood that those who wished to sever the thread that bound the beads, who wanted to build a new society in the air, would entirely fail.[18]

In the Vedic or Upanishad age Maitreyi, Gargi, and other ladies of revered memory have taken the places of Rishis through their skill in discussing about Brahman. In an assembly of a thousand Brahmanas who were all erudite in the Vedas, Gargi boldly challenged Yajnavalkya in a discussion about Brahman.[19]

The Upanishads contain very little history of the doings of any man, but nearly all other scriptures are largely personal histories. The Vedas deal almost entirely with philosophy. Religion without philosophy runs into superstition; philosophy without religion becomes dry atheism.[20]

Children of Immortal Bliss!

'Hear ye children of Immortality! Hear ye Devas who live in higher spheres!' 'I have found out a ray beyond all darkness, beyond all doubt. I have found the Ancient One'. The way to this is contained in the Upanishads.[21]

Go into your own room and get the Upanishads out of your own Self. You are the greatest book that ever was or ever will be, the infinite depository of all that is. Until the inner teacher opens, all outside teaching is in vain. It must lead to the opening of the book of the heart to have any value.[22]

That is what the Vedanta teaches. It does not propose any slipshod remedy by covering wounds with gold leaf and the more the wound festers, putting on more gold leaf. This life is a hard fact; work your way through it boldly, though it may be adamantine; no matter, the soul is stronger. It lays no responsibility on little gods; for you are the makers of your own fortunes. You make yourselves suffer, you make good and evil, and it is you who put your hands before your eyes and say it is dark. Take your hands away and see the light; you are effulgent, you are perfect already, from the very beginning. . . .[23]

Go back to Upanishads

Go back to your Upanishads—the shining, the strengthening, the bright philosophy —and part from all these mysterious things, all these weakening things. Take up this philosophy; the greatest truths are the simplest things in the world, simple as your own existence. The truths of the Upanishads are before you. Take them up, live up to them, and the salvation of India will be at hand.[24]

Read my lectures. . . . It is only the pure Upanishadic religion that I have gone about preaching in the world.[25]

So I preach only the Upanishads. If you look, you will find that I have never quoted anything but the Upanishads. And of the Upanishads, it is only that One idea, strength. The quintessence of the Vedas and Vedanta and all lies in that one word.[26]

Sharp as the blade of a razor, long and difficult and hard to cross, is the way to freedom. The sages have declared this again and again. Yet do not let these weaknesses and failures bind you. The Upanishads have declared, 'Arise! Awake! and stop not until the goal is reached.' We will then certainly cross the path, sharp as it is like the razor, and long and distant and difficult though it be. Man becomes the master of gods and demons. No one is to blame for our miseries but ourselves. Do you think there is only a dark cup of poison if man goes to look for nectar? The nectar is there and is for every man who strives to reach it.[27] □

References

1. *CW*, 3: 237
2. *CW*, 3: 238-239
3. *CW*, 9: 76-77
4. *CW*, 3: 238-239
5. *CW*, 3: 160
6. *CW*, 3: 242
7. *CW*, 3: 443
8. *CW*, 3: 233-234
9. *CW*, 4: 107

10. *CW,* 3: 240-241
11. *CW,* 8: 21
12. *CW,* 1: 453
13. *CW,* 2: 146
14. *CW,* 4: 314
15. *CW,* 2: 305
16. *CW,* 1: 446
17. *CW,* 1: 446
18. *CW,* 2: 117
19. *CW,* 7: 214-215
20. *CW,* 7: 36
21. *CW,* 6: 87-88
22. *CW,* 7: 71
23. *CW,* 2: 184
24. *CW,* 3: 225
25. *CW,* 6: 469-471
26. *CW,* 8: 266-67
27. *CW,* 1: 342

Chapter 3

The Upanishads and Their Origin

SWAMI ASHOKANANDA

Upanishads Means Vedanta

Here we are concerned with the very last part of Vedantic literature, which is called Vedanta—*veda anta*, 'the end of the Vedas'. Many have thought that these portions came last of all in the Vedic age: at first the ancient Aryans practiced rituals; then afterwards, being dissatisfied with rituals, they began to become philosophical and to find philosophical truths, which they embodied in the books generally called the Upanishads, or, in aggregate, the Vedanta. Others have said that this chronological explanation is not right. What *anta* really means is 'the highest' or 'the culmination'. *Veda* means 'knowledge', 'the highest knowledge'.

Orthodox Hindus believe that the second explanation is more appropriate, because the philosophy contained in the Vedanta portion is also found in the hymnal portion. For example, some hymns in the *Ṛg-Veda* and the *Atharva-Veda* cannot be surpassed in their philosophical and mystical depths even by the Upanishads. Of course, Western scholars have said such

25

hymns were afterwards interpolated. Well, orthodox Hindus do not agree with that. They say that from very ancient times both the ritualistic portions and the philosophical portions existed simultaneously.

The Upanishads, in which those truths were expressed, are sometimes called 'secret teachings', and no doubt the word *upaniṣad* has some such implication— not secret in the sense of mysterious, but in the sense that these truths are not found on the surface by the average mind; they are buried deep down and have to be discovered by everyone in his inmost being. Further, when these teachings were given to a pupil, the pupil approached the teacher and sat near him, and the teacher gave this teaching to him alone, not in the presence of others. Even now, these teachings are given in private. Others are not allowed to be present, because it is considered that anything given out publicly can never take root in the deep life of a person. Just as the roots of a plant generally die when they are exposed to the sun or the outside atmosphere, in the same way whenever you express something it fails to go deep into your life, and you hate therefore to speak in public of the deepest things; they should be kept hidden within. On this psychological fact the tradition of privacy was built.

Now, as I said, it probably took two thousand years to develop and consolidate these teachings; that is the orthodox Hindu belief. Many would not agree with it, but when I consider how long it takes to find one single truth, and when I remember that the truths expressed in the Upanishads were not inherited by these people but had to be *discovered* by them—when I consider these facts, I cannot but think that the orthodox Hindu belief is correct.

The Origin of Upanishads

It is said that there are altogether a hundred and eight Upanishads. It is quite obvious that most of these are not true Upanishads at all; that is to say, they did not form a part of the original Vedas but were written afterwards. From that you should not conclude that they are worthless; as a matter of fact, some are highly illuminating and explain many things not found in the original Upanishads, which some scholars have said number twenty-eight.

Of these twenty-eight, some say twelve and others say ten are the principal ones. Shankaracharya, to whom we owe the revival of Vedanta after Buddhism degenerated, commented upon ten Upanishads, and therefore many think that these ten must have been the most authoritative. Two of them—the *Chāndogya* and the *Bṛhadāraṇyaka*—are very large and in many places very abstruse. In fact, one is compelled to confess that some passages cannot today be explained at all. Other Upanishads are smaller; some are composed of just a few verses. But all of them have been considered of exceeding value, and as century has followed century very great authority has been ascribed to them.

Some Upanishads are written in verse, and others in prose and some are mixed prose and verse. The language, which is the Vedic rather than the classical style of Sanskrit, is sometimes obscure, but more often it is very straight and direct. As you read the texts you feel an atmosphere of sunlight, of open spaces, of the frankness, the innocence, and the purity of childhood. You feel that the people who dwelt upon these thoughts and experiences and gave expression to them were sturdy men, strong men, but not violent. (Violent people are weak; truly strong people are gentle, pure, and innocent, and their gentleness is not associated with any kind of weakness.) You also feel that there was not much restriction in their life. By that I do not mean there was licence, but that there was no rigidity about them, and you feel that you would rather like to go back to those people; you cannot escape the feeling that they represented the highest expression of life on earth; that they were highly civilized and highly cultured.

How the Ṛsis Lived

The life they lived, these people who taught the Upanishads, was a very simple life, mostly. But sometimes these teachings were originally given by kings who lived in the luxury of a palace. There is a theory, which Swami Vivekananda himself held to some extent, that the Vedanta, or the Upanishads, really originated among the *kṣatriyas,* the warrior caste, rather than among the *brāhmins.* And in support of this we often find in the history of India that the most liberalizing thoughts in religion or philosophy came not from the first caste, not from the *brāhmins,* but from the second caste, the *kṣatriyas*. For example, Sri Krishna was not a *brāhmin*; he was the son of a *kṣatriya*, and Buddha, who democratised the teachings of the Vedanta and spread them broadcast, was the son of a *kṣatriya* king. We do not consider this to be a reflection on the *brāhmins*; we say that just as two opposite forces create a balance, so in every community or every system of knowledge there have to be two forces working— one conservative and the other liberal. If liberalism has complete freedom in its own experimentation, it is apt to kill itself; therefore, there has to be a conservative force that will challenge it. When liberalism can stand that challenge it is gradually embodied into the accepted authority. In India the *brāhmins* have represented that conservative force, and in the matter of Vedanta we find that some of the teachers were *brāhmins*, others were *kṣatriyas*. So we sometimes find *brāhmins* going to *kṣatriyas* to learn this most excellent truth, the truth about the Atman and Brahman.

Well, whatever that might be, most of these teachers lived a simple life in an *aśrama*, which can be translated as 'retreat'. Just as modern retreats are located outside the cities in a solitary place in the midst of nature, so in those olden days there were many such retreats or hermitages all over the country, particularly in the Himalayan region. And many of these teachers— who were generally called ṛṣis, which literally means 'seers', because they directly perceived supernatural truths—were established in these *aśramas* and were supported by the rich or by kings, who considered it their duty to protect them and to supply their needs.

Those needs were very simple. They lived in huts; they would get up at what they called the *brahma-muhūrta*, the 'hour of God', an hour before dawn, and would go in the dark or semi-dark to a nearby stream and bathe; then they would sit around a fire, which was always burning, but which at that time was burning brighter because the disciples had put more logs on it, and they would plunge into meditation. After long meditation some teachings would be given, and then they would all go to their respective duties. Later, classes would be held in the different branches of learning, particularly in the Vedas and the Upanishads; the ṛsis would teach their pupils the art of meditation; they would teach them what is called *brahma-vidyā*—the 'science of Brahman', or the 'science of God-realization', and they would teach them philosophy, so that their intellect would be trained in accordance with their spiritual findings. There were also other teachings, sometimes called *vedāṅgas*, which were essentially secular subjects like astronomy, prosody, grammar, and so on.

The pupils themselves had to live a life of utmost asceticism, of which the most essential condition was the practice of celibacy. Many rules are given in the old books for this rigorous life. The pupils would live many years with the teachers, whose examples were considered very important as a part of their training. Then some of them would return to the world, get married, and live as ideal citizens. They would not give up their spiritual practices; rather, they would carry them on, and when they were fifty years old they were supposed to retire from the world and plunge again into a life of contemplation and meditation. And then, after some time, they would embrace the life of utter renunciation and become *sannyasins*, or wandering monks. That was the general picture.

It goes without saying that although there might have been hundreds and hundreds of such hermitages, not all the ṛṣis were equally proficient. It is but natural that there were differences among them, and you find that some became very well-known as great spiritual teachers and as great scholars of the Vedas or Vedanta. Of course, more people would come to them than to others, and one to whom thousands and thousands of people would flock used to be called *kula-pati*, the 'chief of the clan', the clan of spiritual aspirants. Such 'chiefs' were very highly regarded, and necessarily used to receive great respect from all. And of course the kings and the nobles of a kingdom considered it their special duty to support them.

Discovering Inner Truths

You can understand why the people amongst whom Vedanta originated lived in a very quiet place where their meditation would not be disrupted or interrupted, where there would not be even the slightest noise, for only in that silence, external and internal, were they able to discover inner truths unknown before. They practised hard austerities; you can see why that had to be so: how would they know there were deeper states of mind to begin with? Only the other day in the West you began to talk about the subconscious mind and to recognize that there are many things hidden in the mind which have great meaning for our conscious life. You see, even the science of the mind seems to be a modern thing with us. So in order to find ultimate truths, these ṛṣis had to work very hard. No doubt many of them came up with wrong knowledge. They thought they had found something extraordinary, but the mind is a very subtle and complicated thing. When you think you have found something new and begin to talk about it, others find that it was not new or anyhow not valid.

So while there must have been many experimenters who found something true, there were also many who became deluded. You can well see that it must have taken centuries and centuries before enough authoritative knowledge was gleaned, out of which a system of mysticism and a system of philosophy took birth. ☐

Chapter 4

The Message of the Upaniṣads

SWAMI RANGANATHANANDA

Swami Vivekananda says:

'Religion deals with the truths of the metaphysical world just as chemistry and the other natural sciences deal with truth of the physical world. The book one must read to learn chemistry is the book of (external) nature. The book from which to learn religion is your own mind and heart. The sage is often ignorant of physical science because he reads the wrong book—the book within; and the scientist is too often ignorant of religion, because he, too, reads the wrong book—the book without.'[1]

Śruti versus Smṛti

The Upaniṣads are an impressive record of this 'reading of the book within'. The scriptures of every religion are such records. But all of them, except the Upaniṣads, contain also a good bit of extraneous matter, not only myths and legends and cosmological theories, which the Upaniṣads also contain, but also a large number of rules and regulations, with their do's and don'ts, to guide the individual and collective conduct and behaviour of their respective followers. The significance of these latter being merely local and temporary, they are not capable of universal application and are not relevant for all time; the fundamental message of all religions, however, derive from their central core of essential spiritual truths which are universal and for all time. The Upaniṣads are *the only* sacred books which addressed themselves exclusively to the discovery of these essential spiritual truths and to leading man, irrespective of creed and race, to their realization in his own life.

The Sanātana Dharma: Its Uniqueness

This explains the very high authority and prestige of the Śruti in the Indian tradition; it derives from the verified and verifiable character of its truths and their universality. Accordingly, the Smṛtis is always subordinate to the Śruti in spiritual matters. Smṛtis come and go; they change age after age; but the Śruti, according to the penetrating analysis of Śaṅkara[2], contains *vastutantrajñāna,* 'knowledge of reality as it is', whereas Smṛti contains *puruṣatantrajñāna,* 'knowledge depending on the person', which 'can be modified or altered by human effort': *kartum akartum anyathākartuṁ śakyate.* A Smṛti that sustained society in one age may choke it in another age.

Regarding all Smṛtis in general, Rama-krishna's pithy utterance correctly conveys the Indian idea: 'Mughal coins have no *currency* under the (East India) Company's rule.' Referring to this, the mathematician-philosopher, A.N. Whitehead says:[3]

'Religion will not regain its old power until it can face change in the same spirit as does science. Its principles may be eternal, but the expression of those principles requires continual development.'

Historian Arnold Toynbee also stresses this point:[4]

'In the life of all higher religions, the task of winnowing is a perennial one because their historic harvest is not pure grain. In the heritage of each of the higher religions, we are aware of the presence of two kinds of ingredients. There are essential counsels and truths, and there are non-essential practices and propositions.

'The essential counsels and truths are valid at all times and places, as far as we can see through the dark glass of mankind's experience up to date. . .'

The philosophy and religion that India developed out of the Śruti bears, therefore, a significant title, namely, sanātana dharma, 'Eternal Religion'. It derives its authority from its truth-character and not from any person, be he a saint or even an incarnation; and the truth-character of a teaching demands that it be verifiable by all irrespective of dogma, creed, and race, and at all times.

Throwing light on this unique character-istic of the Sanātana Dharma as derived from the Upaniṣads, Swami Vivekananda says:[5]

'Two ideals of truth are in our scriptures; the one is what we call the eternal, and the other is not so authoritative, yet binding under particular circumstances, times, and places. The eternal relations between souls and God are embodied in what we call the Śrutis, the Vedas. The next set of truths is what we call the Smṛtis, as embodied in the words of Manu, Yājñavalkya, and other writers, and also in the Purāṇas, down to the Tantras. . .

'Another peculiarity is that these Śrutis have many sages [ṛṣis] as the recorders of the truths in them, mostly men, even some women. Very little is known of their personalities, the dates of their birth and so forth, but their best thoughts, their best discoveries, I should say, are preserved there, embodied in the sacred literature of our country, the Vedas. In the Smṛtis, on the other hand, personalities are more in evidence. Startling, gigantic, impressive, world-moving persons stand before us, as it were, for the first time, sometimes of more magnitude even than their teachings.'

By Śruti is generally meant the Vedas; specifically, it means the Upaniṣads, they being the Vedānta, the *anta*, literally the end or concluding portion, but in a deeper sense, the very *gist* or *essence*, of the Vedas. Clarifying this idea in his address at the Parliament of Religions, Chicago, Swami Vivekananda says[6]

'By the Vedas no books are meant. They mean the accumulated treasury of spiritual laws discovered by different persons in different times. Just as the law of gravitation existed before its discovery, and would exist if all humanity forgot it, so is it with the laws that govern the spiritual world. The moral, ethical, and spiritual relations between soul and soul, and between individual spirits and the father of all spirits, were there before their discovery, and would remain even if we forgot them.'

Meaning of the Term 'Upaniṣad'

That this is the traditional view is evident from what Śaṅkara says on the etymology of the term 'Upaniṣad'. The term means knowledge received by the student 'sitting close to' the teacher. Explaining the derivation of the term in the introduction to his commentary on the *Kaṭha Upaniṣad*, Śaṅkara says:

'By what etymological process does the term *upaniṣad* denote knowledge? This is now explained. Those who seek liberation, being endowed with the spirit of dispassion towards all sense objects, seen or heard of, and *approaching* this knowledge indicated by the term *upaniṣad* presently to be explained, devote themselves to it with one-pointed determination—of such people, this knowledge *removes, shatters,* or *destroys* the *avidyā* (ignorance or spiritual blindness), which is the seed of all relative existence or worldliness. By these etymological connections, *upaniṣad* is said to mean knowledge.'

Education involving the student 'sitting close to' the teacher means the most intimate student-teacher communion. The higher the knowledge sought, greater is this communion and greater the silence accompanying the knowledge-communication. These values reach their maximum when the knowledge that is sought and imparted is of the highest kind, namely, *ātmajñāna* or *brahmajñāna* knowledge of the Ātman or Brahman.

Truth versus Opinion

The Upaniṣads discovered very early in history what Thomas Huxley refers to as the difference between opinion and truth, between 'I believe such and such' and 'I believe such and such *to be true.*' Says Huxley:[7]

'The longer I live, the more obvious it is to me that the most sacred act of a man's life is to say and feel, "I believe such and such to be true". All the greatest rewards and all the heaviest penalties of existence cling about that act.'

Such truths are far different from the private beliefs of an individual or a group, a sect or a church, held with all emotional intensity and projected for other people's acceptance with equal fervour. Such beliefs cannot claim 'the greatest reward' because they have not paid 'the heaviest penalty' involved in being subjected to the rigorous scrutiny of reason and being thrown open to universal verification. Referring to this unique characteristic of Vedānta, Romain Rolland says:[8]

'The true Vedāntic spirit does not start out with a system of preconceived ideas. It possesses absolute liberty and unrivalled courage among religions with regard to the facts to be observed and the diverse hypotheses it has laid down for their co-ordination. Never having been hampered by a priestly order, each man has been entirely free to search wherever he pleased for the spiritual explanation of the spectacle of the universe.'

The Mental Climate of the Upaniṣads

I have referred before to the fearless quest of truth characteristic of these Upaniṣads. Any reader of this literature cannot also escape being struck by the rational bent and speculative daring of these sages of ancient India.

The spirit of inquiry which possessed them led them to question experience, to question the environing world; it also led them to fearlessly question their gods and tenets of their traditional faiths.

The Upaniṣads do not disclose any details as to the personal histories of their thinkers; but they provide us with a glimpse of the working of their minds; we can study in this literature the graceful conflict of thought with thought, the emergence of newer and newer thought more satisfactory to reason and more in accord with experience at deeper levels, and the rejection of the less adequate ones without a tear. Hypotheses are advanced and rejected on the touchstone of experience and reason, and not at the dictate of a creed. Thus thought forges ahead to unravel the mystery of man and the universe in which he finds himself; and we can watch this developmental movement of thought and, if we are sensitive enough, also experience, in the words of the *Muṇḍaka Upaniṣad*,[9] this onward march of being carried along in its current to the one ocean of truth and beauty and delight, and realize our oneness with the One behind the many:

'Just as rivers, as they flow, merge in the ocean giving up their (separate) names and forms, so the knowing one, freed from (separateness arising from) name and form, attains the luminous supreme Self, which is beyond (even) the (other) supreme (namely, nature in its undifferentiated state).'

The Upaniṣads reveal an age characterised by a remarkable ferment, intellectual and spiritual. It is one of those rare ages in human history which have registered distinct break-throughs in man's quest for truth and meaning and which have held far-reaching consequences for all subsequent ages. The mental climate of the Upaniṣads is saturated with a passion for truth and a similar passion for human happiness and welfare. Their thinkers were 'undisturbed by the thought of there being a public to please or critics to appease', as Max Müller puts it.[10] They considered no sacrifice too heavy in their quest for truth, including not only earthly pleasures and heavenly delights, but also what is most difficult to achieve and what every truth-seeker is called upon to achieve, namely, the sacrificing of pet opinions and pleasing prejudices. Referring to this characteristic of the Upaniṣads in his book *Six Systems of Indian Philosophy*, Max Müller says:[11]

'It is surely astounding that such a system as the Vedānta should have been slowly elaborated by the indefatigable and intrepid thinkers of India thousands of years ago, a system that even now makes us feel giddy, as in mounting the last steps of the swaying spire of a Gothic cathedral. None of our philosophers, not excepting Heraclitus, Plato, Kant, or Hegel, has ventured to erect such a spire, never frightened by storms or lightnings. Stone follows on stone after regular succession after once the first step has been made, after once it has been clearly seen that in the beginning there can have been but one, as there will be but one in the end, whether we call it Ātman or Brahman.'

An impressive procession of students and teachers, earnest and sincere; a moving record of their animated discussions and graceful thought conflicts here in small groups and there in large assemblies; a flight of thought now and then into sublime heights of experience recorded in songs of freedom and delight, graceful and direct; an effective use of beautiful metaphors and telling imageries serving as feathers to its arrows of thought in flight; a singular absence of an atmosphere of coercion, open or veiled, secular or sacred, inhibiting the free pursuit of truth or its communication; the constant summons to man to verify for himself the truths placed before him for his acceptance; and the treatment of man as man and not as cut up into creeds, races, and sex—these and other varied features invest the Upaniṣads with the enduring greatness and strength of a perennial philosophy and the beauty and charm of an immortal literature.

Unlike philosophies elsewhere and other systems here, Vedānta is a living philosophy; and from the time it was first expounded in that dim antiquity down to our own times, it has been the spiritual inspiration behind the vast and varied Indian cultural experiment.

The Upaniṣads and Indian Culture

Without understanding the Upaniṣads, it is impossible to get an insight into Indian history and culture. Every subsequent development of philosophy and religion in India has drawn heavily on the Upaniṣads. The path of *bhakti* or devotion to a personal God, the path of *karma* or detached action, and the synthesis of all spiritual paths in a comprehensive spirituality, expounded by the *Gītā*, are all derived from the Upaniṣads. Emphasizing this pervasive influence of the Upaniṣads of Indian religions, Swami Vivekananda says:[12]

'In the Upaniṣads, also, we find all the subsequent development of Indian religious thought. Sometimes it has been urged without any grounds whatsoever that there is no ideal of *bhakti* in every Upaniṣad. Those that have been students of the Upaniṣads know that that is not true. There is enough *bhakti* in every Upaniṣad, if you will only seek for it; but many of these ideas which are found so fully developed in later times in the Purāṇas and other Smṛtis are only in the germ in the Upaniṣads. The sketch, the skeleton, was there, as it were. It was filled in some of the Purāṇas. But there is not one full-grown Indian ideal that cannot be traced back to the same source—the Upaniṣads.'

In the words of Bloomfield:[13]

'There is no important form of Hindu thought, heterodox Buddhism included, which is not rooted in the Upaniṣads.'

Every creative period in India's long history has behind it the impact of this Vedāntic inspiration in a concentrated measure. The drying up of this fount of inspiration, similarly, has always seen the setting in of the low tide of her culture and life. The ages of the *Gītā*, Buddha, and Śaṅkara in the past, and of Sri Ramakrishna and Swami Vivekananda in the present, are such landmarks in India's ancient and modern history.

Hence their constant summons to man is to wake up and march on: 'Arise! Awake! And stop not till the goal is reached!', as conveyed by Swami Vivekananda, adapting the powerful words of the *Kaṭha Upaniṣad: Uttiṣṭhata jāgrata prāpya varān nibodhata.*

A Message of Fearlessness

Before Swami Vivekananda's time, very few people knew about the Vedānta, about the philosophy of the Upaniṣads. He took it upon himself to proclaim these truths from the housetops, both in the East and in the West:[14]

'Let me tell you that we want strength, strength, and every time strength. And the Upaniṣads are the great mine of strength. Therein lies strength enough to invigorate the whole world; the whole world can be vivified, made strong, energized through them. They will call with trumpet voice upon the weak, the miserable, and the downtrodden of all races, all creeds, and all sects, to stand on their own feet and be free. Freedom, physical freedom, mental freedom, and spiritual freedom are the watchwords of the Upaniṣads.'

Śaṅkarācārya (A.D. 788-820) was the first teacher in historic times to make the Upaniṣads popular in this country. Before that, only a few select people, largely of the monastic community, knew the glory of the Upaniṣads. But Śaṅkarācārya opened up these treasures to householders and to all citizens. It will do them good, he said. But still the Upaniṣads reached only a small minority. Today, however, thanks largely to the work of Swami Vivekananda, they are the property of one and all.

The Upaniṣads, however, require close study. A newspaper is also a kind of literature; but it is read in the morning and thrown away in the evening, and thus stands at the lowest level of the literary spectrum. The Upaniṣads are not like that; they stand at the highest end of that spectrum. They must be read again and again; every step in growth of mental maturity and clearness brings us closer and closer to the heart of this great literature. The more we read them, the more we get out of them, because their words come from the depths of the heart. 'Where words come out from the depth of truth', says Tagore in his *Gitāñjali*. The words of the Upaniṣads come out from the depth of truth. The sages experienced Truth; they *saw* something profound in man and nature, and they tried to capture and communicate this vision in snatches of poetry. The sublime poetry of the Upaniṣads has moved the hearts of thinkers and poets from ancient times to the present. [Take for instance this verse]:

> 'The wise ones [*dhīra*] realize Him everywhere, inside as
> well as outside, Him whose form is bliss and immortality
> and whose glory overflows as the visible universe.'

The word *dhīra* in the text means 'the wise one' and indicates a combination of intelligence and courage. The Upaniṣads speak of man's greatness in two forms: first, his intelligence by which he understands the facts of the outer and inner worlds; second, his courage, heroism, by which he not merely knows but also achieves truth and excellence. Mere intelligence is not enough; courage is also necessary. Their combination makes for the highest character where the power of knowledge becomes transmuted into the energy of vision.

The capacity to scale the Everest of experience, to scale the highest peak of truth, comes to intelligence only when it blazons forth as courage. He is the *dhīra*, the wise one; he alone is entitled to realize the Ātman. What is the form of that realization? *Paripaśyanti*, 'he realizes Him everywhere', inside as well as outside, in man as well as in nature. The whole of nature becomes ablaze with divinity to his purified vision. He realizes Him as *ānandarūpam amṛtaṁ yadvibhāti*, 'of the form of bliss and immortality which has overflown as nature, as the visible universe'. The universe becomes transformed into waves of bliss, *ānandalaharī*, and waves of beauty, *saundaryalaharī*, as expressed by Śaṅkarācārya. The Ātman shines in man and nature, in the sun and moon and stars, in every particle of dust. Now here is a vision captured in a snatch of poetry. This is just a sample; there are scores of such in the Upaniṣads.

So there is great need for us to study this legacy, to understand it. The whole country will become galvanized with a new energy, a new resolve, a new discipline, even if only a little of the wisdom of the Upaniṣads can come into our lives. We read in the *Bhagavad-Gītā* (II. 40): *Svalpamapyasya dharmasya trāyate mahato bhayāt*—'Even a little of this *dharma* will save us from great fear.' Here is the message of fearlessness, of strength, of growth, development, and realization. Man must rise higher and higher and reach out towards perfection which is the unity of all-encompassing love and knowledge. This is the message, the clarion call, of the Upaniṣads—a call to dynamic action in the pursuit of Truth and total excellence, a call to carry forward evolution to the level of total life fulfilment through spiritual realization. What a hopeful message it is! □

References

1. *CW, 6: 81*
2. Commentary on the *Brahma Sūtra*, I. 1. 2
3. *Science in the Modern World*, p. 234
4. *An Historian's Approach to Religion*, pp. 262-64
5. *CW, 3: 248-51*
6. *CW, 1: 6-7*
7. Quoted by J.Arthur Thomson in his *Introduction to Science*, p.22
8. *The Life of Vivekananda and the Universal Gospel*, Third Impression, 1947, p. 196
9. *Muṇḍaka Upaniṣad*, III. 2. 8
10. *Three Lectures on Vedānta Philosophy*, p. 39
11. *Six Systems of Indian Philosophy*, Max Müller, p.182
12. *CW, 3: 230-31*
13. *The Religion of the Veda*, p. 51
14. *CW, 3: 238*

Chapter 5

Peace Chant in Upanishads

SWAMI SRIDHARANANDA

Introduction

All Upanishads begin with peace invocations called *shanti patha*. The Mundaka Upanishad, for instance, opens with two peace invocations. The significance is that, knowing full well that nothing happens in the world without the sanction of the Divine the Vedic *rishis* humbly seek guidance and blessings from the Divine so that their efforts may be fruitful. In all the Upanishads the first words invoke peace, not only for oneself but also for maintaining balance in the whole universe. Brahman, which is denoted by *Aum*, the *satyam* (the Real), the *ritam* (the cosmic order) is in equilibrium and in peace.

The Vedic *rishis* experienced the fact that an individual is at peace with himself when he is at peace with his surroundings, when the *jivatma* (individual soul) has established an inseparable bond with the *Vishvatma* (Universal Soul). We are one with the universe and the universe is one with us; as long as this Oneness is not realised, there will be lack of balance and peace. The Brahman is in continuous communion with Itself to be at peace with Itself and with the whole universe. Let us consider this *Shanti patha*:

47

ॐ भद्रं कर्णेभिः शृणुयाम देवाः भद्रं पश्येमाक्षभिर्यजत्राः ।
स्थिरैरङ्गैस्तुष्टुवाग्ंसस्तनूभिः व्यशेम देवहितं यदायुः ॥

Aum! O gods, the effulgent ones, may we with our ears hear what is propitious! While engaged in sacrifices, may we behold with our eyes what is propitious! May we, with firm and strong body and mind, lead a life full of worship working for the Divine. *Aum!* Peace Peace Peace!

Understanding Aum

This is the first part of the *Shanti patha*. Everything starts with *Aum*. It consists of three letters – 'a', 'u', 'm' and the *bindu*. When 'm' is uttered with the mouth closed then there is an inner vibration known as the *nada-bindu*. This vibration is due to the short vowel (*ā*) which is a nasal sound similar to the resonance which follows the striking of a gong or bell. The main purpose here is to make the study fruitful to us. *Aum* has been defined in the Vedas in various ways because it symbolizes the whole gamut of spiritual wisdom relating man and the universe.

Aum can be subjectively interpreted in terms of the individual self. Corresponding to the four 'parts' of *Aum*, there are four states of the individual soul or *jivatma*. The *aham*, or 'I', fluctuates between these four states of awareness. In the waking state we are awake and alert. After some hours of hard work we are tired and go to sleep in which there are dreams. This state is called the dream state. While dreaming we are not aware that we are dreaming; for us the dream is as real as the waking experience. We know we were dreaming only when we wake up and compare our surroundings with the dream experience. Then we realize that the latter was not real.

The third state is deep, dreamless, undisturbed sleep. On waking from this it takes a few moments to remember where one is and what the circumstances are, for in deep sleep one is not aware of the space, time and causation; only gradually do they soak into our consciousness again on waking. Then one says of his experience: 'Oh, I had such a joyous deep sleep. I was not aware of anything.' Unlike the dream state, in deep sleep the person experiences immense joy which is remembered after returning to waking state. We are ignorant about the source of the joy, so we say 'I knew nothing' though we experience the joy during that state. The veil of *avidya* or ignorance covers our real nature; still the bliss percolates through.

There is a fourth stage of awareness called *turiya-avastha* (*turiya* means transcendental). Going into *nirvikalpa samadhi*, (absolute concentration free of any differentiation), the individuality merges with Brahman, and the experience is—'This Self is Brahman, I am Brahman' (*Ayam atma brahma, Aham brahma asmi*). The aspirant experiences immense bliss in the glory of the Self. This occurs only through one's continued disciplined effort under the guidance of the guru, and with the grace of the Divine. It cannot be described as it is beyond the realm of relativity where alone words can be used. In this state the phenomenal world totally disappears and one is identified with the Essence of the universe, which is symbolized by the dot (*nada-bindu*) of the *Aum*.

Aum can also be seen as suggesting the forty-nine letters of the Sanskrit alphabet in their various permutations and combinations as 'a' is the starting point which ends with 'm' and 'u' rolls over representing the other alphabets. Then the dot stands for the ultimate purpose of language, which lies beyond language itself: 'failing to reach which i.e., Brahman, speech falls back together with the mind.' Language is a vehicle through which man can attain to a level which is beyond language—this is how one can look at *Aum*.

Another Meaning of Aum

Aum can also be objectively interpreted, as the foundation on which the concept of the Oneness of the creation or universe is based. The universe can be classified into three categories. The first letter 'a' symbolizes the gross, physical, material aspect of universe which is perceived by the senses. It is called *jagat* because it changes constantly (*gaccati iti jagat*). Like the water of a fast flowing river the *jagat* or physical universe is never the same; it flows as a continuous stream in time-space-causation (*desha-kala-nimitta*) which is its underlying strata.

The second letter 'u', stands for the subtle aspect of the universe, which exists behind the things of the gross world. The senses have an upper and lower range beyond which they cannot perceive, though we can find ways to increase this range. For example, we have been able to increase or decrease the wavelength of sound to bring it within hearing level. Still, sounds exist which we do not hear with our ears. So it is with these subtle objects beyond the gross form. The subtle world, which is behind the manifested gross world, is not readily perceivable unless one's faculties or instruments are developed to bring it within the boundaries of our experience. The principles of time-space-causation, on which the gross world functions, are also part of the subtle world.

The third letter 'm', denotes the causal principle, the cause of both gross and subtle aspects of this universe. Why does one see the world as tangible when in fact it is not? Why does one seek permanency in this transient world? Everyone knows that being born they will die but none is prepared to accept it and face the truth. It is because of the non-perception of the Real Substratum that we take the appearance as true. We are unable to grasp the Truth underlying the world. However, we import and impose the permanence of the Reality onto the objects of this impermanent world. This ignorance is the fundamental cause of all misery. Everything in this universe depends on this divine Cause, or Source. Thus our inability to analyse this world correctly and to thoroughly grasp the truth behind the whole play of the universe is the cause of all suffering. Ultimately, not understanding the truth of the Oneness of *jivatma* and *paramatma* is known as primal cause or primal ignorance.

But by explaining the gross, subtle and causal aspects of the universe nothing positive has been suggested about their source the Absolute. The Ultimate Reality exists. It is both immanent and transcendent. When one sees someone as a human, it is partial seeing. When seen as a manifestation of the Divine, that perception is a little more complete. And when Absolute Knowledge dawns then one experiences the oneness of the seer, the seen and all the aspects of the universe. The Absolute, which is manifested in so many names and forms, is in its absoluteness beyond all diversity. This is suggested by the *nada-dhvani*, the concluding nasal sound of the *Aum*. It suggests that there is only One Reality in the universe, and that It is manifesting as everything. The causal principle is what prevents one from seeing the Absolute in its totality as the immutable, without alternatives, formless Self, which is Absolute Existence (*sat*), Consciousness (*chit*) and Bliss (*ananda*).

The significance of the symbol '*Aum*' is not confined to the scriptures alone, but applies to all knowledge, science and technology, called the *apara-vidya* or lesser knowledge. All branches of knowledge, both scientific and philosophical, take into consideration the gross, subtle and causal aspects but the substratum of everything is the Spirit or Self. Thus, the purpose of the study of the Upanishads is to experience the Truth denoted by *Aum* in the *shanti-patha*, the prayer for inner peace, and not simply to recite it. The Upanishads ask for nothing apart from peace—neither success, nor wealth, nor victory nor any other-worldly object, because it is the peaceful mind alone which can fathom the secrets of Nature.

Understanding the Way to Peace

The invocation is addressed to *devas*, or lords of the universe. The concept of *devas* in the Upanishads should be harmonized with the concept of the universe we have today. To our ancestors at the Upanishadic time *devis* and *devatas* were not glorified human forms but were addressed as the principles controlling Nature. The word *Deva* here is derived from the verb *dyu dyotane* meaning 'to shine'. It refers to the 'effulgent ones', implying not only bright light but also that which removes lack of understanding. Each branch of learning follows a certain principle; get hold of it and that whole branch is within your grasp. In the invocation the principles of the universe governing sound, etc., are being addressed:

'O Principles of the universe! You who guide and conduct the cosmic affairs in a rhythmic manner, we pray to you to help us to use the hearing organ to hear only that which is inspiring, so that we may become worthy and adequately qualified to know the meaning of the sacred word *Aum*, the Truth.'

1. The prayer to the *devas* is a request that we may hear only the *bhadra*, the good. *Bhadra* also means grace. It means hearing, by the grace and guidance of the *devas*, all the truths in the world that are gracious, uplifting and ennobling. For only this will help us to experience the total meaning of the symbol *Aum*. Therefore worship starts with this prayer that we may be granted the blessing of hearing the good. We are endowed with five senses, and we beg the *devatas* to

help us put those senses to use only in order to attain to Oneness, through the experience of the meaning of *Aum*.

2. Then follows the second part of the prayer:

'Let our eyes develop the power of seeing everything in the world that ennobles us, inspires us, and makes us full of grace.'

The eyes, which now only see the various ordinary forms, should be enabled to see the unified essence of these forms. The Divine is to be seen everywhere by disciplining the organ of vision. The sages say that when the body-consciousness of an individual is absolutely melted away, he then experiences non-difference between himself and *Paramatman*, the Supreme Self, wherever his mind may roam.[1]

The performance of offerings or sacrifice, *yajna*, was an obligatory duty of life. It was more than merely the performance of a sacrifice with fire and other materials. It symbolized our obligation to parents, teachers, friends, society, spouse, children, other creatures, natural resources—to all the things that enable us to live and be comfortable. Above all, it symbolizes our obligation to ourselves, to be the knower of the Self. Such an obligation is *yajna*, and its application is universal. Seeing and hearing the good while performing the duties of life, does not hinder or stop the flow of our lives. The mistake we make is to equate spirituality with other-worldliness. But nowhere in the Upanishads is one asked to run away from the realities of life. In fact, the command is to perform *yajña*, sacrifice, as a daily duty in the world. This was relevant in the past and it is more so today.

3. Now we come to the third part of the prayer:

'May we, with firm and strong body and mind, lead a life full of worship doing work for the Divine.'

Most psychologists say that the movements of the body are controlled, motivated or guided by the movements of the mind. The Upanishad highlights the same in a different manner. Until you are physically stable and have got rid of your bodily restlessness, your mind too will jump around like a monkey that has been given wine and then been attacked by a swarm of bees. Thus the purpose here is to control all the limbs of the body and thereby gain control of the mind. For example sitting relaxed and still in *padmasana*, a yoga posture suitable for meditation, helps one to control the erratic movements of the mind. So the prayer is that the body and mind may be strong and calm. This will let us enjoy a long life for *devahita*, that is to say for the good of the many through the *devas*, the effulgent principles of the universe.

Vyashema means to enjoy, not selfishly but by dedicating oneself to the welfare of society under the guidance of the Divine.

The ancient philosophers were greatly introspective, no doubt, but they also gave importance to the world in which they lived. There was no question of living in disharmony or in isolation, or for one's own self-interest. So they prayed for a life beneficial to one and all, and also in harmony with the principles of the universe, so as to be able to contribute to them and not to clash with them. They desired to be part and parcel of the symphony and equilibrium of nature and thus attain Eternal Bliss which is the purpose of human life. This comes only when one has grown beyond the demands of the body and mind and is no longer bound by them. Now let us consider the second part of the Shanti patha:

स्वस्ति न इन्द्रो वृद्धश्रवाः । स्वस्ति नः पूषा विश्ववेदाः ।
स्वस्ति नस्ताक्ष्र्योऽरिष्टनेमिः स्वस्ति नो बृहस्पतिर्दधातु ॥
ॐ शान्तिः शान्तिः शान्तिः ॥

'May Indra confer undisturbed prosperity on us. May Vriddhashrava (the ancient), Pushan, Vishvaveda (sustainer of the world and all-knowing one), Tarkshya (celestial bird), Arishtanemi (protector from harm), Brihaspati (preceptor of devas), bestow on us undisturbed sustenance to grow in our endeavour. *Aum!* Peace Peace Peace!'

This is the second part of the peace-chant. In the earlier prayer the word *shanti* was used. In this verse the key word is *svasti*. The nearest meaning of *svasti* is 'absence of disturbance.'

Further, in this verse Indra, Pusan and Brihaspati are mentioned by name, whereas in the earlier verse only principles of nature were spoken of. Those principles are now personalized, so as to make communication with them easy. The sages must have thought that the principles by which rain, thunder, and lightning occurred needed to be identified and given names, so that prayers could be offered to them. Indra is thought of as the mastermind behind all the natural forces which either help or trouble the insignificant human being. He is the master-controller of all the forces of nature that can make life enjoyable and free from danger.

Vriddhashrava means the most ancient, the most powerful and revered. So the prayer is to Indra, the master of all the gods, to let us live free in *svasti*, from any disturbance.

Pushan is the *deva* or god who manages the affairs of Mother Earth—the fertility of the land, the flow of the rivers, the atmosphere on which our existence depends, and so on. Let it be auspicious and propitious so that life is undisturbed.

Arishtanemi is the *deva* who protects us from the evil influences that come between us and attainment of the Divine, and who helps us understand the secret of the Upanishads, which is our goal.

Brihaspati is the god of wisdom and we pray to him to prevent us from losing our balance and wisdom, to help us control ourselves, and thus to allow us to live undisturbed. In this way the prayer is that the forces of the universe may give us peace and the opportunity to manifest fully our creative talents.

Conclusion

This two-part *shanti-patha*, though ancient, is very modern and relevant to our times, for it is a prayer for peace. And it makes it clear that this human life has not been given to us to be lived as if we were simply a biological creature, but as a *manava*, a human being, who has the capacity to control the movement of the *manas* or mind. In this way we are differentiated from the animal world.

The purpose of our being born is to realise our true nature as well as the origin of Nature and the relation or equation of the two. This is clearly the purpose of the first part of the *shanti patha*. And the second part tells us of the struggle necessary to emancipate ourselves from the bondage created through innumerable births. Thus we pray for help to the *devas* of the universe who are stronger and wiser than us. ☐

Reference

1. *cf. Drigdrishya-viveka*, 30, *Sarasvatirahasyopanishad*, 55

Chapter 6

Spiritual Experiences of Sri Ramakrishna: Upanishads Revitalised

SWAMI ADISWARANANDA

Central Theme of the Upanishads

The Upanishads present a vision of truth that is profound, universal and limitless like the sky. Saints and savants are enchanted by this grand vision of truth, and sincere spiritual seekers draw inspiration from this vision. Schopenhauer wrote,

'In the whole world there is no study so beneficial and so elevating as that of the Upanishads. It has been the solace of my life; it will be the solace of my death.'[1]

All the philosophical systems of Hinduism invoke the teachings of the Upanishads as their authority and support. According to the seers of the Upanishads, truth is one without a second. It is immutable, incorporeal, all-pervading pure consciousness, known as Brahman or the Supreme Self. This Self has no name, no form, no epithet, and no limitations whatsoever. The various names and forms of the Supreme Self are feeble attempts by the human mind to name the nameless and attribute form to the formless. The Self is Knowledge-Existence-

Bliss absolute. Realization of the Self is more than blind belief, intellectual conviction or emotional exaltation. It is the result of direct perception that is vivid, purifying, transforming, and conducive to the welfare of all beings. Self-knowledge is bliss. Tasting the intoxicating bliss of the Self, a person achieves infinite expansion of the soul that embraces all beings and things of the universe as one with itself. Only knowers of the Self, not philosophers or theologians, demonstrate the reality of God and the validity of the scriptures.

Self-knowledge is the central message of the Upanishads. Seers of the Upanishads maintain that the Self is the Reality of all realities, Truth of all truths, and Consciousness of all consciousness. Anything in the universe that does not reflect the light of the Self is shadowed by death and destruction. Self-knowledge is realizing that our individual soul is the focus of the all-pervading Supreme Self. Pursuit of Self-knowledge is the highest form of worship. All our prayer, meditation, self-control, vows, charity and austerities culminate in Self-knowledge.

The seers of the Upanishads exhort us to sacrifice everything for the realization of the Self. Self-knowledge is the goal of all goals of life. It is the essence of liberation. Only by realizing the deathless Self within can one overcome death and attain true immortality. Those who leave this world without attaining Self-knowledge go from death to death. Whenever the Upanishadic teachings were neglected, Hinduism experienced the proliferation of dogmas and the rise of sectarianism and bigotry.

Decline in Religion

Nineteenth century Hinduism experienced a severe crisis that brought about a spiritual eclipse of its soul. The message of the Upanishads lost its fire and vigour and ceased to be a practical reality. That which is the teaching for the strong-minded became a refuge for the weak, escapists, fatalists, and miracle-mongers. Hinduism ignored the grand vision of the Upanishadic seers and drifted toward anthropomorphism and polytheism. There arose diverse schools of thought, each claiming its superiority over the others. Glorification of local myths and beliefs, adherence to outdated customs and traditions, and mechanical observance of rituals and ceremonies became the order of popular Hindu spirituality. The Upanishadic virtues of renunciation, dispassion, self-control, and longing for the divine were looked upon as extreme practices meant only for monks and ascetics living in the forests and mountains. Upanishadic verses were memorized and chanted with perfect accent and intonation in the seminaries but were rarely practiced in everyday life.

Hinduism of the time encouraged a morbid inwardness, a flight from the world in despair over life and its problems. Passivity became its keynote and self-withdrawal its prime virtue. Inertia passed for tranquillity and hopelessness for dispassion. Once a teaching of hope and strength, Hinduism exaggerated human weakness, unworthiness, and sinfulness, focusing only on human limitations and not on human possibilities. It tilted too much toward a form of pseudo-mysticism that saw God only in the temple and prayer room, and not outside. Hinduism became a hollow philosophy of life that produced fake reformers, dreamy idealists, idle philosophers, and so-called knowers of truth who sought transcendental solutions for earthly problems. It created pessimists who proved life intolerable yet continued to tolerate it. Devotion became cheap sentiment and knowledge became mere rationalization. Devout Hindus prayed for personal gain and personal liberation but looked upon the sufferings of others as the deserved result of their past karma. The message of the Upanishads was lost in the wilderness of superstition, false piety, eroticism, and occultism.

Sri Ramakrishna and His Experiences

At this moment of crisis Sri Ramakrishna (1836-1886) was born. His life, his epoch-making spiritual adventure, his daring and determined search for truth, his blazing spiritual experiences stemmed the tide of degeneration and changed the thought current of the time. In his spiritual search Sri Ramakrishna walked alone. Very few were able to understand that his spiritual realizations would set in motion a tidal wave of spiritual regeneration and revival. Sri Ramakrishna's life was one of uninterrupted contemplation of the divine. To a world that indulged in distraction and chatter Sri Ramakrishna brought news from a world in which communion with the Self imparted the highest bliss. What he saw, others could not see; what he understood, others failed to comprehend.

The nineteenth century, taken over by the delirium of dry philosophy and cold reason, was challenged by this unknown temple priest who rose to superhuman greatness by his direct perception of the divine. His spiritual realizations gave him power to visualize the invisible, and the keenness of his observation enabled him to describe the indescribable truth with extreme precision. The universe of beings and things appeared to him not as a framework of illusion but as the manifestation of Brahman in time and space. The gulf between heaven and earth was bridged. Psychologists describe only two levels of the human mind, conscious and subconscious. But Sri Ramakrishna directs our attention to another level, the superconscious that transcends belief and reason. For psychologists, the master urge in a human individual is the sex-drive or the pursuit of power or pleasure. For Sri Ramakrishna, the master urge is the desire for everlasting life, unlimited bliss, and absolute knowledge. Purity was Sri Ramakrishna's life-breath. His high spiritual states were observed with awe not only by believers but also by sceptics, agnostics, and atheists, and his samadhis were tested for genuineness by medical doctors. After reaching Brahman, Sri Ramakrishna remained in samadhi for six months. He said:

> For six months at a stretch I remained in that state from which ordinary men can never return; generally the body falls off, after three weeks, like a sere leaf. I was not conscious of day and night. Flies would enter my mouth and nostrils just as they do a dead body's, but I did not feel them. My hair became matted with dust.[2]

The Upanishads declare that by realizing Brahman one goes beyond all sorrow and suffering. The chronicler of *The Gospel of Sri Ramakrishna* records how even when suffering from the excruciating pain of cancer in his last days, his mind would soar into ecstasy:

Sunday, March 14, 1886... That day Sri Rama-krishna was feeling very ill. At midnight the moonlight flooded the garden, but it could wake no response in the devotees' hearts. They were drowned in a sea of grief. They felt that they were living in a beautiful city besieged by a hostile army.... In a very soft voice and with great difficulty he said to M: 'I have gone on suffering so much for fear of making you all weep. But if you all say: "Oh, there is so much suffering! Let the body die", then I may give up the body.' These words pierced the devotees' hearts. And he who was their father, mother, and protector had uttered these words! What could they say? All sat in silence. Some thought, 'Is this another crucifixion—the sacrifice of the body for the sake of the devotees?'

Monday, March 15, 1886... [The devotees] sat speechless and looked grave, thinking of the Master's suffering of the previous night.

Master *(to the devotees):* 'Do you know what I see right now? I see that it is God Himself who has become all this. It seems to me that men and other living beings are made of leather, and that it is God Himself who, dwelling inside these leather cases, moves the hands, the feet, the heads. I had a similar vision once before, when I saw houses, gardens, roads, men, cattle—all made of One Substance; it was as if they were all made of wax. I see that it is God

Himself who has become the block, the executioner, and the victim for the sacrifice.' As he describes this staggering experience, in which he realizes in full the identity of all within the One Being, he is overwhelmed with emotion and exclaims, 'Ah! What a vision!' Immediately Sri Ramakrishna goes into samadhi. He completely forgets his body and the outer world. The devotees are bewildered. Not knowing what to do, they sit still. Presently the Master regains partial consciousness of the world and says: 'Now I have no pain at all. I am my old self again.' The devotees are amazed to watch this state of the Master, beyond pleasure and pain, weal and woe.[3]

The Upanishadic verse, 'His hands and feet are everywhere; His eyes, heads, and faces are everywhere; His ears are everywhere; He exists compassing all'[4] was often thought to be a poetic imagination of the Upanishadic seers until it was exemplified in the life of Sri Ramakrishna.

Pundit Shashadhar [a renowned religious leader of the time] one day suggested to Sri Ramakrishna that the latter could remove the illness by concentrating his mind on the throat, the scriptures having declared that yogis had power to cure themselves in that way. The Master rebuked the pundit. 'For a scholar like you to make such a proposal!' he said. 'How can I withdraw the mind from the Lotus Feet of God and turn it to this worthless cage of flesh and blood?'

'For our sake at least,' begged Narendra and the other disciples.

'But,' replied Sri Ramakrishna, 'do you think I enjoy this suffering? I wish to recover, but that depends on the Mother.'

Narendra: 'Then please pray to Her. She must listen to you.'

Master: 'But I cannot pray for my body.'

Narendra: 'You must do it, for our sake at least.'

Master: 'Very well, I shall try.'

A few hours later the Master said to Narendra: 'I said to Her: "Mother, I cannot swallow food because of my pain. Make it possible for me to eat a little." She pointed you all out to me and said: "What? You are eating through all these mouths. Isn't that so?" I was ashamed and could not utter another word.'[5]

Sri Ramakrishna perceived Brahman in samadhi with eyes closed, and he perceived the same Brahman with eyes open. For him the image of Mother Kali was not stone but a transfiguration of Brahman. He said, 'Kali is verily Brahman, and Brahman is verily Kali.'[6] He saw the manifestation of Brahman in the Divine Mother worshipped in the temple and the same manifestation in a fallen woman on the street. Seeing drunkards in a grog shop, he would be overwhelmed with divine inebriation.

Samadhi was so intense in Sri Ramakrishna that he saw the presence of Brahman in everything and everywhere. Coming down from the superconscious level of samadhi, he would often be unaware of his surroundings. In his exalted spiritual state he would feel identified with all beings and things and experience intense pain at the suffering of others. During his worship in the temple, he would often put the flowers on his own head instead of offering them at the feet of the image of the Mother. The distinction between the Mother in his heart and the Mother in the image had disappeared for him. Sri Ramakrishna's God-consciousness transcended the limits of all sects, denominations, traditions and conventions. Everyone who came to him felt uplifted by his profound God-consciousness and boundless love. It was as if every particle of Sri Ramakrishna's body was filled with God-consciousness. Greatly amazed to see Sri Ramakrishna's continual God-intoxication, Mathur, the proprietor of the Kali temple, lovingly told Sri Ramakrishna, 'Father, there is nothing inside you but God.'[7]

Revitalizing the Upanishads

Through his life and realizations, Sri Ramakrishna revitalised the Upanishads. The great teachings of the Upanishads again became practical and life giving. For Sri Ramakrishna the real temple is the human heart where the great Self shines. The real ingredients for worship are the virtues of purity, self-control, physical and mental austerities. The essence of all austerity is the conquest of lust and greed. True pilgrimage is communion with this inmost Self through concentration and meditation. Bathing in ordinary waters does not purify our soul unless we bathe in the waters of the divine Self.

Truth is to be known by realizing the divine Self within through prayer and meditation and also through action and expression in daily life. Being good and doing good go together. Self-knowledge becomes complete when it expresses itself as the spirit of service to all living beings. Selfless service to all beings is the true worship of God. Oneness of existence is the basis of all love and charitable feelings. For Sri Ramakrishna different religions are different natural pathways to reach the same truth.

Conclusion

The great Master of nineteenth century India did not found a new religious system or philosophy. He liberated spirituality from religiosity. His luminous life attracted hundreds of pure souls who dedicated their lives to spread the message of the living God in the human heart. Temples of lifeless ceremonies and rituals became temples of concentration, meditation and selfless service to all. The God in every human heart that had been trampled underfoot was re-established in its full glory.

Sri Ramakrishna reminds us that everything becomes dark when we become cut off from our true Self, the centre of our being. The maladies of life are primarily spiritual. Wealth and prosperity when not used for the attainment of Self-knowledge breed delusion. Art and aesthetics that do not reflect the greatness of the Self lapse into sensuality. Intellectual knowledge when it does not consummate in Self-knowledge creates egotism. Achievements of science and technology when they are not for the attainment of knowledge of the Self prove to be dangerous weapons of self-destruction. The quest for the Self is not a choice but a vital necessity. When we neglect this Self we become lost in the world of delusion and distraction and face the same Self as the unforgiving realities of sorrow and suffering. Only Self-knowledge can save us from the great terrors of life and guarantee everlasting peace and happiness. □

References

1. Quoted in Swami Nikhilananda, *The Upanishads,* vol. 1 (New York: Ramakrishna-Vivekananda Center, 1990), p. 11.
2. Introduction to *The Gospel of Sri Ramakrishna,* trans. Swami Nikhilananda (New York: Ramakrishna-Vivekananda Center, 2000), p. 32.
3. *The Gospel of Sri Ramakrishna,* Pp. 941-942.
4. *Svetasvatara Upanishad* 3.16, in *The Upanishads,* vol. 2, trans., Swami Nikhilananda (New York: Ramakrishna-Vivekananda Center, 1990), p. 103.
5. Introduction to *The Gospel of Sri Ramakrishna,* pp. 69-70.
6. *The Gospel of Sri Ramakrishna,* p. 134.
7. *ibid.,* p. 359.

Chapter 7

Sri Sarada Devi
in the Light of the Upanishads

PRAVRAJIKA ATMADEVAPRANA

There is an interesting incident about how we perceive things. Lord Buddha once pointed to a flower and asked each one of his disciples present to say something about it. One of them pronounced a lecture, another a poem, yet another a parable. Each outdid the other in depth and erudition. Mahakashyap, an eminent disciple, however, only smiled and kept quiet. It is said that only he had *seen* the flower. Others were mere 'label makers.'

Indeed, in our quest for experiencing God, we think too much, reflect too much, talk too much. As Swami Vivekananda said,

'Our great defect in life is that we are so much drawn to the ideal, the goal is so much more enchanting, so much more alluring, so much bigger in our mental horizon, that we lose sight of the details altogether.'[1]

Engrossed in feverish action, we are apt to overlook the real significance of simple things in life—whether it is a flower or a flower-like simple pure life. One such example is Sri Sarada Devi's life. It is a simple life, nay simplicity itself. But as Sister Nivedita wrote in a letter to Holy Mother once,

'Surely the wonderful things of God are all quiet—stealing unnoticed into our lives—the air and the sunlight and the sweetness of gardens and of the Ganges, these are the silent things that are like you!'[2]

Let us ponder on how this simple life demonstrated the teachings of the Upanishads.

Upanishads in Practice

Though Holy Mother's life looks so simple and commonplace, to understand it is not easy. One needs to make a good deal of spiritual evolution to appreciate the Mother's extraordinary life. One might draw a parallel to what Swamiji said of Sri Ramakrishna:

'The life of Sri Ramakrishna was an extraordinary searchlight under whose illumination one is able to really understand the whole scope of Hindu religion. He was the object-lesson of all the theoretical knowledge given in the Shastras (scriptures). He showed by his life what the Rishis and Avataras really wanted to teach. The books were theories, he was the realisation. This man had in fifty-one years lived the five thousand years of national spiritual life and so raised himself to be an object-lesson for future generations.'[3]

No wonder Chakravarthy Rajagopalachari aptly named Sri Ramakrishna's teachings as 'Ramakrishna Upanishad.' But if Sri Ramakrishna was the living embodiment of the ancient principles of the Upanishads, then Holy Mother's life practically presents the recent reliable commentary on them.

Cosmic Sweep of Divine Vision

One common feature of sages of the Upanishads as well as Mother's life is that they both are shining examples of how to pursue the path of attaining the vision of the One *behind* the many, consummating it with the vision of the One *in* the many, and finally with the One *as* the many. Mother's life is a simple story which explains this profound truth in detail. Her life is an enduring image of fulfilment and joy.

Once a small ocean fish went to an older fish and asked, 'Excuse me, you are older than I, so can you tell me where to find this thing they call the ocean?' 'The ocean,' said the older fish, 'is the thing you are in now.' 'Oh! This? But this is just water. What I am seeking is the ocean,' said the disappointed fish as it swam away to reach elsewhere. The older fish exclaimed, 'Oh little fish! What are you looking for? Just look!' Living in the very ocean and searching for it! That is the irony of human situation—searching for the Infinite while infinite is all around us.

Once a lady went to Holy Mother. She expressed her desire to have some spiritual guidelines from her. But the Mother went on doing her household duties. She did puja, cooking, distributed food and so on. All the while, the lady was following Mother. While taking leave of her, she expressed her disappointment, 'Mother! I thought of getting some instruction from you.' Mother answered, 'Yes my child! I have been instructing you all the while.' That is Holy Mother's message to us— live the life. Her own life demonstrates the glorious fact that right from the humblest household duties to that of guiding the affairs of a spiritual organization, any responsibility could be performed without losing the cosmic sweep of Divine vision. She made no distinction between the sacred and secular nor compartmentalised life in any other way.

A Pitcher of Bliss

Holy Mother used to say that during her days in Dakshineswar, she felt as if a pitcher of bliss was placed in her heart. To us it seems as if Sri Ramakrishna established Her as a pitcher of bliss, in the very heart of our world to guide and provide us succour in this dismal state of affairs. In Sister Devamata's words,

'Those who had the rare blessing of living with Holy Mother learned that religion was a sweet, natural joyous thing; that purity and holiness were tangible realities.'[4]

How to live in this world? By possessing God, by renouncing whatever is not real. For, says the Isha Upanishad, 'The whole universe is filled with God.'[5] Holy Mother showed us how we are to do this. Small, little acts of her life show us how to live in this clumsy, consuming world of hundred little exacting problems, without being affected by them. Her central message is that one can remain unaffected by the worldly cares only by keeping God, and God alone, as the light, solace and goal of life.

The Upanishadic Solution

To perceive the presence of all-pervading God is the highest achievement of all human genius. To strive for this realisation is what the Upanishads guide us to do. Kena Upanishad declares that 'Man achieves great energy through the atman and immortality through its realization,' (*atmana vindate viryam*). Echoing this important truth, Swami Vivekananda said,

> 'Call upon the sleeping soul and see how it awakens! Power will come, glory will come, and everything that is excellent will come, when the sleeping soul is aroused to self-conscious activity.'[6]

Awakening this inner core of our being and aligning our lives to It, is the ultimate solution to present day problems. One may recall here what Arnold Toynbee, the great historian and the Nobel laureate observed some 50 years ago. He said that 'a chapter which had a western beginning will have to have an Indian ending if it is not to end in the self-destruction of the human race.' He further explained,

> 'In the present age, western technology has not only annihilated the distance, but it has armed the people of the world with weapons of devastating power at a time when they have been brought to point blank range of each other without yet having learnt to know and love each other. At this supremely dangerous moment in human history, the only way of salvation for mankind is an Indian way. The primary reason is that this teaching is right and ... is right because it flows from a true vision of spiritual reality. That true vision is to be found in the truth of the Upanishads.'[7]

The Upanishadic vision of life is a holistic vision of life. Says the Mundaka Upanishad:

O adorable Sir, what is by knowing which all this becomes known?[8]

This search for the common denominator of life, in truth, is what life is forcing us to seek. Generally we keep struggling to keep our individuality, our separateness, and that is the cause for unhappiness. If we keep ourselves away from total life, it generates a feeling of insufficiency and emptiness. Separation and differentiation only add to our misery. The solution, therefore, lies in breaking the false barriers and seeking unity and oneness. This is where the absolute contentment and fullness can be found. It is this all-inclusive vision of spiritual reality which Toynbee termed as the 'Indian Way.'

Holy Mother practised this vision of inclusiveness and love in her life. Her oft-quoted words 'Learn to make the whole world your own. No one is a stranger, my child. The whole world is your own,' sum up not only her central message but the message of the Upanishads as well.

Overcoming Inner Obstacles

Though we, the heirs of such immortal wisdom, hear this, it does not stir us; we find these spiritual truths dry and insipid. Why? The problem lies with our attitude towards life. It is only when the field is fertile that the seeds sprout. A handful of wheat, five thousand years old, was found in the tomb of one of the kings of ancient Egypt. Someone planted the grains and to every one's amazement they came to life. Therein lies the secret.

The wisdom of Upanishad can be likened to those seeds. They contain much life and energy. Though they can remain in the form of seeds for centuries, when they are sown in the fertile soil of a receptive heart, their potential is revealed. If our hearts are dry and dead, how could anything take root there? We must introspect and find out how to make our minds spiritually fertile. Holy Mother's God-centred life can be a source of great inspiration in this context. Looking at her life strengthens our faith that this ideal is practical.

Practice of Universal Love

True love is universal. This is what Isa Upanishad (verse7) proclaims, 'One who sees the same self in others, where is sorrow or delusion for him?' The wise man is he who realizes all beings as not distinct from his own self and his own self as the self of all beings. Such a person cannot hate anyone; he can only love. Holy Mother was an embodiment of this truth. Her love was as universal as air, as un-polarized as space, as same-sighted as sunlight.

Be it at her little cottage at Jayrambati or the Udbodhan House in Calcutta, wherever Mother lived, it was a Rishi Ashrama. Whoever came there—no matter if one was a labourer or a cart driver, a hawker or a palanquin bearer, a fisherman or a fish monger —that person was Mother's son or daughter. They all received the same welcome, love and attention from Mother as her own devotees. Hence wherever Mother lived, there came into existence a unique institution which formed in itself a Math, a veritable temple, as well as a house-holder's home—all rolled into one.

If we study Mother's life in depth, we come to understand that true spiritual outlook means to seek the welfare of all. Love should be *universal*, directed towards all people. Such a universal attitude comes only through expansion of heart, through sharing in larger life.

Before leaving for America, at Mount Abu, Swami Vivekananda said to Swami Turiyananda, his brother disciple,

'Hari bhai, I don't know what I got through all these spiritual practices, but this much I am sure, my heart has expanded. I feel for all.' [9]

This is real compassion or true spiritual outlook.

An illustration from Mother's life explains this further. Once someone brought two choice mangoes to the Holy Mother. Mother wanted to give them to Sister Devamata, an American nun, who was on a visit to her. But Sister Devamata refused to accept them saying that it would make her happier if the Holy Mother had them. To this Holy Mother responded with a beautiful meaningful question, 'Do you think it will give you greater pleasure to have me keep them or give me greater pleasure to have you take them?'

Devamata, the wise lady understood the inner meaning of this question and answered, 'Yes, it will give you greater pleasure because you have a larger heart to feel it.' She realized the fact that Holy Mother's love and compassion were not based on ordinary human instincts. They were based on larger awareness.

Later Sister Devamata made this comment: 'Unbounded was Mother's concern for every living being. No human measure could contain it.'[10] Swami Virajananda (later 6th President of the Ramakrishna Order), while commenting about the uniqueness of Mother's divine love says,

> 'While at home I had loved my mother intensely and she too had abundant affection for me. But could that love stand in comparison to that of Holy Mother's? Nay, she is the mother of my innumerable past incarnations—the mother of eternal time the mother of my very being. Earthly love however pure and noble, still binds but Mother's affection had a liberating effect on the bonds of ignorance.'[11]

A Tower of Tolerance

One reads in the Chandogya Upanishad:

> 'Where one sees another, one hears another, so long as there are two, there must be fear, and fear is the mother of all misery. Where none sees another, where it is all one, there is none to be miserable, none to be unhappy.'[12]

Holy Mother, throughout her life, neither excluded nor hated anyone. She included all in the breadth of her love. She accepted all, even criminals, drunkards and thieves, if they but called her 'Mother.' Her boundless tolerance was based on the fact that she thought of the world as ignorant rather than wicked, as unsatisfactory rather than rebellious.

A small incident beautifully expresses this. A young student used to visit Mother quite often to receive her blessings. But in college he had to keep company with all sorts of boys and went astray and gradually came to feel that he was no good. So, one day he went to Mother and said, 'Mother, I will not come here again. I am a misfit here. I am not worthy of this place.' So saying, he tried to run away but Mother ran after him, took him by the shoulders and shaking him said,

'Whenever bad thoughts disturb your mind, think of me.'

Then she let go of him. On his way home, the young man kept repeating, 'Think of me, and remember me.' He could not forget Mother's wonderfully compassionate eyes. Eventually he became a monk.[13]

Thus lived this modern *brahmavadini* of the ancient Upanishads. Conscious of her cosmic divine nature and power, she boldly proclaimed, 'If my child gets covered with mud or dirt, is it not my duty to cleanse him and take him on my lap? . . .I am the mother of the virtuous and also the mother of the wicked.' The fact that Mother's affection had a liberating effect on the bonds of ignorance was literally proved in the case of Radhu, her brother's daughter.

Unlimited Power, Yet No Trace of It!

Though a spiritual giant of great exception, Holy Mother lived like a commoner. There is a moving incident depicting her as an unassuming, simple mother. After visiting Mother at Jayarambati, Swami Nikhilananda then a college student, along with

Gowri-ma and two other devotees were starting for
Calcutta. The Holy Mother asked him again and again
to look after Gowri-ma during the journey and with
tearful eyes prayed repeatedly to Master for their safety.
Gowri-ma in order to assure her asked her vehemently
not to worry about them. Swami Nikhilananda later
recalled:

'The louder Gowri-ma roared not to worry about them, the
more humbly the Mother prayed to God for us. I watched
the scene and said to myself: "Here is a woman who has
not a millionth part of Mother's power and is bubbling
over. And there is the Holy Mother, a veritable dynamo of
power acting like a ordinary mother and restraining it
all."'[14]

Writes Swami Budhananda,

'Such was the tremendous power of her unassuming
renunciation that though she went about attending to daily
duties like an ordinary woman in white sheet, great
sannyasins and Brahmajnanis felt blessed prostrating
before her. She looked upon those self-realized souls as a
mother would on the little ones. Mighty Vivekananda was
at best a robust child before her. Such was the quiet
authority of her renunciation; such was her absolute
assimilation of the purest content of sannyasa.'[15]

The Upanishad Personified

Holy Mother was the embodiment of many ideals
mentioned in the Indian spiritual tradition. One may
recall here the great brahmavadinis (knowers of
Brahman) like Gargi who challenged sage Yajnavalkya

in the learned assembly at the court of King Janaka. There have been many great women seers like Vak, who gave the famous *Devi Suktam* of the Rig Veda. The Upanishads also speak of great wives like Maitreyi, who rejected worldly riches and preferred immortal wisdom. The Puranas describe great mothers like Queen Madalasa who imparted spiritual knowledge to her sons from their very birth. There have been great nuns and great women administrators. But think of any one who has been all these at the *same* time, and yet much more? The name of Holy Mother naturally comes to mind.

Sri Sarada Devi is like the space which contains both atoms and galaxies. That is why even some of the direct disciples of Sri Ramakrishna could not realize her greatness in the beginning. It was comprehended by Swami Vivekananda alone. He was the first one to point out to his brother disciples saying, 'You have not yet understood the wonderful significance of Mother's life. None of you. But gradually you will know.

'Without Shakti there is no regeneration for the world. Mother has been born to revive. . . once more will Gargis and Maitreyis be born into the world.'

To read Holy Mother's life and teachings is to know the Upanishads in practice. Let us conclude with Sri Ramakrishna's glowing eulogy,

'Look, this Sarada is Saraswati herself. She has come down to the world to give knowledge. . . She is no ordinary woman.' ☐

References

1. *CW*, 2:1
2. *Sri Srarada Devi, the Great Wonder*, Advaita Ashrama, Kolkata, Pp. 484-5
3. *CW*, 5.53
4. *Days in an Indian Monastery*, p.228
5. *Isha Upanishad*, 1
6. *CW*, 3: 193
7. Arnold Toynbee, *Vedanta Kesari*, 2004, p. 451
8. *Mundaka Upanishad*, verse 3
9. cf. *The Life of Swami Vivekananda By His Eastern and Western Disciples*, 1: 388
10. *Days in an Indian Monastery*, p. 215
11. *Sri Srarada Devi, the Great Wonder*, p. 124
12. *Chandogya Upanishad*, VII, xxxiii - xxiv
13. cf. *Teachings of Sri Sarada Devi The Holy Mother*, p. 165-166
14. *Sri Srarada Devi, the Great Wonder*, p. 187
15. *Ibid*, p. 449

Chapter 8

Swami Vivekananda's Love of Upanishads

SWAMI GAUTAMANANDA

Swamiji and Upanishads

Swami Vivekananda was an ardent lover of Upanishads. He said that he quoted nothing but the Upanishads in his message. He loved the Upanishads because they contain the essence of Vedas (*vedanta*, or the quintessence of Vedas). The Upanishads are the repository of the direct experiences of innumerable *rishis* about the eternal truth about God, creation, soul, the nature of soul's bondage and the way to its freedom.

Upanishads declare that the goal of human life is neither happiness of the senses nor mind nor seeking money, comforts, name or fame but Absolute Freedom. This Freedom makes one fearless which is the direct outcome of experiencing our own spiritual Self, the Atman, as infinite Life, infinite Knowledge and infinite Bliss (*sat-chit-ananda*).

In reality, everyone of us is eternal. We are ever-free souls, the atman. Since we are ignorant of this central truth of our being, we suffer. Man should strive to experience spiritual truth that he is the eternal and free Atman, the source of infinite bliss, infinite love, infinite knowledge, power and fearlessness.

Swami Vivekananda's teachings to the humanity as a whole centre round this 'Freeing the soul from its fetters of worldliness and bondage born of ignorance.' He placed before everyone *atmano mokshartham jagat hitaya cha*, ('For Self-realization and to live for the welfare of others') as the ideal of life. In order to attain Self-realisation, one should practise renunciation and service which ultimately lead one to self-fulfilment. Through renunciation and service alone can one make the society grow nobler and better.

Therefore Swamiji wanted everyone, specially the youth, to read Upanishads. Swamiji's *Complete Works* record the following conversation with his beloved disciple Sarat Chandra Chakravarty:

In the evening Swamiji called the disciple and asked him, 'Have you got the Katha Upanishad by heart?'

Disciple: 'No, sir, I have only read it with Shankara's commentary.'

Swamiji: 'Among the Upanishads, one finds no other book so beautiful as this. I wish you would all get it by heart. What will it do only to read it? Rather try to bring into your life the faith, the courage, the discrimination, and the renunciation of Nachiketa.'[1]

Swami Vivekananda's love for the Upanishads was born of his innate love for direct knowledge of everything—both secular and spiritual. As a young man, fired with intense desire to know Truth, he went to Sri Ramakrishna. He wanted direct experience of God, and in his very first meeting with Sri Ramakrishna, he asked Sri Ramakrishna, 'Have you seen God?' This incident reminds us of the Upanishads where it is said, 'This Atman is to be directly experienced (*drashtavyaha*) through hearing from the enlightened Guru and then through contemplation and meditation on the same.'[2]

Sri Ramakrishna's reply was exactly like that of an Upanishadic Rishi. He said 'Yes, I have seen God. Others also can see Him, if they earnestly desire to. He who wants him, gets him.' On hearing this, the young Swami Vivekananda at once observed that by saying that 'I have seen, others also can verify it, and the way to do is to intensely long for Him,' Sri Ramakrishna had made religion into a *science*. This is what a scientist would say: 'I have done it, you also can do it and this is the method.' And this is what Sri Ramakrishna too said.

Swami Vivekananda declared:

'The Upanishads are the great mine of strength. Therein lies strength enough to invigorate the whole world; the whole world can be vivified, made strong, energised through them.'[3]

Let us now try to understand why Swami Vivekananda loved Upanishads so much and what makes them so universally relevant and appealing.

Divinity of Man

The first reason why Swamiji admired the Upanishads so much is because the Upanishads teach divinity of man, (*Tatvamasi*, 'You are That Brahman') and the solidarity of all creation in Brahman ('*Sarvam khalu idam brahma*, 'All this creation is Brahman'). Swamiji explains how this knowledge helps one in practical terms. This knowledge confers Absolute Fearlessness, Freedom and Joy. As it makes one realise the unity of the individual with all creation, one loses all fear and hence develops unqualified love towards all. In short, it makes every man or woman a living god—one who loves all and is loved by all.

Paraphrasing what the Upanishads taught, Swamiji said:

'Ye are the Children of God, the sharers of immortal bliss, holy and perfect beings. Ye divinities on earth—sinners? It is a sin to call a man so; it is a standing libel on human nature. Come up, O lions, and shake off the delusion that you are sheep; you are souls immortal, spirits free, blest and eternal; ye are not matter, ye are not bodies; matter is your servant, not you the servant of matter.'[4]

That is why Swami Vivekananda declared Upanishads as a mine of strength—for they preach strength by arousing the inherent divinity. He always stressed the Upanishads' declaration of man as one with God Himself. This idea, that it is 'The one' that appears as 'many' which makes this world a playground where the Lord plays like a child and we are His playmates, however terrible, hideous and dangerous it may appear. Swami Vivekananda saw in the teachings of the Upanishads *manliness*. The Upanishads taught that:

'You make your own destiny. . . "What you have done you can also undo."'[5]

Religion is Realisation

When Swami Vivekananda lectured in the United States and Europe, people were astonished to hear that God can be seen, that soul can be seen. He emphasised the fact that religion was a matter of experience. Religion was realization, not merely believing in dogmas. When he spoke (in California in 1900) that 'It is no good simply to pray to Jesus, but you should yourselves become Jesus,' he was actually speaking the language of the message of Upanishads which says: 'It is good to know Brahman even in this very life.' (*Iha chedavedidatha satyamasti*).[6]

In the Western concept of religion, the 'dogmas' of theologians are the bugbear of the scientists. Reasoning of the scientists is a terror for the theologians. Thus, scientists and religionists have been in constant friction and fight. Swami Vivekananda placed before them the message of Upanishads as 'Realize the Truth directly for yourself; why depend only on reason or belief?' The Upanishads say, 'Atman cannot be realized by reasoning, reading or hearing' (*nayamatma pravachanena labhyo na medhaya na bahuna shrutena*).[7] They declared that 'This atman is really Brahman (*ayam atma brahma*). Therefore the search for God starts with the search of one's own 'soul'. No one can deny the existence of one's own self, the 'I' behind one's ego. By gradually developing purity, dispassion, concentration, this small individual 'I' will itself be experienced as the Infinite 'I' or GOD. That is why Swami Vivekananda said, 'The old religions said he is an atheist who did not believe in God, but the new religion says that he is an atheist who does not believe in himself.'[8] This 'self' refers to our inherent 'Self', the Divine Core of our being.

This Self (the pure 'I') is beyond gender because it is behind and beyond the body-mind complex. Hence, the teachings of Upanishads are addressed to the souls of all men or women of all castes and races and each can practice their teachings in order to realize the highest truth.

Universality of Upanishads

Upanishads declare that God, soul, heaven, immortality, eternal moral laws, and so on are all true because one can 'experience' these through a purified, concentrated mind. This is called the 'Yoga of Atman'. As is said: 'One realizes this Atman through the Yoga of Atman (*adhyatma-yogaadhigamena devam matwa*). In other words, one can realise the atman through following a certain method. Everyone is eligible for it provided he is willing to undergo all the discipline involved in attaining it. Hence the Upanishads are relevant to all—Hindus, Muslims, Christians, and all others. In this, there is no bar of gender or caste either. Indeed the Upanishads can be called a Universal Book of Eternal Religion.

He called the religion of Upanishads as a Universal Religion of the future humanity for the future humanity will be full of knowledge, *both* scientific and spiritual. Upanishads have no fear of any truth whether of external world (science) or of internal world (spirituality).

Swami Vivekananda wanted this universality of the Upanishads to be taught to all so that all people of the earth can come together through a spiritual fraternity. Even as the scientific principles discovered by a person of any nationality are accepted and put into application by the people of any other country, so also the Truth of Divinity as the Core of every human being can be applied by any person of any country and religion. Swami Vivekananda loved Upanishads for this universality and all-inclusiveness.

Upanishads as the Remover of Superstitions

When we add manure for nourishing plants, this often results in lot of wild weeds also sprouting up! So is the case with religion. Soon after a few centuries of the departure of the founding prophet of a religion, many charlatans who fake the original message of their prophet come to the scene. They give false promises and indulge in miracle-mongering. They form secret societies and give esoteric teachings. All these weaken the people unlike the true religion, which always makes one strong, free and fearless.

If one looks at the teachings of the Upanishad in this context, one finds them so free from all such superstitious elements. They are a mine of life giving, transparent and rational ideas. They kill all superstitions even before they come anywhere near them. It is like sunrays that dispel all darkness and give all nourishment and energy to everything on earth. Swami Vivekananda loved Upanishads for this aspect. He told his brother disciple, Swami Premananda, on the last day of his life (4 July 1904) in Belur Math, that a Vedic school where all the Vedas would be taught should be started. Swami Premananda asked, 'Why Vedas?' 'It will kill all superstitions,' replied Swamiji.[9]

Self-experience as the Source of Strength

Since the Upanishads deal with spiritual truths with the authority of *'sva-anubhava'*, or direct (self) experience, they are a terror to all the weakening, mystery-mongering superstitions which thrive on ignorance and human failings. We see that in the science there are no serious disputations because it is based on verifiable truths. Similarly Swamiji held the Upanishad in high esteem as they are based on experiential or verifiable truth.

In the Brihadaranyaka Upanishad, it is mentioned how sage Yajnavalkya encountered a number of people who disputed his views about spiritual truths. But as Yajnavalkya had realised what he was preaching, he could bring all of them round without much difficulty. Says Swamiji:

Strength, O man, strength, say the Upanishads, stand up and be strong. Ay, it is the only literature in the world where you find the word "Abhih", "fearless", used again and again; in no other scripture in the world is this adjective applied either to God or to man. *Abhih*, fearless![10]

Swami Vivekananda wanted all religions to adopt this method of self-experience in preference to holding on to some dogmas or mythologies and fighting over them. Swamiji thought that these Upanishads would pave the way for healthy inter-religious dialogues and evolution of a universal morality and religion in the near future.

Eternal Principles amidst Change

Swami Vivekananda admired Upanishads for they contain the eternal principles of spiritual life of all religions of the world. These principles remain unchanged despite all social or economic changes. The nature of God and soul remains *unchanged* amidst changing times but, the external details like social customs, rituals, forms, dress, food or drink do change. Swamiji says that the latter should be allowed to change with times but always keeping the 'eternal principles' intact. He believed that these changes would be effected by men and women of Self-realization who come at the right time. They come, as if with a badge of authority, and the society also accepts them gladly.

Hence, Swami Vivekananda felt the need of newer and newer prophets, giving fresh interpretation to eternal principles for the changing scenario. Upanishads teach these eternal principles and this has endeared them to Swami Vivekananda.

Real social reformation will come when this Atman is made to manifest in everyone.[11] That is done when selfishness is given up through renunciation and loving service. In carrying out reforms, Swamiji advised:

'Carry the light and hope of Vedanta to every door and rouse up the divinity that is hidden within every soul. In this is centred the salvation of humanity here and hereafter.'[12]

Swamiji saw Upanishads as the unifier of all the philosophies—dualism, qualified non-dualism and non-dualism. He said, 'The belief in Atman, common to all sects, which is the repository of all power, purity and perfection, is your birthright, it is inside you always.'[13] This doctrine of Upanishad he called as 'The science of the soul.'[14]

Hence, Schopenhauer, the great German philosopher of 19th century remarked after reading a rough translation of Upanishads,

'In the whole world there is no study so beneficial and so elevating as that of the Upanishads. It has been the solace of my life, it will be the solace of my death.'

Renunciation or Materialism?

Today many people believe that it is consumerism which is 'good' for human progress. But the Upanishads point out that though it is good to have the least number of worldly things, the real joy in life comes from inculcating control over ourselves. Referring to this, says Swamiji, 'The world-weariness has come upon the West, whereas the followers of renunciation and self-control in India are fresh and young.' In the Upanishads, there is a clear demarcation of the changing rituals and rules from the eternal principles of religion. Hence, Vedanta is beyond 'changes.' And consequently it is Eternal.

Upanishads have made India a land of tolerance, acceptance, peace and spirituality because of their glorious teachings of unity in diversity (*ekam sat vipra bahudha vadanti*, 'Truth is one, sages call it by many names'). How immensely relevant and great this teaching is has been highlighted by the events of 9/11 and after. Vedanta gives to every individual freedom in religion through its principle of *Ishta Devata* (chosen form of God), and in social matters, it offers a rich mix of *culture* or personal refinement—a sure antidote to heartless competition we are caught in, instead of the present caste based on money.

Here is the underlying oneness of all religions, their Gods and angels, sages and seers, prophets and divine incarnations. They are all *one* God, appearing as many, according to time, place, customs and circumstances. It is like one actor in different dresses coming in many roles in a drama on stage.

Steadfastly holding on to any one real prophet, one can reach the highest divine perfection being called variously as Brahman, God or Allah.

Swami Vivekananda pointed to the urgent need of a rational religion for today's world. He declared that Upanishads fulfilled this need. He prophesied that if the West did not orient its materialistic society to these spiritual precepts, it would crumble into pieces before long.

He often repeated *Maharnarayana Upanishad's* words, 'neither through work nor through progeny but through renunciation alone is immortality to be reached (*na karmana na prajaya dhanena tyagenaike amritatva manashuh*).[15] The infinite God cannot be got through clinging to finite sense-pleasures of the world. Hence, renunciation is taught in Upanishads.

Swami Vivekananda notes that Upanishads give us the rational sanction for universal ethics—'Do unto others which you would like others do unto you.' This is based on oneness underlying all creations. Let us remember that 'You hurt another at the risk of hurting yourself because you are the other also'.[16]

This is the message of strength given by the Upanishads. The world needs strength and fearlessness and this comes from realising our oneness with each other in and through God.

Conclusion

Though there is much progress in science and technology today, people in general are not happy both in their social and individual life. Wealth has accumulated but men are decaying. The values like simple living and high thinking, inter-personal love, cooperation, appreciation, service, sacrifice for poor, needy, and weaker sections of society, respect for pure knowledge, and interest in learning spiritual truths are fast vanishing.

The result is the proliferating restlessness, threat of war and violence, terrorism and suicide squads.

Correspondingly there is increase in alcoholism, drug addiction, divorces, suicides, violence against women and children and reckless bloodshed in the name of religion. What is the way out?

Swami Vivekananda sounded the 'death-knell' of all fanaticism and bigotry on Sep 11, 1897 at Chicago Parliament of Religions. The world did not listen to him and the result is the devastation of 9/11 of 2001 at New York!

May we listen to Swami Vivekananda's fervent call to follow the Upanishads: *uttishtata jagrata, praapya varan nibodhatha* (Arise, awake, go to the teacher and be enlightened).[17] Swami Vivekananda made it more direct and dynamic as follows: 'Arise, Awake and stop not till the goal is reached.'

Assures Swami Vivekananda,

'Teach yourselves, teach every one his real nature. Power will come, glory will come, goodness will come, purity will come and all that is excellent will come when this sleeping soul is roused to self-conscious activity.'[18] □

References

1. CW, 6: 456
2. *Brihadaranyaka Upanishad*
3. CW, 3: 238
4. CW, 1: 11
5. CW, 1: 320
6. *Kena Upanishad*, II. 5
7. *Mundaka Upanishad*, III. ii. 3
8. CW, 2: 301
9. *Life of Swami Vivekananda*, 2: 654
10. CW, 3: 237
11. cf. CW, 3: 196

12. cf. CW, 3: 199
13. cf. CW, 3: 159
14. CW, 3: 160
15. CW, 4: 183

16. cf. CW, 3: 189
17. *Kathopanishad,*
18. CW, 3: 193

Chapter 9

Frequently Asked Questions About Upanishads

SWAMI HARSHANANDA

QUESTION: What does the term 'Upaniṣad' mean?

ANSWER: The word 'Upaniṣad' is derived from the verbal root *sad* which has several meanings: loosening, movement and annihilation. Putting all these three senses together, the word 'Upaniṣad' refers to that divine knowledge or wisdom which loosens the bonds of saṁsāra (transmigratory existence) of a being, annihilates his ajñāna or ignorance of his real nature and leads him to Brahman or God, the Absolute. The book or the scriptural work that teaches this wisdom is also called 'Upaniṣad'.

The word may also mean 'sitting devotedly near'. Hence it represents the 'secret teaching, of spiritual wisdom' imparted in private to worthy pupils, but zealously guarded from the unworthy ones.

QUESTION: How old are the Upaniṣads?

The orthodox view is that the Upaniṣads are Revealed Word. They are revealed by God himself at the commencement of each cycle of creation to the worthy few. Hence they are eternal. However, treating them as books of spiritual wisdom, can we assign any date or period, in relation to human history as known till now? Attempts in this direction have rather been frustrating, thanks to that peculiar trait of the Hindu mind which accords much greater importance to the principle than to the person or the period.

The Upaniṣads have been an integral part of the Vedas. Hence, a date assigned to them can as well hold good for the Upaniṣads also. The date of the *Ṛgveda* has varied from 4500 B.C. (B.G. Tilak) and 2400 B.C. (Hang) to 1200 B.C. (Max Muller). Modern European scholars assign the period 700 B.C. – 600 B.C. to the Upaniṣads assuming a gradual evolution to the philosophical ideas from the period of the Vedic hymns to that of the Āraṇyakas and the Upaniṣads. B.G. Tilak, on the basis of an astronomical data provided in the *Maitrāyaṇīya Upaniṣad*, has however, assigned 1900 B.C. as the date of the Upaniṣad. Hence, according to him and the scholars that concur with him, the Upaniṣads belong to the period 2500 B.C. – 2000 B.C.

QUESTION: *Please specify the number of Upaniṣads.*

ANSWER: From among the extant Upaniṣads, only ten to fifteen are considered to be the older ones. They are the basic sources of ancient Hindu philosophy.

The number of works that go by the name 'Upaniṣad' and available in print today exceeds 200. The *Muktikopaniṣad* gives a list of 108 Upaniṣads. Śaṅkara (A.D. 788-820), the earliest commentator, has chosen only ten Upaniṣads to expound. He refers to a few more in his commentary on the *Brahmasūtras*. Rāmānuja (A.D. 1017-1137) has chosen, in addition, two more.

Considering the ones chosen by them as more ancient and authoritative we can now list them (in the alphabetical order) as follows:

Aitareya Upaniṣad
Bṛhadāraṇyaka Upaniṣad
Chāndogya Upaniṣad
Īśāvāsya Upaniṣad
Jābāla Upaniṣad
Kaivalya Upaniṣad
Kaṭha Upaniṣad
Kauṣītaki Upaniṣad
Kena Upaniṣad
Māṇḍūkya Upaniṣad
Mahānārāyaṇa Upaniṣad
Muṇḍaka Upaniṣad
Praśna Upaniṣad
Śvetāśvatara Upaniṣad
Taittirīya Upaniṣad
Vajrasūcikā Upaniṣad

Most of the Upaniṣads, outside the list given above, belong to a much later period in our history and were written to propagate specific cults and sects. The nomenclature 'Upaniṣad' was conveniently added to them to gain respectability, acceptance and authority in the orthodox circles or among the followers. However, it must be conceded that these Upaniṣads also, though sectarian in character, have contributed quite a lot to the propagation of popular religion and ethics as also to the maintenance of the Vedāntic spirit among the people.

These minor Upaniṣads are sometimes grouped as follows:

a) Vedānta Upaniṣads
b) Śaiva Upaniṣads
c) Śākta Upaniṣads
d) Vaiṣṇava Upaniṣads
e) Yoga Upaniṣads
f) Sannyāsa Upaniṣads

The Vedānta Upaniṣads follow the beaten track of the major Upaniṣads as far as the general principles are concerned. The Śaiva, the Śākta and the Vaiṣṇava Upaniṣads deal with the respective cults of Śiva, Devī and Viṣṇu. The Yoga Upaniṣads supply a lot of information about Haṭhayoga and Rājayoga based on the *Yogasūtras* of Patañjali and other works. The Sannyāsa Upaniṣads deal exclusively with monasticism, its ideals and practices.

QUESTION: Considering their vast diversity, do all these Upaniṣads teach a single system of philosophy? Or, do they contain several, mutually conflicting, systems?

ANSWER: The orthodox Hindu tradition has always considered the entire body of the Upaniṣadic literature as one unit ('Śruti') and hence teaching one philosophy. Though this philosophy may contain several aspects, they always form a homogeneous unit. Hindu religious tradition has always accorded the Upaniṣads the status of the highest authority.

A look at the different and divergent teachings of these Upaniṣads does not easily convince us about the soundness of the orthodox standpoint. The traditional commentators have, however, solved this problem by sticking to one view as *the* teaching of the Upaniṣads and explaining (explaining away?) the others in a way that suits their interpretation.

Could it be that, over the centuries, many vital links have been lost and what we now have, are only fragments of the original works leading to this dichotomy of views? Though this is a plausible explanation, there is no clinching evidence to prove it.

Or, can we say that the various sages that we come across in the Upaniṣads—like Gautama Āruṇi, Yājñavalkya, Śvetaketu or Raikva—were great thinkers and mystics in their own right, who have given independent views, based on their own logic and experience? The Truth, Brahman (the Infinite, the Absolute), is too great to be known exhaustively by anyone. One can get only a glimpse of the same, like the six blind men touching the same elephant. Hence, could it not be that the views of these sages, though apparently different, reflect the several facets of the same Brahman?

QUESTION: *Who is a ṛṣi?*

ANSWER: Derived from the verbal root *'ṛṣ jñāne'*, the word *'ṛṣi'* means any person possessing knowledge and expertise in any field. Thus Caraka and Susruta of Āyurveda (Health Sciences), Bharata of Nāṭyasāstra (Dramaturgy, including music and dancing) or Kauṭilya of Arthasāstra (Political Science including Economics) are all ṛṣis. However, the word is commonly used to indicate persons of spiritual eminence.

QUESTION: *How many ṛṣis Upaniṣads mention?*

ANSWER: We come across a good number of ṛṣis or sages in the Upaniṣads. Some like Yājñavalkya are extraordinarily great geniuses. Others like Gautama Āruṇi are excellent teachers. A few others like Śvetaketu are hard task-masters. Sacrifices conducted by rich and powerful—but noble—kings provided opportunities to these sages not only to exhibit their skills but also earn wealth and fame.

A selected list of sages that occur in the major Upaniṣads may now be given just for the sake of information:

Aṅgiras, Bhṛgu, Gārgī, Ghora Āṅgirasa, Hāridrumata, Mahidāsa Aitareya, Nārada, Pippalāda, Raikva, Sanatkumāra, Śāṇḍilya, Satyakāma Jābāla, Uddālaka Āruṇi, Vāmadeva and Varuṇa.

Yama, the god or death, Prajāpati, the creator, great kings like Janaka, Ajatāstru and Pravāhaṇa Jaivali also appear in the role of teachers. One thing that strikes us is that these teachers were revered for their knowledge and excellence, irrespective of their birth, caste or gender.

QUESTION: *How have the Upaniṣads influenced Hinduism?*

ANSWER: If there is one mass of scriptures that has inspired and sustained the Hindus over the millennia, it is the Upaniṣads. By advocating the ultimate triumph of the spirit over matter, of man over nature, the Upaniṣads have created, strengthened and preserved a great tradition of spirituality. This they have done, not only by a fearless spirit of inquiry to its logical conclusions, but also by intuitive mystical experiences beyond the ken of the intellect, these experiences almost always converging to a unitive principle.

No school of thought, no religious movement, of the subsequent periods in the history of India has remained untouched by their influence, if not pervaded by them. In fact, many of these schools and movements could gain respectability or acceptance only because they tread the path lighted up by the Upaniṣads.

Scholars of Indian thought have discovered the influence of the Upaniṣads on the religio-cultural life of other nations far beyond the boundaries of India, whether it is Japan, China and Korea in the East or Central Asia in the West.

QUESTION: *What do the Upaniṣads contain?*

ANSWER: The Upaniṣads contain the quintessence of Vedic religion and philosophy. The Ṣaḍḍarśanas or the six systems of Indian Philosophy derive their strength and inspiration from them. The Vedānta systems are entirely an outcome of their study. The idea of mokṣa as the primary goal of life, which has permeated the Indian religions and culture of the succeeding centuries, owes its origin entirely to the Upaniṣads. And, they are the basis of the *prasthānatraya* (the three foundational scriptures), the other two being the *Bhagavadgītā* and the *Brahmasūtras*.

The depth as well as the catholicity of their thought has attracted the attention of the savants of other religions and societies also, resulting in their being translated into other languages too.

QUESTION: *What is the basic teaching of the Upaniṣads?*

ANSWER: The Upaniṣads say that the basic cause of the universe, the cause of all causes, is called as 'Brahman'. Ātman, Sat, Akāśa and Bhūmā are the other appellations used for this Brahman. The world rises out of him, is supported by him and gets dissolved back into him. He is omniscient, omnipotent and omnipresent. He is greater than the greatest, smaller than the smallest and is also the inmost Self of all. He is immanent in this world even as salt is, in saline water. He is beyond all wants and limitations. He is the lord as well as the substratum of the whole creation. He sees, hears and knows although none can see or hear or know him. He is the very personification of all the great virtues to their perfection. It is he who responds to the prayers of his votaries and grants them whatever they seek. He is the ultimate goal of all.

QUESTION: *What is atman?*

ANSWER: The atman is the core of all living being. He is neither born nor does he die with the birth and the death of the body. He is unborn and eternal. He is different from the body, the senses, the vital airs, the mind and the ego-sense and is ever free. All of them are enlivened by Him, made to work by Him, for Him. The defects and the infirmities in them, or even their loss, can never affect Him.

QUESTION: *Why are we born?*

ANSWER: Though ever-free as atman, it is also a fact of experience that we are born and we die. This atman has been, as it were, encased and bound in this corporeal frame and has lost much of his freedom. In this state, he is called as 'jīvātman' or simply as the 'jīva'. The answer to the question as to why and how he has come to such a pass is 'karma,' the inexorable consequence of his past actions. For the question, how and when the very first karma started this chain of bondage; there is no answer, since the Upaniṣads accept creation as an eternal process, without beginning or end.

QUESTION: *What is saṁsāra or relative existence?*

ANSWER: Atman's involvement in the cycle of birth and death, and consequent suffering, has been called 'saṁsāra.' Mokṣa or liberation from this bondage of saṁsāra has been presented before him as the goal of his life. And, this can be achieved by jñāna, or knowledge and, bhakti or devotion, which includes upāsanā or meditation. Karma or action as prescribed in the scriptures is an aid to this mokṣa.

QUESTION: *How to be free from saṁsāra?*

ANSWER: An aspirant seeking spiritual freedom should first cultivate certain moral and ethical virtues as the first step. Through discrimination he should understand that the Vedic rituals can never lead him to the eternal Truth and hence renounce them. He must be ever ready to reject the *preyas* (the pleasant) and choose the *śreyas* (the good). By eschewing evil conduct and by practicing self-control, he should turn back his mind from outside, into himself, the region of the heart, the seat of the atman, and meditate on it. He should show compassion to all the living beings. He should try to give them what they need and should never be greedy. He must be vigilant forever and should always speak the truth and act according to dharma or righteousness, by following the scriptural injunctions. Study of the Upaniṣads, performing austerities and observing brahmacarya or celibacy are also invaluable aids in his inner struggle.

QUESTION: *How to begin this inner journey?*

ANSWER: He should approach a competent guru or spiritual teacher in all humility and learn the truth about the atman from him, through proper questioning and sevā or service to him. The Upaniṣads make it incumbent on the guru to teach spiritual wisdom to a worthy disciple, after testing him if necessary.

The disciple should then practise manana (reflection) and nididhyāsana (meditation) on the atman which will result in anubhūti or realization.

QUESTION: *What is the nature of the spiritual experience that an aspirant gets when he realizes the atman?*

ANSWER: He sees all beings in himself and himself in all. Hence he feels neither special attraction nor repulsion for others. Behind every thought of his, he is able to feel the power of the atman, the pure consciousness. He clearly perceives that all the bonds of his heart which had him tied down to this mundane existence, have broken down. He experiences great joy and bliss within himself. When he directs his attention outside, there too he sees the same spirit, the atman or the Brahman. Spiritual experience, thus, leads to same-sightedness and resultant love for all.

QUESTION: *In practical terms, what kind of happiness does an aspirant experience when he realizes atman?*

ANSWER: The bliss he experiences is incomparably superior to any other happiness one can get in this world. And he will never have any type of regret for anything in life. He may even roam about the world in a joyous state, declaring his experiences for the benefit of others.

QUESTION: *When such a one, the jīvanmukta (one who is liberated even while living here in this body), gives up his body, what happens to him?*

ANSWER: According to one view, his physical body and the subtle body disintegrate at death and get absorbed into the five elements. And, he gets merged in Brahman, like a river entering into the ocean. Losing his separate identity, he attains complete and perfect unity with Brahman.

However, a large body of the Upaniṣadic lore propounds the theory of the liberated soul travelling by the Arcirādimārga or the Bright Path (also called Devayāna and Uttarāyaṇa) to the Brahmaloka (also known as Satyaloka) and reside there permanently in infinite peace and bliss. The various stations on the path are fire, day, bright fortnight, the six months of the northern solstice, the year, the sun, the moon and the lightning. All these actually represent the guardian deities of these stations. From the last station, the vidyut or lightning, an 'amānava puruṣa,' a non-human (divine) being, leads the liberated soul to the Brahmaloka.

Anyone reaching Brahmaloka will not return to mundane existence.

QUESTION: *What kind of society existed during the time of Upaniṣads?*

ANSWER: Gleaning through the various Upaniṣads it is possible to have a fairly good idea of the type of society that existed during the period of the Upaniṣads.

The country extended up to Gāndhāra (Afghanistan) in the northwest, and included several kingdoms like Madra (Sailkot), Kuru (Delhi), Kekaya (Punjab), Pāñcāla (Bareilly, Kanauj in Uttar Pradesh), Kosala (Ayodhya in Uttar Pradesh), Videha (Tirhut in Bihar), Kauśāmbi (Kosam, in Uttar Pradesh) and Kāśī. The kings who ruled over these countries were all kṣatriyas who were experts in warfare and administration, as also in the Vedic lore. In fact, they were the traditional custodians of some types of esoteric sciences. They not only sheltered learned brāhmaṇas and sages but also strove to propagate the Vedic dharma. They were ruthless in enforcing the highest standards of satya (truth) and dharma (righteousness). The varṇa system was very much in vogue. As for the āśrama system, brahmacarya, gārhasthya and vānaprastha were more common though there is enough reason to believe that sannyāsa was also being practiced. Great stress was laid on the purity and integrity of personal life, irrespective of a person's station in life.

QUESTION: *Some more details about the Vedic society?*

ANSWER: Apart from religion, ethics and philosophy, a number of secular sciences like grammar, music, dance, archery, astrology, exorcising the evil spirits, preparing of perfumes, toxicology and so on, were also well-known.

Vedic sacrifices were very common. If they provided an occasion for the kings to earn merit and show their generosity, it was also an opportunity to the scholars to display their knowledge and earn name and fame, as also some wealth.

On the whole, people seemed to be contented with whatever they could earn by right means. They believed that their sorrows and misfortunes were caused by their own karma in their previous lives and hence did not hold others responsible for the same.

QUESTION: *It is said that the Upaniṣads are full of stories. Please tell us something about them.*

ANSWER: Strangely enough, the Upaniṣads, though teaching abstruse philosophy, also give us some interesting stories.

The *Kena* describes how the gods in heaven, under the leadership of Indra, were taught a lesson by Brahman in the guise of a yakṣa or demigod (3.1 to 11).

Major part of the *Kaṭha* is devoted to the story of Naciketas and Yama.

The *Chāndogya* contains the following stories: Dogs singing the udgītha (1.12); the king Jānaśruti learning

from the sage Raikva (4.1 to 3); the story of Satyakāma
Jābāla approaching Hāridrumata for knowledge (4.4 to
9); the story of Satyakāma and his disciple Upakosala
(4.10 to 15); Śvetaketu the proud boy, his humble father
Gautama and the king Pravāhaṇa Jaivali (5.3 to 10);
Sanatkumāra teaching Nārada (7.1 to 26); Indra and
Virocana approaching Prajāpati for the knowledge of
the atman (8.7 to 12).

QUESTION: How are the Upanishads relevant in
today's context? How to practise thier teaching in our
day-to-day life?

ANSWER: The greatest problem of the modern man
is lack of inner peace and constant conflict with the
outside world. By stressing meditation on the inner
incorporeal self (called Ātman or God) and harmonious
relationship with others—in whom too the same God
dwells—in the outside world, the Upaniṣads are very
relevant even today. This solution which has worked
for five millennia (or more)—as indicated by the men
who lived such a life—can work even today if taken
seriously and implemented sincerely.

*An earnest study of the Upaniṣads, without preconceived
notions and prejudices, is bound to inspire one to aspire for
the life of the spirit. Swami Vivekananda said that Upaniṣads
are a mine of strength, and anyone who reads them will derive
strength and succour. Unlike earlier times, now they are
available to all.* ☐

Chapter 10

Direct Disciples of
Sri Ramakrishna:
the Living Upanishads

SUDESH

Introduction

Upanishads! An ocean of precious gems of our ancient spiritual Wisdom, profound and inexhaustible! The aim of all Upanishads is to impart the Knowledge of Self, which when realized, leads man from death to immortality. Seeing the One Self in all, the aspirant can neither hate nor be attached to anyone in finite human relationship. He loves all—the saint and the sinner, the virtuous and the wicked with same impartial love. If one could look at Sri Ramakrishna from this perspective, Sri Ramakrishna was like a huge tree with its root fixed in transcendental heights of *nirvikalpa samadhi*. His young pure-souled devotees, the direct disciples, were the sweet and ripe fruits of this miraculous tree— sweetened through pure bhakti and ripened into the Knowledge of Self. This divine tree has been the shelter of the numerous men and women seeking solace, succour and peace in life.

Once when someone said that he will teach Upanishads to the novices, Swami Premananda, a direct disciple of Sri Ramakrishna, said,

'What other Upanishads would you teach them when there is the living Upanishad? The life of the Master is the living, flaming Upanishad. None could have understood the meaning of the Radha-Krishna cult if Sri Chaitanya had not been born and demonstrated it in his life. Even so, the Master is the living demonstration of the truths of the Upanishads. The Upanishads have been current for many centuries and people also have been reading them. And yet they bow down to our illiterate Master and accept his words as gospel truths. He never read the Upanishads or any other book. Yet how is it that he could explain those subtle and complex truths in so simple and straight a manner? If you want to read the Vedas, you have to commit the grammar to memory and read various commentaries, in which every commentator has sought to explain the texts in his own way. Innumerable scholars have been arguing over the texts without coming to any conclusion. Our Master, however, has in very simple language explained all those truths, and his words are extant. When you have such a living fountain before you, why dig a well for water?'[1]

Cast in the same mould as their Guru, all the direct disciples of Sri Ramakrishna were also living embodiments of the Upanishads. They were men of intense renunciation, self-control and filled with love and compassion. In their early twenties, when the grip of maya is strongest, drive to enjoy sense pleasures intense, ambition to improve worldly prospects high, they renounced their hearths and homes and went out in quest of the Divine. Almost starving and barely having a piece of cloth each, they plunged head-long in practising austerities, meditation, reading scriptures, and singing devotional songs. Embracing monasticism, they set up a monastery in a dilapidated house (because of its low rent) at Baranagore, reputed to be haunted by ghosts and infested with snakes. In their later lives they brought succour to the afflicted and illuminated the hearts of many.

The natural inclination of most mystics is to remain in uninterrupted communion with Self, hidden from the world. Yet their lives can tell more about the joy of communion with Self, than all the discourses we may hear or any number of scriptures we may read. One day a monk told Shivananda, 'I want to study the Upanishads with you.' Shivananda replied:

'Can you study our lives? Our lives are verily Upanishads. Here you will find the quintessence of the scriptures.'[2]

Let us consider a few instances from the lives and teachings of some of the direct disciples, which demonstrate how they were ingrained into this Upanishadic ideal of oneness and love.

Earnestness Alone Matters

Says Mundakopanishad,

'This Atman cannot be attained by the study of scriptures or by intelligence or by much hearing of sacred books. It is attained by him who earnestly seeks it. To him the Atman reveals its true form.[3]

The life of Swami Adbhutananda, Latu Maharaj, is a demonstration of this verse to the scholars and pundits who take pride in their scriptural knowledge without imbibing their spirit in their lives. Latu Maharaj, an unlettered, unsophisticated village boy through intense yearning of the soul and the divine touch of his Guru, Sri Ramakrishna, attained the highest state of illumination. Guileless and simple, his mind was uncluttered by intellectualism and not trained to doubt. He absorbed the teachings of his Guru unquestioningly and in *toto*. In later life highest wisdom of Vedas and Vedanta poured from his lips. Swami Turiyananda said,

> 'Many of us had to go through the muddy waters of intellectual knowledge before we attained God, but Latu jumped over that like Hanuman. . . . His life teaches us how to live in God without touching the dirt of the world.'[4]

Swami Adbhutananda was the greatest miracle of Sri Ramakrishna. Without ever studying Vedanta philosophy, he answered abstruse questions about Vedanta. One day Shashadhar Ganguly, a teacher from Malda, asked him, 'Can the Atman be an object of knowledge?'

Latu Maharaj: 'An object is something that cannot be known without the help of something else, but the Atman is self revealing.'

Shashadhar: 'Then why should we want to know the Atman?'

Latu Maharaj: 'Because the Atman is our real nature.'

Shashadhar: 'If the Atman is our real nature, then why are we not aware of it?'

Latu Maharaj: 'Man's real nature is covered by a dense cloud of ignorance. . . Dip your mind in the jar of Lord's name, and all the unclean stuff will be washed away. Then dip it in the jar of Lord's grace. You will see how beautifully your real nature will shine forth.'[5]

Though he had no book-learning, Latu Maharaj could instinctively see the inner significance of scriptures because of his spiritual realizations. Once a pundit was reading the Kathopanishad. He read the following verse:

'The Purusha of the size of a thumb, the inner soul, dwells always in the heart of beings. One should separate Him from the body with patience as the stalk from a grass.'

Latu Maharaj was overjoyed and exclaimed, 'Just the thing', as if he was giving out his own inner experience of life.[6]

Going Beyond All Sorrow

Says the Upanishad,

'Whoever knows the Supreme Brahman... he goes beyond sorrow and sin and attains immortality.'[7]

In January 1926 Swami Shivananda, a direct disciple and second President of the Ramakrishna Order, visited the Ramakrishna Mission Vidyapith, at Deoghar. There he caught a chill that developed into a bad cold accompanied by asthmatic spells.

One night it was so bad that he could not sleep. Next morning, he cheerfully greeted everyone as usual. He told them his experience:

'I suffered a great deal last night. I felt almost suffocated. . . Being at a loss what to do, I started meditating. . . my mind soon became absorbed within. I noticed then that there was no pain or suffering and the mind became quiet and placid. . . . . After remaining in that state awhile my mind came down to the external world.'

Curious, a monk asked: 'What is that Maharaj?' The Swami replied: 'That is the Atman.' Swami Shivananda's experience substantiates this verse of the Katha Upanishad:

'The Purusha, not larger than a thumb, the inner Self, always dwells in the hearts of men.'[8]

As to his own realization, Swami Shivananda once exclaimed: 'I am happy. I have realized the purnam (the Infinite) by the grace of the Master.' He then joyously chanted the peace mantram of the Brihadaranyaka Upanishad:

'All that is invisible is verily the Infinite. All that is visible is also the Infinite. The whole universe has come out of the Infinite, which is still the Infinite.'[9]

No Hatred, Only Love

In Isha Upanishad we read:

He who sees all beings in the very Self, and the Self in all beings, feels no hatred by virtue of that (realization).[10]

Here is an incident describing how Swami Shivananda, embodied this principle in practice. One morning, solemn and indrawn, Swami Shivananda asked his attendant to see if there was someone who wanted initiation. The attendant went downstairs and found that a woman was waiting, keen to get initiation. He was startled when he learnt that though born in a brahmin family, she had kept bad company and fallen into sinful ways. She implored him to be allowed to see Mahapurshji.

The attendant told the Swami that it was a lady who wanted to be initiated. But before he could say anything, the Swami was ready to shower his blessings upon her after she had bathed in the Ganges and visited the shrine. When she came for initiation he said, as if he knew everything about her: 'What is there to fear, my daughter? You will certainly be blessed, since you have taken refuge in Sri Ramakrishna, our Master and Saviour...'[11] After initiation, the woman appeared to be an altogether new woman.

Tara, an actress in Girish Ghosh's theatre described in her memoirs of Swami Brahmananda how one day, depressed and dejected in mind she went to Belur Math along with Binodini, another actress whom Sri Rama-krishna had blessed. She touched the holy feet of Swami Brahmananada in great hesitancy, afraid that she might offend him. It was past noon and lunch was over in the Math. But Maharaj immediately ordered fruit prasad, and arrangements were made to fry luchis for them. She said later,

Maharaj asked me, 'Why don't you come here often?' I replied, 'I was afraid to come to the Math.' Maharaj said with great earnestness, 'Fear? What fear can there be? Whenever you wish you come here. Daughter, the Lord does not care about the externals. He sees our inmost heart.'

I could not hold back my tears. My lifelong sorrow melted…and I realized: Here is my refuge. Here is someone to whom I am not a sinner, I am not an outcast.[12]

The above incidents show that the consciousness of men of realization becomes universal. Having realized that Atman is ever-pure and all-pervasive, that sin and virtue are things of mind and body, they become the channels of divine love and mercy. All hatred and repulsion comes to one who sees others as bad and different from oneself. But for one who sees only the absolutely pure Self in all, how can he despise or criticize anybody?

Once Sarat (later, Swami Saradananada, another direct disciple of Sri Ramakrishna and the first General Secretary of the Ramakrishna Math and Mission) discovered that one of his neighbour's maid-servant had been stricken with cholera and that her master, fearing contagion, had moved her up to the roof and left her to her fate. Sarat rushed to the dying woman and did what he could for her. When she died, he made all the necessary arrangements for her last rites.

Swami Saradananda's concern for others knew no limits. He offered his services without reserve. In 1893, he nursed Swami Abhedananda who was seriously ill from a severe infection in his feet. Abhedananda recuperated after three months under Swami Saradananda's care. Saradananda also took care of Yajneswar Bhattacharya, a householder devotee of the Master, who was dying of tuberculosis. When he went to Gangotri, while walking down a one-mile slope, Swami

Saradananda saw an old woman who was losing her balance because she did not have a walking stick; he gave his own stick to her risking his life.[13]

Swami Vivekananda says:

'All this universe is the reflection of the One Eternal Being, the Atman and as the reflection falls upon good or bad reflectors, so good and bad images are cast up. . . It is the same, the one Existence of the universe that is reflecting itself from the lowest worm to the highest being.'[14]

One finds an expression of this timeless vision of the Upanishads reflected in the lives of all direct disciples of Sri Ramakrishna.

Unshakable Under All Situations

Swami Turiyananda, a direct disciple, was a deep student of the Upanishads. His mind was bent towards the Advaita Vedanta, and he strove sincerely to live up to that ideal. The story goes that once when he was bathing in the Ganga, something looking like a crocodile popped up in the river, and a shout was raised around asking the bathers to run up. His first reaction was to leave the water and come to the bank for the safety of his life. At once the thought occurred to him: 'If I am one with Brahman, why should I fear? I am not a body. And if I am Spirit, what fear have I from anything in the whole world, much less from a crocodile?'

This idea so much stirred his mind that he did not leave the spot. Bystanders thought he was foolishly courting death. But they did not know that he was testing his faith.[15]

In Varanasi, a doctor operated on Swami Turiyananda. Referring to the finger that was operated, his attendant asked, 'Don't you feel any pain?' The Swami replied:

'Look, the mind is like a child; we must hold it tight. But like a youngster it will go on crying "Let me go! Let me Go!" Once in the midst of surgery I let my mind loose. Immediately I felt pain...so I had to catch hold of the mind once more.'... 'Do you know how it is? In the Bhagavad Gita we read: "Where in established in the bliss of his inmost being he is not shaken even by the heaviest sorrow."(6.22) This verse is explained by Shankara, "A man of realization is not shaken even by the pain caused by the application of a sharp weapon."'

The doctors who came in contact with Swami Turiyananda became his devotees.[16]

Swami Vivekananda returned to Belur on 9 December 1900, after his second visit to the West. He was not well. Owing partly to this and partly to the fact that he wanted to see the work progress as quickly as possible during his lifetime, he was now and then very severe in his dealings with brother disciples. During this time no one dared go near Swamiji except Saradananda, whose steadiness and mental poise could freeze anybody's hot temper. Once Swamiji sent Saradananda to Calcutta on an errand. When he learned that it had not been done, he rebuked him with harsh language. Saradananda remained as motionless as a statue. When tea was served, he began to drink it as if nothing had happened. Swamiji commented in a lighter vein: 'Sarat's veins carry the blood of fish, it will never warm up.'[17]

Once when Swami Brahmananda was living in Belur Math he was suffering from an abscess and needed minor surgery. Swami Saradananda accompanied Dr. Kanjilal (a devotee of Holy Mother) from Calcutta, and they left for the monastery by boat. In the middle of the Ganges, a heavy storm arose and the boat began tossing violently. Swami Saradananda was calmly smoking his hubble-bubble, but panicky doctor could not control himself. Angrily he threw the hubble-bubble into the Ganges, and told Saradananda: 'You are a strange man! The boat is about to sink, and you are enjoying your smoke!' The Swami calmly said: 'Is it wise to jump into the water before the boat sinks?' Gradually the storm subsided and the boat safely reached the Belur ghat.[18]

We come across in Mundakopanishad: 'The Self is not gained by men of weak spirit.'[19] Knowing that the Self does not suffer nor perish, the other disciples also remained tranquil and undaunted in spirit during extreme suffering. After returning from pilgrimage in 1895, Swami Trigunatitananda, another direct disciple, stayed at Calcutta and gave classes at various places on the Gita and the Upanishads. There he developed a fistula which needed surgery. Swami Trigunatita told the doctor to do the surgery without chloroform. The doctor spent half an hour removing the fistula cutting nearly six inches. The doctor and the nurses did not see any change in Trigunatita's face. He was as calm as if he were in deep meditation.[20]

This state of attaining fearlessness and immortality of Self is expressed in Brihadaranyanka Upanishad:

> That infinite, birthless, undecaying, indestructible, immortal and fearless Self is Brahman. He who knows (the Self) indeed becomes fearless Brahman.[21]

The night before his passing away, Swami Turiyananda said to his attendants, 'Tomorrow is the last day.' Towards the end he chanted, 'Om Ramakrishna, Om Ramakrishna', and then asked his attendant to make him sit up. Then he folded his hands in salutation, drank a little holy water and summed up his life's experience: 'Everything is real. Brahman is real. The world is real. The world is Brahman. The life force is established in Truth. Hail Ramakrishna! Hail Ramakrishna! Say that he is the embodiment of Truth, and embodiment of Knowledge.' He then recited an Upanishadic mantram along with Swami Akhanadananda:

> *'Satyam jnanam anantam Brahma'* (Brahman is Truth, Knowledge, and Infinity).

Slowly he closed his eyes, as if merging into Brahman.[22]

In Conclusion

All the monastic disciples of Sri Ramakrishna through their lives and teachings have enjoined upon us the importance of renunciation. Let this not frighten us, the lay devotees. Let us not think that it is for the sannyasins alone. For, they do not ask the householders to renounce their homes and families, their work and worldly duties. They only ask us to renounce the false and adore the Real; renounce our false individuality with all our anger, hatred, jealousy, lust and greed; our unripe ego which says 'my' and 'mine', 'I act', 'I am wealthy', 'I am a scholar'; our narrow conventionality which makes us pray for power and wealth, name and fame, sons and comrades. They ask us to renounce the desire for fleeting pleasures of the world which makes us forget our true nature and becomes the cause of repeated births and deaths in this *samsara* of *maya*. They ask us to pray instead to root out all desires. If a tree is pulled out with its roots it does not spring again. They ask us to love and look upon our husband, wife, son, friend, etc., as our own Self playing with us and not in transitory, finite, human relationship.

Swami Ramakrishnananda, another direct disciple, explained the mystery of renunciation:

'Those who give up the world for spiritual life are giving up the uncertain for the certain, the passing for the permanent. . . Only when we have given up our lives do we begin to live. . . As soon as a man finds out. . . that these little pleasures of the flesh are nothing compared with the infinite pleasures of spirit, he wants to renounce; not for the sake of renunciation, but because he has found something better. . . Renunciation means giving up a lesser thing for a greater.'[23] □

References

1.   *Spiritual Talks*, Advaita Ashrama, Pp. 81-82
2.   *God Lived with Them*, Swami Chetanananda, Advaita Ashrama, Mayavati, 1998, 169 Hereafter: *God Lived With Them*.
3.   *Mundakopanishad*, 3.2.3
4.   *God Lived with Them*, p.393
5.   *ibid*, 433-434
6.   *Apostles of Ramakrishna*, Pp. 288-89
7.   *Mundakopanishad* 3.2.9
8.   *Katha Upanishad*, 2.3.17
9.   *God Lived With Them*, Pp.168-69
10.   *Isha Upanishad*, Verse 6
11.   *God Lived With Them*, Pp. 170-171
12.   *ibid*, 117
13.   *ibid*, Pp. 311,324,322
14.   *The Complete Works of Swami Vivekananda*, Advaita Ashrama: Calcutta, 1963, 2: 249
15.   *Apostles of Ramakrishna*, p. 304
16.   *God Lived With Them*, p. 162
17.   *ibid*, 331-332
18.   *ibid*, 343-344
19.   *Mundakopanishad*, 3.2.4
20.   *God lived With Them*, p.500
21.   *Brihadaranyaka Upanishad*, 4.4.25
22.   *God Lived With Them*, p. 392
23.   *ibid*, Pp. 300-301

Chapter 11

An Overview of the Upanishads in the West

SWAMI TATHAGATANANDA

India's Antiquity

'It cannot be denied', said Friedrich von Schlegel[1],

'that the early Indians possessed a knowledge of the true God; all their writings are replete with sentiments and expressions, noble, clear, and severely grand, as deeply conceived and reverentially expressed as in any human language in which men have spoken of their God... Even the loftiest philosophy of the Europeans, the idealism of reason, as it is set forth by Greek philosophers, appears, in comparison with the abundant light and vigour of Oriental idealism, like a feeble Promethean spark in the full flood of heavenly glory of the noonday sun—faltering and feeble, and ever ready to be extinguished...'

Friedrich von Schlegel was not alone in paying such glowing tributes to India's pursuit after the Ultimate Truth. More than one hundred western scholars devoted themselves to the arduous pioneering work of bringing India's eternal philosophy to the West. We can name the greatest of these savants and cite the achievements of very *few* in the brief space of this article. These include Max Müller, Paul Deussen, and Franz

Bopp among those in **Germany**; Sir William Jones, Sir Charles Wilkins, Monier Monier-Williams, Sir Edwin Arnold, and some others among those in **Great Britain**; Louis Renou among those in **France**; Charles R. Lanman, Maurice Bloomfield and Edward W. Hopkins in **America**; and Count Novarov and Pitirim A. Sorokin among those in **Russia**.

During the early 1920s, many philosophers and thinkers drew inspiration from great French savant Romain Rolland's biographies of Sri Ramakrishna and Swami Vivekananda, *The Life of Ramakrishna* and *The Life of Vivekananda and the Universal Gospel* (French, 1929; English, 1931).

In antiquity, India's civilization and spiritual culture left its powerful influence in many countries. Most Scholars acknowledge that Plato's ideas were shaped by Hindu thought. Max Müller noted many similarities between Indian ideas and Platonic thought:

'It cannot be denied that the similarity between Plato's language and that of the *Upanishads* is very startling. . . There must have been some kind of historical contact even at that early time between the religious thought of India and the

Max Müller

philosophical thought of Greece. We cannot deny the possibility of such a view.'[2]

In the first half of the seventeenth century Abraham Roger, a missionary from Holland, published the first translation of an Indian text into a European language (Dutch).[3] His work on the 'religion of the Brahmins' influenced German scholars later. Around the same time, Prince Dara Shukoh, the eldest son of Mogul Emperor Shah Jahan, first translated fifty *Upanishads* into the Persian language in 1656. The Prince was assisted in this work, titled *Sirr-i Akbar*, by pundits from Benares living in Delhi.

Early Indologists systematically mastered Sanskrit, collected and interpreted data, and preserved rare and valuable manuscripts for shelter in western museums and libraries. Asiatic, Oriental and Vedanta Societies, academic Sanskrit chairs, and comparative philology, linguistics and religion—all disseminated India's spiritual knowledge in the West, where it is now firmly established.

Sir Monier Monier-Williams' Sanskrit-English and English-Sanskrit dictionaries as also Sanskrit grammar books by many eminent scholars helped in creating a new interest in the great spiritual classics of Upanishads. Let us have a look at the brief history of Upanishads' influence on the West and how they have influenced some of the best minds over the last few centuries.

France's Significant Role

In the eighteenth century, some broad-minded European scholars learned of the Sanskrit language and the wisdom of the Upanishads. Inspired, they wholeheartedly dedicated themselves to the daunting study of eastern languages, literature, religion and culture. In 1760, Voltaire received the *Ezour-Vedam* (*Yajur-Veda*) from a knight returning from India. In *The Hinduism of the Upanishads* (1950), J. V. Nayadu writes that Voltaire saw in it 'the most precious [gift] for which the West was ever indebted to the East.' Voltaire recognized Europe's need for ideas from India. Desiring to awaken western minds to the vast perspective of Indian thought he brought attention to historical Indian accounts, particularly Major Alexander Dow's *The History of Hindostan*, which was translated into many languages and reached a broad audience.

In 1754, the spirited Frenchman and most eminent linguist of his century, Abraham Hyacinthe Anquetil-Duperron, traveled to India in search of her spiritual knowledge. His translation of the Upanishads into French and Latin (1801-02) immensely inspired a steady stream of western scholars, poets, writers and others seeking to understand the soul of India. They included German philosophers Friedrich W. Joseph von Schelling and Arthur Schopenhauer. Although Anquetil's *Oupnek'hat* (*The Upanishads*) was partially translated into German in 1808, his Latin translation highly influenced Schopenhauer and Paul Deussen later in Germany.

In 1821, Paris became the first European city to officially teach Sanskrit, following the example laid down by the *Asiatic Society* in Calcutta. Eugène Burnouf, an expert in Vedic language and literature, was a fountainhead of Sanskrit and Indological studies. A very enthusiastic member of the *Socimtm Asiatique*, he contributed many articles to its *Journal Asiatique* which began in 1823. It evolved into a series of expository works, to fulfil 'the scientific and literary concerns' of European scholars.[4] Slowly Paris became 'the capital of nascent Indology.'

There were many French translations of significant Sanskrit works by late eighteenth century: Of the many texts published then, Burnouf's *Bhagavata-Purana* and extracts from the *Brihadaranyaka Upanishad* remains an important resource. Baron Ferdinand Eckstein translated the *Aitareya* and *Katha Upanishads* into French. Other French translations include Charles d'Harlez's *Kaushitaki Upanishad*, Herold's *Brihadaranyaka Upanishad*, F. Marcault's translation of Mead's English rendering of nine Upanishads, and some expository treatises on the Upanishads by some notable writers.

England's Contribution

Alexander Dow's essay, *On the History and Culture of India* (1768) introduced England's noteworthy study of abundant Sanskrit works waiting to be revealed to the world. Two significant events followed. First, the *Asiatic Society of Calcutta* was founded by Sir William Jones in 1784. Second, Sir Charles Wilkins published his English translations of the *Bhagavad Gita* and *Hitopadesa* in London and his authoritative Sanskrit grammar soon after in 1785 and 1787, which became the basis for all later Indological work.[5]

Sir William Jones

Sir William Jones invited thirty eminent Europeans to become members of the Asiatic Society.[6] From the outset, this epoch-making event brought about the intellectual and spiritual meeting of minds, east and west. The Society published twenty volumes of proceedings and research in its reputed journal, *Asiatic Researches*. The first generation of Indic scholars was vigorously interested in the work of the *Asiatic Society*.

Upanishads and the Bhagavad Gita

The Upanishads made their greatest impact in the West through the Bhagavad Gita. Sir Charles Wilkins was the first employee of the East India Company to learn Sanskrit.[7] Wilkins' *Bhagavat-Geeta* was published in London (1785).[8] In 1787, Abbe Parraud re-translated Wilkins' version into French. Also in 1787, the first Russian translation of Wilkins' English version of the Bhagavad Gita by N. I. Norikov[9] was introduced in Russia. The Upanishads and the Bhagavad Gita profoundly influenced Leo Tolstoy. Later Indologists liberally referred to Wilkins' translation of the *Bhagavad Gita*.[10]

A Greek translation of the *Bhagavad Gita* by Demetrios Galanos was published posthumously in 1848.

One hundred years after the publication of Sir Wilkins' English translation of the Bhagavad Gita, Sir Edwin Arnold published his blank verse translation, *The Song Celestial* (1885). Mahatma Gandhi considered it the best translation and wrote in his autobiography that it inspired his lifelong study of the *Gita* in his search for truth.[11] Arnold also rendered a part of the *Katha Upanishad* in a free metrical style.

George Augustus Jacob added an important resource to the serious study of the Bhagavad Gita. He edited the *Mahanarayana Upanishad* (1888) and translated some of the Upanishads in *Eleven Atharvan Upanishads* (1891). He published an alphabetical index of the main words of sixty-six principal Upanishads and also the Bhagavad Gita in his *Concordance to the Principal Upanishads and Bhagavadgita*.

In 1908, a retired English civil servant in Bengal and Sanskrit scholar, Charles Johnston, published from New York, his translation of the Bhagavad Gita titled 'The Songs of the Master', with a lengthy tribute in the General Introduction to the historical and eternal significance of the scripture.

England's novelist and critic Aldous Huxley was transformed by his association with Vedanta. His novels, *The Near and the Far* and *Island*, respectively explored the concepts of *moksha* and *nirvana*. He wrote the introduction to *Bhagavad Gita, the Song of God* (1944), translated by Swami Prabhavananda and Christopher Isherwood.

The poems of American-born British citizen T. S. Eliot reflect his knowledge and regard for the Upanishads. In his monograph on Dante (1974) he wrote, 'The *Bhagavad Gita*. . . is the next greatest philosophical poem to the *Divine Comedy*, within my experience.' The *Gita*'s revelations about the function of the ego in human affairs are reflected in his drama, *Murder in the Cathedral*. Becket's speech at the height of his spiritual crisis, 'To do the right deed for the wrong reason. Ambition comes behind and unobservable. Sin grows with doing good,' indicates Eliot's understanding of *niskama karma* as Sri Ramakrishna explained it:

> 'For those who serve the greater cause may make the cause serve them, still doing right; and striving with political men may make that cause political, not by what they do but by what they are.'[12]

Robert Ernest Hume, the only American Sanskritist born in India, taught there and at Oxford. Recognizing the *Upanishads* as the first written evidence of India's philosophical system, he published his remarkably clear English translation, *Thirteen Principal Upanishads* (1921), which has had many reprints.

Role of Germany

The *Bhagavad Gita* played a vital role in Germany's spiritual life. The modern German Indologist Jacob Hauer described it as

> 'a work of imperishable significance' that contains 'the classical presentation of one of the most significant phases of Indo-German religious history. . . It shows us the way

as regards the essential nature and basal characteristics of Indo-Germanic religion. Here Spirit is at work that belongs to our spirit.'[13]

August Schlegel, founder of Sanskrit philology in Germany, first occupied the chair of Sanskrit and Indology at the University of Bonn[14] and first published standardized Latin text editions of the Bhagavad Gita with the original Sanskrit text (1823).[15]

One of the earliest treatises (1827-1833) on the Upanishads investigated the antiquity of the Upanishads based on the use of grammar by Karl Windischmann and his son Friedrich Windischmann. In 1844 Ludwig Poley produced translations of five *Upanishads*.[16] Then in 1847 he translated the *Katha Upanishad* into German. Max Müller's landmark work in the history of Sanskrit studies is his English edition of the *Rig-Veda with Sayana's Commentary* (Oxford, 1849-1875).[17] His epoch-making series, *The Sacred Books of the East* (Oxford, 1879) was the first authoritative and comprehensive translation of twelve principal Upanishads.

Paul Deussen contributed monumental works, including *Sixty Upanishads*, an annotated and cross-referenced German translation (1897),[18] a German translation of the *Oupnek'hat* (*The Upanishads*, 1897), *The Philosophy of the Upanishads*, which formed the second of six volumes of his *General History of Philosophy* (1899). It is a systematic and scholarly work that still enjoys singular prestige today. The Sanskrit professorships in universities throughout Germany also had great significance. Many of these devoted Sanskrit scholars travelled to other countries and shared their expertise.

The Transcendental Movement in America

In the nineteenth century, Germany's English translations of India's sacred texts and the works of Charles Wilkins and William Jones inspired the leaders of the American Transcendental Movement. Ralph Waldo Emerson, an eminent leader of the Movement, recorded in his *Journal* that he was reading the Bhagavad Gita and Colebrooke's *Essays on the Vedas*.[19]

According to Swami Vivekananda, Emerson's greatest source of inspiration was 'this book, the [*Bhagavad*] *Gita*. He went to see Carlyle, and Carlyle

 made him a present of the Gita; and that little book is responsible for the Concord [Transcendental] Movement. All the broad movements in America, in one way or other, are indebted to the Concord party.'[20] The only book Carlyle showed to Emerson during their first visit together, was an English translation of *The Bhagvat-Geeta* by Charles Wilkins. He told Emerson,

Ralph Waldo Emerson

'This is a most inspiring book; it has brought comfort and

consolation in my life—I hope it will do the same to you. Read it.'[21]

Thanks largely to Emerson and Thoreau, Indian studies advanced in New England through Harvard University. Henry David Thoreau lived in Emerson's household during his early twenties and absorbed himself with Indian literature from Emerson's study. His lifelong inspiration from the Bhagavad Gita began when he read Charles Wilkins' English translation. Thoreau's gift collection of forty-four Oriental books that included a copy of the Gita and the Upanishads[22] became one of the first Oriental libraries in America. In his well-known book, *Walden*, Thoreau wrote,

'How much more admirable the Bhagavat Gita than all the ruins of the East.'

In fine, we can safely conclude that Upanishads, along with Gita, have made a significant change in the western thoughts and philosophy. And this is a continuing process. As the days go by more and more people are appreciating the timeless wisdom of the Upanishads. This rediscovering the 'Perennial Philosophy' is the source of all. Considering the increasing violence and

Henry David Thoreau

restlessness the world over, in the west in particular, one is reminded of Swami Vivekananda's words,

'Europe, the centre of the manifestation of material energy, will crumble into dust within fifty years if she is not mindful to change her position, to shift her ground and make spirituality the basis of her life. And what will save Europe is the religion of the Upanishads.'[23] □

References

1. Müller quoted from Friedrich von Schlegel's work (p. 471) in his lecture, "Origin of the Vedanta Philosophy," *Three Lectures*, pp. 10-11.

2. Swami Ashokananda, *The Influence of Indian Thought on the Thought of the West* (Mayavati, 1931), pp. 37-8. [Hereafter *Influence*]

3. *Influence*, p. 18.

4. Raymond Schwab, *The Oriental Renaissance: Europe's Discovery* of India and the East, 1680-1880 (N.Y, 1984), pp. 82-4, [Hereafter *Oriental Renaissance*]

5. Klaus K. Klostermaier, *A Survey of Hinduism* (New York, 1994), p. 21. [Hereafter *Survey*]

6. Gauranga Gopal Sengupta, *Indology and Its Eminent Western Savants* (Calcutta, 1996), p. 15. [Hereafter *Indology*]

7. *Indology*, p. 29.

8. *Oriental Renaissance*, p. 51.

9. *Indology*, p. 163.

10. *Survey*, p. 21.

11. Mahatma Gandhi, *The Story of My Experiments with Truth*, Mahadev Desai, trans. (Washington, D.C., 1948), Part I, XX: 90.

12. *Studies on Sri Ramakrishna, Commemorative Volume,* Swami Lokeswarananda, ed. (Gol Park, Calcutta, 1988), pp. 269-70.

13. Cit. from S. Radhakrishnan's Introductory Essay in *The Bhagavadgita,* 1997 (New Delhi, 1993). See *Prabuddha Bharata,* August 2001, p. 25.

14. *Survey,* p. 22.

15. *Influence,* p. 20.

16. *Oriental Renaissance,* p. 93.

17. *Prabuddha Bharata,* Oct. 2000, p. 41. See *Indology,* p. 108; p. 119, n. 6.

18. *Art, Culture and Spirituality: A Prabuddha Bharata Centenary Perspective,* (Calcutta, 1997), p. 363.

19. Sachin N. Pradhan, *India in the United States, Contributions of India & Indians in the United States of America* (Bethesda, MD, 1996), p. 12.

20. CW, 4: 95

21. Swami Abhedananda, *Thoughts on Sankhya Buddhism and Vedanta* (Calcutta: Ramakrishna Vedanta Math, 1989), Appendix I, p. 118.

22. *Oriental Religions,* p. 69.

23. CW, 3: 159

Chapter 12

Upanishads and the Science of Yoga

N.V.C. SWAMY

Indian Philosophical Systems

Indian Philosophy is generally studied through its six systems, called Shat Darshana. These are: Nyaya of Gautama, Vaiseshika of Kanada, Sankhya of Kapila, Yoga of Patanjali, Purvamimamsa of Jaimini and Uttaramimamsa of Badarayana Vyasa. They deal respectively with Logic, Atomism, Evolution, Involution, Ritualism and Supreme Consciousness.

Our interest in this article is focused on the fourth and the last of these systems, viz., Yoga and Uttaramimamsa (or Vedanta). The standard texts of these two are, respectively, Yogasutras and Brahmasutras. The first text is attributed to Sage Patanjali, who is surmised to have flourished between the 2nd century BCE and the 2nd century CE. He is not the inventor of this science. Rather, he is the compiler of this experiential knowledge in the form of a textbook (known as *Patanjali Yogasutras* or the Yoga Aphorisms of Patanjali).

The second text is attributed to Badarayana Vyasa and its date of compilation is still a matter of speculation.

It was written down to summarize all extant knowledge about Superconsciousness or Brahman. The scriptures that deal with this subject are the Upanishads, forming the knowledge portion of the Vedas.

When one goes through the Upanishadic texts in detail, especially the major Upanishads, one is sometimes struck by dichotomous statements made by them. This is because the revelations constituting the Upanishads occurred to different sages at different periods of history and have been expressed in words consonant with the era in which they lived. Hence,there was a need to reconcile these apparent contradictions to show the inner consistency of Upanishadic knowledge. This is the purpose served by the Brahmasutras.

A study of the Brahmasutras needs a prior acquaintance with the Upanishads, the Gita and some rudiments of Jaina and Bauddha philosophies. On the other hand, the only prerequisite for a study of Yogasutras is an understanding of Sankhya. In this sense, it is a much easier subject to approach. Sankhya provides the theoretical foundation for the much more practice-oriented Yoga.

Theoretically, Yoga and Vedanta (the topic of the Upanishads and the Brahmasutras) are treated as two entirely different systems of philosophy. This is only a matter of convenience from the point of view of study. But in essence they have a common goal viz., *Svanubhuti*, realization of one's own true nature.) The paths may appear to be different, but in practice they tend to feed upon each other.   Everything eats and is food

It is said that there are about 220 Upanishads which have been identified. Most of them are now considered to be either of recent origin or spurious. The texts of 108 of them have been published by several publishing houses. Of these, at least 21 Upanishads deal with topics related to Patanjali's Yoga. Even though they claim to belong to the Vedic literature, a cursory glance through them shows that they just paraphrase some of the important sutras of Patanjali. Scholars dealing with the dating of the Upanishads have relegated them to a lower order of importance. Hence, we focus our attention here on only what are called major Upanishads.

Are Yoga and Upanishads Contemporaneous?

Before attempting a comparative study of the Upanishads with Patanjali's Yoga, an important question needs to be addressed. Are these two branches of knowledge contemporary in time? Till recently, there had been a feeling that the Vedic people had no knowledge of Yoga at all and that the latter is a later invention.

However, a closer examination of some of the seals and tablets found in excavations in the Saraswati Valley indicate that some of these tablets show postures like yogic asanas. The most famous of them shows a yogi, identified with Pashupati or Siva, sitting in the posture of Mulabandhasana, which is an advanced asana recommended in textbooks of Hathayoga as a means of closing Ida and Pingala and opening the Sushumna for the smooth movement of Kundalini. These seals have been dated to circa 3000 BCE, thus giving rise to a speculation that the Vedic sages did know about this art of entering the superconscious stage and that most of their revelations recorded in the Vedas and Upanishads occurred to them in this state of Consciousness. This is, to a certain extent, substantiated by modern sages, commencing with Sri Ramakrishna himself.

Two more instances can be cited for the contemporaniety of the Vedic literature and Yoga. Every Mantra of the Rigveda is associated with a Rishi, a Devata, a Chandas and a Viniyoga. The first is the composer, the second is the deity addressed, the third is the metre and the last one is the objective to be achieved. One of the most famous and popular Vedic Mantras is the Gayatri or Savitru Mantra. The composer is Sage Vishwamitra, the deity is Savitru or Surya, the metre is Gayatri and the objective is Pranayama. The Rigveda is itself now dated to circa 3500 BCE. This is a clear indication that Pranayama was known and practised even at the time of Rigveda.

Swami Vivekananda was as active on the 4th of July 1902, the day of his Mahasamadhi, as on any other day. During the course of the day he instructed his disciple, Swami Shuddhananda, to fetch the Shukla Yajurveda. Swamiji then asked him to read the fortieth verse of the eighteenth chapter of the Madhyandina recension of the Vajasaneyi Samhita beginning with the words 'Sushumnah suryarashmih', along with the commentary of Mahidhara. Swamiji then remarked,

'This interpretation of the passage does not appeal to my mind. Whatever may be the commentator's interpretation of the word *Sushumna*, the seed or the basis of what the Tantras, in the later ages, speak of as the Sushumna nerve-channel in the body, is contained here, in this Vedic Mantra. You, my disciples, should try to discover the true import of these Mantras and make original reflections and commentaries of the Shastras.'[1]

Mahidhara had interpreted the word as another name of Chandra, the Moon God, but Swamiji had felt that the word actually refers to the canal through which the Kundalini moves.

It is thus seen that there is ample evidence to show that Yogic practices are as old as the Vedic era. Hence, it is no wonder that we encounter the word Yoga explicitly in some of the major Upanishads.

Upanishadic Texts and Yoga

Even though the Vedic and Yogic knowledge systems are contemporaneous, it is not true of the texts, viz., the Upanishads and the Yogasutras. The Upanishads have come down to us through an oral tradition that strived to maintain its original and authentic form. The Yogasutras of Patanjali, on the other hand, were compiled only about 2000 years ago. The system itself might have undergone quite a few changes since the Vedic times, since it emphasizes practice over theory. Hence, it becomes difficult to make a guess as to what kind of Yoga might have been practised by the Vedic people. Thus, our comparison between these two systems has to depend heavily upon the brief references to Yoga in the Upanishadic literature.

Texts ever — distilling down to practice...

The theoretical basis for Yoga is considered to be Kapila's Sankhya. The latter is supposed to be the oldest philosophical system, but is silent on the question of Brahman, either Nirguna or Saguna. But, Patanjali, in his yoga text, appears to make a concession by introducing the concept of Iswara as a *Purusavisesha* (a special type of purusha or person). The symbol or Pratika for this is Pranava or Omkara. Even though there is no elaboration of this point in the text, practising yogis consider Om as the most important symbol to meditate upon. For Yoga practitioners, Om represents that which Vedantins call Brahman.

Upanishads also give equal importance to Pranava. There are many major Upanishads where this word is mentioned explicitly such as Katha Upanishad and Mundaka Upanishad. According to the Kathopanishad, Om is that which is praised by all the Vedas, it is that which is uttered by all spiritual aspirants and it is that desiring to reach which people practice Brahmacharya. Om stands for both the Saguna Brahman and the Nirguna Brahman, serving as a bridge spanning the two. It is the best support one can have in life to reach one's goal.

The Mundakopanishad describes Omkara through an allegory. In the second Mundaka, Section 2, the Upanishad says in Mantras 3 and 4,

'Taking hold of the bow, the great weapon familiar in the Upanishads, one should fix on it an arrow sharpened with meditation. Drawing the string, O Sowmya, hit that very target that is the Imperishable, with the mind absorbed in

Its thought. Om is the bow, the soul is the arrow and Brahman is called its target. It is to be hit by an unerring man. One should become one with It just like an arrow.'

In his commentary, (Adi Sankara says that Om is the bow that brings about the soul's entry into the Imperishable.) Thus, Omkara is a means for self-realization.

The shortest Upanishad, the Mandukya, with only 12 Mantras, is all about Omkara. The letter 'A' represents the waking state, the letter 'U' stands for the dreaming state, the letter 'M' represents the dreamless sleeping state, and the combination of these three, Om, is the Fourth or Turiya, the state of Samadhi.

But, it is in a later Upanishad, the Shvetashvatara, that one comes across an explicit description of Rajayoga. Perhaps nowhere else in the Upanishads can one find such a detailed description. This could be because it is a later Upanishad and by that time the oral tradition of yogic practices gradually came to be written down to become a part of literature.

The Upanishad says in its second chapter:

In order to attain ecstasy, one who is practising yoga will raise high the three parts of his body – the head, the neck and the chest. They should also be in a straight line. With the help of his mind, he should focus all his senses in his heart and then use Brahman (i.e. Pranava, the symbol Om) as a raft to cross the frightful currents of the river of life.[2]

(Now some hints are being given on how to practice Pranayama.) Anyone practising yoga has to be meticulous about what

he should and should not do. (That is, he should follow the rules laid down by the yoga scriptures regarding food and other things,) He should also control his breath with great care. He may release his breath only when he feels exhausted. The mind is like restless horses harnessed to a chariot. Like a charioteer, the wise person has to control his mind and fix it (on some deity)[3].

(But what sort of place is congenial for the practice of yoga? Here is the answer to this question.) The place should be even, holy, without pebbles, fire and sand, without noise, such as coming from a crowd, and not too close to lakes and other sources of water. It should be pleasing to the mind and not repulsive to the sight. It should be a place such as a cave where there are no strong winds. Practise yoga in such a place.[4]

(Some signs of progress in yoga.) Shortly before a yogi has his experience of Brahman, he will begin to see the following signs, all suggestive of that experience: snow, smoke, the sun, air, fire, fireflies, sparks, crystal and the moon.[5]

The gross elements—earth, water, fire, air and space—are no longer gross to the yogi. They are only their qualities (i.e. smell, taste, form, touch and sound). His body is transformed in that it loses its grossness, and he is no longer susceptible to disease, old age or death. His death is at his will.[6]

Lightness of the body, absence of any ailment, no craving for enjoyment, a bright complexion, a sweet voice, a pleasant body odour, and urine and faeces in small quantities – these are the first signs of a successful yogi.[7]

The rest of the Mantras in this chapter deal with the final stage of Samadhi, which is the constant refrain of all Upanishads.

One can already see here the seeds of the thought process that later blossomed out into their fullest form in the 6th Chapter of the Gita and some chapters of texts on Hathayoga.

Apart from this Upanishad there are several other Upanishads also which deal with this subject. But they are more recent in origin and need not be taken too seriously because they essentially repeat whatever is found in Sivasamhita and Gherandasamhita.

Summary

The points that emerge from this study can be summarized as follows. The Upanishads and Rajayoga are contemporary developments. Both were originally propagated through an oral tradition, but the Upanishads came to be gradually written down. Yoga, on the other hand, still retained its oral tradition, because it is a highly practice-oriented science. Only later, when oral traditions became difficult to maintain, was this knowledge put into writing, whose earliest expression is in the Shvetashvatara Upanishad.

Even though it has become customary to consider Rajayoga as a separate philosophy, it is always advisable to remember its close connection to the Upanishadic literature. ☐

References

1. *Life of Swami Vivekananda by his Eastern and Western Disciples*, Advaita Ashrama, Kolkata, Vol. 2. p.653
2. *Shvetashvatara Upanishad* translated by Swami Lokeshwarananda, RMIC, Kolkatta, Verse 8
3. *ibid*, verse 9
4. *ibid*, verse 10
5. *ibid*, verse 11
6. *ibid*, verse12
7. *ibid*, verse13

Chapter 13

The Story of Prajapati and Its Meaning

SWAMI DAYATMANANDA

The Upanishads are called Vedanta. The purpose of the Upanishads is to teach man his real nature and the way to know it. A man is what his core is and the Upanishads say that man's core is divine and knowledge of this core—Self—is the purpose of human life. Not only is man's core divine, the whole creation is, in essence, divine. Says Swami Vivekananda, the modern *rishi*, 'We believe that every being is divine, is God.'[1]

Explaining this, Swamiji further said:

'The whole universe is one. There is only One Self in the universe, only One Existence, and that One Existence, when it passes through the forms of time, space, and causation, is called by different names.

Everything in the universe is that One, appearing in various forms. Therefore the whole universe is all one in the Self, which is called Brahman. That Self when it appears behind the universe is called God. The same Self when it appears behind this little universe, the body, is the soul.'[2]

The Use of Stories

In order to simplify this highest knowledge and make it available to a commoner, the Upanishads often clothed it in stories and similes. The stories of Nachiketa in Katha Upanishad, Uma Haimavati in Kena Upanishad, Bhrigu's quest for Brahman in the Taittiriya Upanishad, and Prajapati's instructions to Indra in Chandogya Upanishad are some the best known examples.

Here is a charming and highly inspiring story from the Chandogya Upanishad.[3]

Once Prajapati, a knower of Brahman, declared:

'The Atman which is free from evil, free from old age, free from death, free from sorrow, free from hunger and thirst, whose desire is of the truth, whose resolve is of the truth, he should be sought, one should desire to understand. He who has found out and who understands that Atman attains all the worlds and all the desires.'

Both gods and demons heard this proclamation. Indra among the gods and Virochana among the Asuras, then approached Prajapati and said :

'We have heard that the Atman has to be known, the Atman that is not touched by sin, or old age or death or sorrow or thirst or hunger, the Atman whose desires are always true (*satyakama*), whose resolutions are always firm. Please instruct us about this Atman'.

Prajapati asked them to practise austerities and celibacy for thirty-two years, and then instructed them thus: 'The Purusha (the Self) visible in the eyes, reflected in the water or in the mirror is the Atman.

Look at yourselves in water and let me know what you see.'

When they did this Prajapati asked them, 'What did you see ?' 'We saw the whole body', they said. Prajapati asked them to dress well and again look at the image and they said that the images also looked well-dressed. Prajapati said, 'This is the Atman that you seek', and they went away satisfied.

Virochana went back to the Asuras and proclaimed, 'The body is the Atman, serve it well and you will obtain all your desires here and hereafter'. To this day people generally say, 'He is a *demon*' when a person has no charitable nature, no faith in the supernatural realms, who never worships gods, who does not perform sacrifices, who is selfish, and body-centred. Those who are identified with the body and think that the body is very valuable, and cater to its whims, falsely thinking that it is the true self of man—in other words, those who identify themselves with the body and worship it are called Asuras, the children of Virochana.

Now let us follow Indra. As a result of living a right type of austere life, Indra became endowed with intelligence, the power of discernment. On his way back he reflected, 'If the Atman becomes lame if the body is lame, and blind if the body is blind, and is well-dressed if the body is well-dressed, and is destroyed if the body is destroyed—I see no good in this teaching.'

So he went back to Prajapati who asked him to live a life of celibacy for another thirty-two years. Then he said: 'He who moves about as the Lord in the state of dream, is the Self, the Atman.' Indra, again reflected on the way back:

'Though this dream Purusha is not affected by any damage to the body, yet at times he is being chased or hurt or that Purusha feels pain or weeps. This certainly cannot be the Self.'

Again he went back to Prajapati. After thirty-two years more of celibacy, Indra was told, 'The Self in the state of deep sleep is the Atman, immortal, fearless, he is Brahman'. Indra again expressed doubt: 'The Self is not affected by dream, or damage to or destruction of the body, but it seems not to know itself, and is, as it were, dead in this state of deep sleep (sushupti). I do not see any real good in this.'

He again went to Prajapati and was told to practise celibacy for five more years. Thus he lived a spiritual life for a total of one hundred and one years. This indicates one should devote, if necessary, one's whole life for spiritual practice.

At last Prajapati found Indra fit to receive the true teaching and instructed him:

'O Indra, mortal indeed is this body, held by death. But it is the support of this deathless, bodiless Atman. Verily, the embodied self is held by pleasure and pain. Surely, there is no cessation of pleasure and pain for one who is embodied. But pleasure and pain do not indeed touch one who is bodiless.

'Bodiless is air; and white cloud, lightning, thunder, these also are bodiless. Now as these arise out of the yonder sky, reach the highest light and appear each with its own form, even so this serene one rises out of this body, reaches the highest light and appears in his own form. He is the Highest Person. There he moves about, laughing, playing, rejoicing with women, vehicles or relations, not remembering this body in which he was born. As an animal is attached to a chariot, even so is the life attached to this body.

Now, where the sight merges in space (inside the eye, i.e., the black pupil of the eye), there exists that which is the person in the eye; and the eye is only for seeing. And he who knows 'I smell this' is the Atman; the nose is for smelling. And he who knows 'I speak this', is the Atman, the organ of speech is for speaking. And he who knows 'I hear this' is the Atman; the ear is for hearing.

And he who knows 'I think this', is the Atman, the mind is his divine eye. Through this divine eye of the mind he verily sees these desired objects which are in the Brahman-world, and rejoices.

Verily, this is the Atman whom the gods worship. Therefore all the worlds and all the desired objects are held by them. He obtains all the worlds all the desired objects, who having known that Atman (from the teacher and the scriptures) understands it.'

The Moral of the Story

The story above is instructive in many ways.

Some people criticise Prajapati saying that deliberately he misled his students by not speaking of the Atman outright. This view is not correct. He was leading his students gradually from a lower to a higher state of understanding. A good teacher always suits his teaching to the receptivity of his student. Had he given the highest truth at the very outset, they would not have understood it.

This becomes clear if we reflect on the life of Sri Ramakrishna. He used to say that no one could achieve anything until the right time comes. A mother-bird will not break open the shell until the chick is fully formed and is ready to come out. Here 'right time' means acquisition of fitness to receive what is given.

We may recollect that Sri Ramakrishna awakened the spiritual consciousness of many of his devotees on first January 1886 by his divine touch. But on that day he did not bless two devotees saying they will have to wait but will receive his grace later on. We may also recollect that the great Swami Vivekananda was also not able to withstand Sri Ramakrishna's touch on his first visit to Dakshineswar. So also Mathur could not sustain the ecstatic state granted to him by Sri Ramakrishna.

Likewise, the same teaching was given to both Indra and Virochana. While Indra's education continued, Virochana's progress stopped because he did not reflect on the teaching properly but was satisfied with what he (mis)understood. This shows us that much depends on our aspiration, sincerity and receptivity. Austerities purify the mind and that is the only way to develop our receptivity.

Both Indra and Virochana were asked by Prajapati to live the life of celibacy (*brahmacharya*) for thirty-two years. Both of them did as they were instructed. Yet Virochana was unable to grasp the teaching clearly. Just as we can infer the cause by observing the effect, we can guess that though Virochana did perform austerity, it did not serve the purpose for he could not grasp his teacher's words rightly.

In Hindu mythology we come across many instances of demons like Ravana, Narakasura or Bana who performed rigorous austerities. Instead of making their minds pure, their austerities only intensified their worldly desires like lust, greed, jealousy and anger. As a result, they did immense harm to others and in the end had to be vanquished. Swami Yatiswarananda (1889-1966), Vice President of the Ramakrishna Order, used to say that the development of concentration without some amount of mental purity can only harm us and others.

What is True Tapasya?

We find in the Upanishads the idea of tapas acquired a variety of meanings such as knowledge, meditation or concentration of the mind and the control of the senses. Sri Ramakrishna used to say that 'Truthfulness is the greatest austerity for this age', because Truthfulness leads to the realisation of Truth.

Once Swami Brahmananda was asked about austerity. He replied:

'It is to direct the mind towards God in order to taste divine bliss. Sri Ramakrishna's message in this age is renunciation of lust and gold. Real austerity consists in the control of the passions. It is very difficult to renounce lust and greed, to give up the desire for name and fame. Real austerity is based upon these three principles: First, take refuge in the truth. Truth is the pillar to which you must always hold while performing any action. Second, conquer lust. Third, renounce all cravings. Observe these three principles. That is real austerity, and the greatest of these is to conquer lust.'[4]

Clearly, the purpose of Tapasya or austerity is to purify the mind and direct it towards God.

If after performing austerity one becomes a slave to passions that cannot be called austerity. Apparently Virochana did live a life of brahmacharya but obviously it did not bring about the right result. Had he lived a right type of life, his mind would have become pure and he would have been able to reflect on the instruction of his teacher correctly. He would have come to the same conclusion as Indra that the body could not be the Atman, for the body is subject to the six-fold changes like growth, old age, disease, death and so on. Had he understood the teaching properly, like Indra, he too would not have stopped until he realised Brahman.

Vedanta, however, assures that no one is lost forever. Everyone will, in due course, turn towards higher life. Many spiritual aspirants fall into the same trap as Virochana. While we find them doing so much japa, pilgrimage, study of scriptures and charities, we do not find them much changed. In fact, sometimes, we find them even more self-centred, uncaring, and blissfully unaware of their behaviour.

Understanding the 'Three States'

One of the favourite themes of the Upanishads is the analysis of three states (*avastha traya*) of our normal life. Prajapati's instructions also mention these three states of the self: the waking state (*jagrata*), the dream state (*svapna*) and the state of deep-sleep (sushupti). By mentioning them, he gradually leads his pupils to Turiya, the stateless state.

Every being experiences these three states. The Atman as the lower self functions in these three different states : the waking state, which experiences gross objects; the dream state, which experiences subtle objects; and the state of deep sleep, in which it experiences rest and relaxation. Brahman as *chit* or Absolute Consciousness illumines the activities of the senses and mind during their states of waking and dreaming, as well as their inactivity in dreamless sleep.

Through proper analysis we can conclude that deep sleep, dream and waking are three distinct and independent states, each with its peculiar characteristics and each implying the absence of the other two, though Pure Consciousness is present in all the three states all the time. We infer Pure Consciousness because conscious beings can never conceive of unconsciousness. Some circumstances, which are present in one of the states, are absent in other states. Naturally, what is present in one state but is absent in another is inessential and does not form part of the real Self. Each state clearly contradicts the other two states.

All the time we are changing from one state to another state. Whatever is changeable cannot be real. What then is real? The unchangeable alone is real. There must be an entity which remains unchangeable which at the same time is the knower, the cogniser, the witness of these states. It is to this unchanging being which is the Self or Atman to which Prajapati leads Indra.

This is how the process of self-analysis takes an aspirant to the Knowledge of the Self. Sri Ramakrishna summarises the essence of this story so succinctly through a beautiful parable:

'Yes, all one's confusion comes to an end if one only realizes that it is God who manifests Himself as the atheist and the believer, the good and the bad, the real and the unreal; that it is He who is present in waking and in sleep; and that He is beyond all these.

'There was a farmer to whom an only son was born when he was rather advanced in age. As the child grew up, his parents became very fond of him. One day the farmer was out working in the fields, when a neighbour told him that his son was dangerously ill—indeed, at the point of death. Returning home he found the boy dead. His wife wept bitterly, but his own eyes remained dry. Sadly the wife said to her neighbours, "Such a son has passed away, and he hasn't even one tear to shed!" After a long while the farmer said to his wife: "Do you know why I am not crying? Last night I dreamt I had become a king, and the father of seven princes. These princes were beautiful as well as virtuous. They grew in stature and acquired wisdom and knowledge in the various arts. Suddenly I woke up. Now I have been wondering whether I should weep for those seven children or this one boy." To the followers of Jnana Marga the waking state is no more real than the dream state.'[5]

When one reaches the state of Turiya then one becomes free; only then does one truly understand Prajapati's declaration. He then reaches a state of blessedness and remains immersed in Eternal Bliss. □

References

1.   CW, 4: 357
2.   CW, 2: 461
3.   cf. *Chandogya Upanishad*, VIII. vii - xii
4.   cf. *The Eternal Companian*, p. 205
5.   *The Gospel of Sri Ramakrishna*, p. 236

Chapter 14

So Began the Story

PREMA NANDAKUMAR

Uniqueness of Indian Culture

There is something unique about Indian culture which can be identified with a single word: Integration. Sanatana Dharma has never seen life as a compartmentalized experience. Here life, religion, society, the material, the spiritual, youth, old age, the past, the present and even the future are seen as an integralised whole. This was also true of the ancient Indian educational system.

We are struck with amazement at the achievements of ancient India. The highest heights were scaled with ease whether it was arts or sciences. Surely the reason lay in the manner in which the young mind was educated and moulded helping the youth to become achievers. But this was never done consciously. The inspiration was there and the aim pointed out from a distance. High importance was given to the building up of character. The rest would follow, the elders thought. And they were not disappointed.

From all this it becomes clear that the ancient Indians had certainly mastered the art of education. What was their education like? How did they build strong foundations in the psyche of the young student? Surely not by masses of books, instruments or computers! Nolini Kanta Gupta, a great thinker and educationist says:

'The basic point is that education begins with the student and not with the subjects. Education must be allowed to blossom from within the student, from the heart of the student—everything lies only there, the external ingredients have to be provided as and when needed as props and guides. For this, it is not enough to know the general nature of the student, the general psychology of the child—this is a truth which some people have begun to realise only recently. But every student has to be dealt with individually: the nature of the person, the force, the inspiration, the yearning that lies hidden in him, the specific quality with which he has come into this world—all these have to be observed and thoroughly comprehended. He has to be awakened to his soul, and, this is termed as initiation. He who has got initiation and has found his own strength, his own individuality, the divine being within him, will be able to discover easily his own wealth of knowledge.'[1]

The Upanishads give us a clue to how this was managed by the teachers residing in their forest dwellings long, long ago. The Upanishads, coming after the ritualistic part of the Vedas, are among the most ancient texts that we possess. Known as Vedanta, they have been the starting point of all our Darsanas. The highest reaches of Vedantic thought reaching out to the knowledge of the Brahman are to be found in these works. Often referred to as 'the Himalayas of the soul', they teach us all we need to know about our conscious life and the layers of consciousness within, the various upasanas which help us master the technique of meditation to gain personal experience of the received knowledge. Since there is always the teacher with his students close by listening to him, one gains the 'feel' of education all the time. But this is education without tears. Nay, this is education with positive joy. For the Upanishads are never dry argumentation and the meaningful stories carefully imbedded in them light up our pathways to self-discovery in a big way.

As we progress with the Upanishad, the teacher and the taught appear to merge, the story and philosophy become integrated while intellect is subsumed by poetry. Unrivalled images are scattered by the seers through these teachings which flash brilliances:

'The face of Truth is covered with a golden lid.'

(Isa Upanishad)

'This earth is like honey for all beings, and all beings are like honey for this earth.' (Brihadaranyakopanishad)

'In this Brahmapuri there is a lotus-house; and within it there is a little space.' (Chandogya Upanishad)

And unforgettable are the stories. None of them forces knowledge down the throats of the disciples, but the message comes over clearly, with silken gentleness. At a time when we are making confused noises over reservation comes the story of Raikwa the cart-puller from the *Chandogya Upanishad*, and never have I come across a tale so powerful that chases away pride in one's attainments by birth, by endowment and by education. Here is the story.

The Story of King Janasruti

Once upon a time a king called Janasruti was ruling over the kingdom of Mahavrisha. The Upanishad says that he was knowledgeable, pious, charitable, one who prepared plenty of food to feed people. He had also mastered the languages of birds and beasts. It is in the nature of things that from the obscure spaces of the soul rises the plant of pride and soon overwhelms the person with its evil fruits. Such a plant rose within Janasruti and he told himself: 'Ah, this is good. Everywhere people are eating my food'. *My food!* This is the very height of pride for who is the 'I' that says 'my'?

One night he lay in the upper storey of his palace, enjoying the beauty of the evening twilight. He found two swans flying fast, all the time conversing with each other. One of them said: 'Are you so myopic that you do not see the brilliant light of Janasruti, the great grandson of Janasruta spread across? Don't you dare touch it lest it scorch you. Skirt from it carefully!'

Swift came a reaction from the other swan. 'Goodness gracious! You speak as if this Janasruti was greater than Raikwa the cart-puller!'

The first swan was taken aback and asked: 'Who is this Raikwa who is just a cart-puller yet is apparently greater than the great Janasruti?'

The second swan replied: 'As the lower throws of dice all go to the highest throw, to the winner, so whatever good things creatures do, all goes to him. I say the same thing of whoever knows what he knows.'[2]

The king Janasruti lay there musing on the conversation while the swans flew out of sight and night closed in on the city. The message had been delivered to him in no uncertain terms. He was eager to gain fame and had become proud of his generosity. Now the swan had said that he may be a rich king performing lots of *anna dana* (food offerings), but in effect, his achievement was insignificant compared to that of a mere cart-puller. Obviously this Raikwa is a poor fellow. And yet he has gained the respect of even swans. Swans are said to be symbols of spiritual attainment and what they say must be true.[3] They would speak highly of a person only when he was worthy, noble and above all at peace with himself. Swans could separate water from milk; surely they would know the nature of good and evil very well.

The more he mused on it, the greater became Janusruti's desire to find out this Raikwa and learn from him the secret of his spiritual attainment which had drawn praise from the swans. For, by nature Janasruti was full of humility and was a very good man. His character is placed before us by the Upanishadic seer to let us know how easily the best of us can go astray and become proud if we do not care to be conscious of our place in this wide creation. And how easily we can be flattered and come to think very highly of ourselves. On the following day, Janasruti's first action was to stop his attendant from praising him, saying there was one better than him, the cart-puller Raikwa. He then dispatched the servant to find the great-souled cart-puller.

It was not an easy task for the servant. We tend to associate high thinking, knowledge, spirituality and other attainments of this kind with persons in ashrams, who are in high positions. After sometime, the servant did find Raikwa who sat scratching himself under a cart. The servant asked him whether he was Raikwa. 'Yes, I am,' was the quiet and dignified reply. The servant went back to the palace and reported to Janasruti.

Janasruti was not fazed when he came to know that Raikwa was no more than an ordinary cart-puller whom everybody ignores except when they wish to have something hauled from one place to another. He made elaborate preparations and went to Raikwa with six hundred cows, a chain of gold and a mule-driven carriage. He offered them all at the feet of Raikwa and said: 'Sir, be pleased to accept all this and teach me spiritual knowledge.'

Raikwa's reaction was short and snappy. 'Take back the chain and the carriage and the cows! Knowledge of the Self is not for sale!'

Janasruti went back and returned after a while, this time with a thousand cows, a chain of gold, a mule-driven carriage and his daughter. He offered all this and prayed that he may be taught the higher truths of existence. Raikwa was not moved by the gifts. But he was moved by Janasruti's persistence and complete sincerity. One who has these two virtues is eminently suited to be a perfect disciple. Raikwa then gave the desired instruction to the king:

In this creation there are many elements which are worshipped as gods. There is the wind that sweeps everything. The fire burns up whatever comes in contact with it. There is also the vital breath which activates a living being. But all these are moved by the Spirit within. This Spirit is not created by anyone. It exists by itself. And yet it creates and sustains the creation. Thus the entire creation is a complex instrument that is carrying out the behests of the Spirit.

When this is so, how can Janasruti think that it is he who has fed the people or he is the one who has brought gifts to his instructor? When it is the Spirit which does all, how can an individual have the pride to say, I am doing? When Janasruti feeds a person, he must realise that it is the Spirit within him and which pervades the entire creation that is giving food. By thinking in these terms and meditating on the Indwelling Universal, he will not be stained with pride. One who has this realization will not sorrow. He will remain ever content, self-fulfilled, happy.

With this true knowledge of the Spirit, Janasruti shone with a deep joy. When he now offered the thousand cows, the mule-drawn carriage, the golden chain and his own daughter in a totally self-less manner, Raikwa accepted. For all future time, the cluster of villages in this blessed area came to be known as Raikwaparna.

Speaking of this Brahman-knowledge, the Upanishadic teacher thinks that not even human beings but the gods themselves are occasionally veiled by pride in their own power. This is how another charming story underlines the conclusion arrived at by the Janasruti-Raikwa legend.

The *Kena Upanishad* as its name implies, opens with a series of questions (*Kena* in Sanskrit means how or why).

'By whom missioned falls the mind shot to its mark? By whom yoked moves the first life-breath forward on its paths? By whom impelled is this word that men speak? What god set eyes and ears to their workings?'[4]

The young mind should ask such questions. The desire to know is the foundation for a future of achievement. But questions should not be flung idly to frustrate a speaker or to score a point. When a student puts questions, it should be obvious that he desires to know sincerely about man, nature and Brahman. With equal anxiety the teacher should try to give clear answers and not befuddle the young mind with big words. The teacher in the *Kena Upanishad* first tries to answer but then how can one define the indefinable?

'That which breathes not with the breath, that by which the ear's hearing is heard, know That to be the Brahman and not this which men follow after here.'

The teacher says that this Spirit that is inexpressible is in a place that cannot be known to us for our sight or speech or mind can never travel to it. All that we know about it is what we have heard from our elders (*iti susrooma purveshaam*). Did the teacher see his disciples nod as if he had made it all clear? Swift comes a warning:

'If thou thinkest that thou knowest It well, little indeed dost thou know the form of the Brahman. That of It which is thou, that of It which is in the gods, this thou hast to think out.'

Easily said! The fact is that not all lectures and classroom teachings can give us Brahman knowledge. But shall we never know the Spirit and how it functions? The teacher suggests that the Brahman can be known by one's own experience. The *Parajnana* is an experiential knowledge. One experiences the truth of it. Towards explaining this idea, the teacher tells a graceful story.

The Story of Uma Haimavati

The gods and demons had fought one of their many wars and the former had emerged victorious. The Brahman had battled and conquered the day for the gods but the gods thought it was *they* who had achieved the victory. Brahman decided to humble their pride and appeared before them but they could not recognize the Spirit. Who is this Yaksha, they wondered. The gods then called upon Agni to find out for he is the knower, the priest of the sacrifice, the prime witness. Agni immediately rushed towards the Brahman which asked him who he was that he should rush so fast. 'I am Agni' was the answer: 'I am he that knows all things born.' Asked about the force which was in him which seemed to make him so very proud, Agni said that he had the power to burn everything that came into contact with him. Is that so? Everything? The Spirit wondered and placed a blade of grass before him. 'Burn this up!' But Agni could not. The fire in him was too cool to burn the blade of grass which had been placed there by the Brahman. Agni turned away and simply said he could not make out who this Spirit was that was able to help a mere blade of grass withstand his heat.

Vayu was then asked to go, and he told the Spirit that he can take everything by his force. The Spirit asked him to take the blade of grass but he could not even move it. A mere blade of glass to defy him! So it was a superior power that they had encountered, he thought and came back and told the gods that he could not make out who this Yaksha was. Finally Indra, the chief of gods was deputed to find out the name and nature of the Spirit. Even as Indra moved towards the Yaksha, the image vanished. Instead there was a beautiful woman, Uma Haimavati. Indra asked Uma about the Spirit that had now disappeared. She identified it as Brahman:

'It is the Eternal. Of the Eternal is this victory in which ye shall grow to greatness.'

Mark the words of the golden goddess. She does not chide the gods for thinking they are the powerful ones who defeated the asuras. She gently teaches them the humility needed to free oneself of the delusion that this body is all. By recognizing that it is the Brahman within which moves them all, the gods and men are freed of all delusion. While the experience of the Brahman is like a flash of lightning or the winking of the eye, one who realizes the truth about the Eternal would be blessed with a settled Ananda. The teacher concludes that this holding on to the experience of Brahman is possible through tapasya and lists the limbs of such askesis:

'Of this knowledge austerity and self-conquest and works are the foundation, the Vedas are all its limbs, truth is its dwelling place (satyamaayatanam). He who knows this knowledge, smites evil away from him and in that vaster world and infinite heaven finds his foundation, yea, he finds his foundation.'

If truth is the dwelling place of Brahman, what is truth? Again the Upanishads place before us an enduring tale in the *Chandogya Upanishad*. Considered the most ancient of the available Upanishads, the *Chandogya* opens with a description on the right way to chant the Pranava, OM, referred to as Udgitha.

The Story of Satyakama

There was a young boy called Satyakama who wished to join the ashram of a teacher and learn the sacred knowledge. Knowing well that the teacher would ask him for his antecedents, Satyakama asked his mother about his *gotra*. The mother, an honest, hard-working lady who had experienced the sorrow and struggle of earthly life, told him simply:

'This I know not, my son, of what *gotra* thou art; resorting to many as a serving-woman in my youth, I got thee, therefore I know not of what *gotra* thou art. But Jabala is my name and Satyakama is thine, Satyakama Jabala therefore call thyself.'[5]

Satyakama chose Haridrumata Gautama as his teacher. He went to Gautama and saluted. Then he expressed a desire to gain Brahman-knowledge from him. The teacher asked the expected question about Satyakama's family. Satyakama spoke the simple truth:

'This alas, I know not, of what *gotra* I am; I asked my mother and she answered me, "Resorting to many in my youth as a serving-woman, I got thee, therefore I know not of what *gotra* thou art; but Jabala is my name and Satyakama is thine", Satyakama Jabala therefore am I'.

The teacher realised at once that this was no ordinary boy. One who could stand on his own base of truth with such poise and self-confidence must needs have a noble inheritance. He said: 'None who is a not a Brahmin can be strong enough to say this; gather the firewood, my son, I will take thee under me, for thou didst not depart from the truth.'

Under Haridrumata Gautama's tutelage, Satyakama became one of the finest teachers of his times. Sri

Aurobindo has expertly drawn out the significance of this exceptional tale to prove that casteist touch-me-not-ism (Swami Vivekananda's phrase) has no place in India's Sanatana Dharma:

> 'Satyakama, as we gather from other passages was one of the great Vedantic teachers of the time immediately previous to the composition of the Chhandogya Upanishad. But his birth is the meanest possible. . . It appears from this story as from others that, although the system of the four castes was firmly established, it counted as no obstacle in the pursuit of knowledge and spiritual advancement. The Kshatriya could teach the Brahmin, the illegitimate and fatherless son of the serving-girl could be *guru* to the purest and highest blood in the land. This is nothing new or improbable, for it has been so throughout the history of Hinduism and the shutting out of anyone from spiritual truth and culture on the ground of caste is an invention of later times.'[6]

Raikwa the cart-puller, Uma Haimavati and Satyakama Jabala do not exhaust the rich treasure-chest of the Upanishads. Blessed is our motherland that has always gifted such brilliances for us to shape our lives and walk the sunlit path. □

References

1. Translated by Amarnath Dutta, *Education and Initiation* (2003), p. 6.
2. Translated by H.O. Hume
3. This is why spiritual luminaries are referred to with the sobriquet, Paramahamsa. Sri Ramakrishna is known as Ramakrishna Paramahamsa.
4. Translations from the *Kena Upanishad* are by Sri Aurobindo
5. All translations from the *Chandogya Upanishad* are by Sri Aurobindo
6. *The Upanishads* (2000), p. 365

Chapter 15

Call of the Upanishads

Some Practical Guidelines from the Upanishads for Daily Living

Begin Your Day with Prayer

ॐ तत्सवितुर्वरेण्यं भर्गो देवस्य धीमहि धियो यो नः प्रचोदयात् ।। ॐ ।।
—Mahanarayana Upanishad

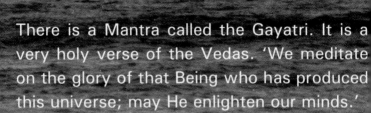

There is a Mantra called the Gayatri. It is a very holy verse of the Vedas. 'We meditate on the glory of that Being who has produced this universe; may He enlighten our minds.'

—Swami Vivekananda, CW, I: 192

172

Seek the Infinite

यो वै भूमा तत्सुखं नाल्पे सुखमस्ति भूमैव सुखं
भूमा त्वेव विजिज्ञासितव्य ।

That which indeed is the Infinite, that is joy. There is no joy in the finite. The Infinite alone is joy. But the Infinite indeed has to be sought after.

—CHANDOGYA UPANISHAD

Why weepest thou, brother? There is neither death nor disease for thee. Why weepest thou, brother? There is neither misery nor misfortune for thee. Why weepest thou, brother? Neither change nor death was predicated of thee. Thou art Existence Absolute. . . . Be your own Self.

—Swami Vivekananda, CW, 5: 275

You Are What You Think

मन एव मनुष्याणां कारणं बन्धमोक्षयोः ।
बन्धाय विषयासक्तं मुक्तं निर्विषयं स्मृतम् ॥

It is indeed the mind that is the cause of men's bondage and liberation. The mind that is attached to sense-objects leads to bondage, while dissociated from sense-objects it tends to lead to liberation. So they think.

—AMRITABINDU UPANISHAD

Whatever you think, that you will be. If you think yourselves weak, weak you will be; if you think yourselves strong, strong you will be.   —Swami Vivekananda, CW, 3: 130

How to Live in the World

ॐ ईशा वास्यमिदग्ं सर्वं यत्किञ्च जगत्यां जगत् ।
तेन त्यक्तेन भुञ्जीथा मा गृधः कस्यस्विद्धनम् ॥

Om. All this—whatsoever moves on the earth—should be covered by the Lord. Protect (Your Self) through that detachment. Do not covet anybody's weatlh.

—Isha Upanishad

Work incessantly, holding life as something deified, as God Himself, and knowing that this is all we have to do, this is all we should ask for. God is in everything, where else shall we go to find Him? He is already in every work, in every thought, in every feeling. Thus knowing, we must work... Thus the effects of work will not bind us.

—Swami Vivekananda, CW, 2:50

Cultivate Positive Attitude

ॐ भद्रं कर्णेभिः शृणुयाम देवाः भद्रं पश्येमाक्षभिर्यजत्राः ।
स्थिरैरङ्गैस्तुष्टुवागंसस्तनूभिः व्यशेम देवहितं यदायुः ॥
स्वस्ति न इन्द्रो वृद्धश्रवाः । स्वस्ति नः पूषा विश्ववेदाः ।
स्वस्ति नस्ताक्ष्यो॓ऽरिष्टनेमिः स्वस्ति नो बृहस्पतिर्दधातु ॥
ॐ शान्तिः शान्तिः शान्तिः ॥

**Om. O Gods! may we hear with our ears
what is auspicious. O Ye adorable ones!
may we see with our eyes what is
auspicious. May we sing praises to Ye
and enjoy with strong limbs and body the
life allotted to us by the Gods. Om Peace,
Peace, Peace.** —MANDUKYA UPANISHAD

Let positive, strong, helpful thought enter into their
brains from very childhood. Lay yourselves open to
these thoughts, and not to weakening and paralysing
ones. . . .Drive out the superstition that has covered
your minds. Let us be brave. Know the Truth and
practise the Truth. The goal may be distant, but
awake, arise, and stop not till the goal is reached.
— Swami Vivekananda, CW, 2: 87

How to Build Character

सत्यं वद । धर्मं चर । स्वाध्यायान्मा प्रमदः ।
सत्यान्न प्रमदितव्यम् । धर्मान्न प्रमदितव्यम् ।
कुशलान्न प्रमदितव्यम् । भूत्यै न प्रमदितव्यम् ।
स्वाध्यायप्रवचनाभ्यां न प्रमदितव्यम् ॥

Speak the truth. Follow the path of virtue. Swerve not from the study of the scriptures. Never swerve from truth. Never swerve from the path of virtue. Do not deviate from what is beneficial. Do not deviate from the path leading to your welfare. And do not stray away from the study and teaching of the scriptures. —TAITTIRIYA UPANISHAD

Doing good to others is virtue (dharma); injuring others is sin.

Strength and manliness are virtue; weakness and cowardice are sin.

Independence is virtue; dependence is sin.

Loving others is virtue; hating others is sin.

Faith in God and in one's own Self is virtue; doubt is sin.

Knowledge of oneness is virtue; seeing diversity is sin.

—Swami Vivekananda, CW, 5: 419

The Essence of Spiritual Struggle

समाने वृक्षे पुरुषो निमग्नो5-
नीशया शोचति मुह्यमानः ।
जुष्टं यदा पश्यत्यन्यमीश-
मस्य महिमानमिति वीतशोकः ॥

Seated on the same tree, the individualised being is deluded and grieves over his helplessness. But when he beholds the other—the worshipful Lord—as also His glory, he becomes free from all grief.   —MUNDAKA UPANISHAD

Man catches a glimpse, then again he forgets and goes on eating the sweet and bitter fruits of life; perhaps after a time he catches another glimpse, and the lower bird goes nearer and nearer to the higher bird as blows after blows are received. If he be fortunate to receive hard knocks, then he comes nearer and nearer to his companion, the other bird, and as he approaches him, he finds that the light from the higher bird is playing round his own plumage; and as he comes nearer and nearer, lo! the transformation is going on. The nearer and nearer he comes, he finds himself melting away, as it were, until he has entirely disappeared. . . He then becomes fearless, perfectly satisfied, calmly serene.
                —Swami Vivekananda, CW, 3: 236

Life is a Journey

असतो मा सद्गमय । तमसो मा ज्योतिर्गमय ।
मृत्योर्मा अमृतं गमय ।।

From untruth lead me to Truth. From darkness (of ignorance) lead me to light (of knowledge). From death lead me to immortality.

—BRIHADARANYAKA UPANISHAD

From the unreal, lead us to the Real.
From darkness, lead us unto Light.
From death, lead us to Immortality.
Reach us through and through our self.
And evermore protect us, O Thou Terrible!,
From ignorance, by Thy sweet Compassionate Face.

— Swami Vivekananda, *Life*, 2: 356

The Conquest of Selfishness

दाम्यत दत्त दयध्वमिति; तदेतत् त्रयं
शिक्षेत्दमं दानं दयामिति

Subdue the senses, do acts of charity, be compassionate. Practise these three virtues—control of the senses, charity and compassion.

—BRIHADARANYAKA UPANISHAD

Selfishness is the chief sin, thinking of ourselves first. He who thinks, 'I will eat first, I will have more money than others, and I will possess everything', . . . is the selfish man. The unselfish man says, 'I will be last, I do not care to go to heaven, I will ever go to hell if by doing so I can help my brothers. This unselfishness is the test of religion. He who has more of this unselfishness is more spiritual

—Swami Vivekananda, CW, 3: 143

Integration of Personality

ॐ वाङ् मे मनसि प्रतिष्ठिता मनो मे वाचि प्रतिष्ठितम्
आविरावीर्म एधि वेदस्य म आणीस्थः श्रुतं मे मा
प्रहासीरनेनाधीतेनाहोरात्रान् संदधामि

**Om! May my speech be based on (i.e. accord
with) the mind; may my mind be based on
speech. O Self-effulgent One, reveal Thyself
to me. May you both (speech and mind) be
the carriers of the Veda to me. May not all
that I have heard depart from me. I shall join
together (i.e. obliterate the difference of)
day and night through this study.**

—AITAREYA UPANISHAD

Live for an ideal, and that one ideal alone.
Let it be so great, so strong, that there may
be nothing else left in the mind; no place
for anything else, no time for anything else.
— Swami Vivekananda, CW, 5: 251-52

Look Upon Others as Divine

त्वं स्त्री त्वं पुमानसि त्वं कुमार उत वा कुमारी ।
त्वं जीर्णो दण्डेन वञ्चसि त्वं जातो भवसि विश्वतोमुखः ॥

**Thou art the woman, Thou art the man,
Thou art the youth and the maiden too.
Thou art the old man who totters along,
leaning on the staff. Thou art born with
faces turned in all directions.**

—SHVETASHVATARA UPANISHAD

If you cannot see God in the human face, how
can you see him in the clouds, or in images
made of dull, dead matter, or in mere fictitious
stories of our brain? I shall call you religious from
the day you begin to see God in men and
women. . .Whatever comes to you is but the
Lord, the Eternal, the Blessed One, appearing to
us in various forms, as our father, and mother,
and friend, and child—they are our own soul
playing with us.

— Swami Vivekananda, CW, 2: 326

The Secret of Meditation

प्रणवो धनुः शरो ह्यात्मा ब्रह्म तल्लक्ष्यमुच्यते ।
अप्रमत्तेन वेद्धव्यं शरवत्तन्मयो भवेत् ।।

Om is the bow; the soul is the arrow;
and Brahman is called its target. It is to
be hit by an unerring man. One should
become one with It just like an arrow.

—Mundaka Upanishad

Concentration of the powers of the mind is
our only instrument to help us see God. . .
The concentrated mind is a lamp that
shows us every corner of the soul.

—Swami Vivekananda, CW, 7: 59-60

Think of Strength Always

ॐ आप्यायन्तु ममाङ्गानि वाक्प्राणश्चक्षुः
श्रोत्रमथो बलमिन्द्रियाणि च सर्वाणि ।
. . . तदात्मनि निरते य उपनिषत्सु धर्मास्ते
मयि सन्तु ते मयि सन्तु ।

May my limbs, speech, vital force, eyes,
ears, as also strength and all the organs,
become well developed. . . May all the
virtues that are (spoken of) in the Upanishads repose in me who am engaged in the
pursuit of the Self; may they repose in me.

—Kena Upanishad

Think of your own body, and see that it is
strong and healthy; it is the best instrument
you have. Think of it as being as strong as
adamant, and that with the help of this body
you will cross the ocean of life. Freedom is
never to be reached by the weak. Throw
away all weakness. Tell your body that it is
strong, tell your mind that it is strong, and
have unbounded faith and hope in yourself.

—Swami Vivekananda, CW, 1: 146

Self-discipline is the Key to Success

तपसा ब्रह्म विजिज्ञासस्व । तपो ब्रह्मेति ।

Know Brahman by means of tapas; that is, by means of penance, austerity, meditation and control of the senses. Tapas is Brahman.

—TAITTIRIYA UPANISHAD

No force can be created; it can only be directed. Therefore, we must learn to control the grand powers that are already in our hands, and by will power make them spiritual, instead of merely animal.

—Swami Vivekananda, CW, 8: 46

The Way is Difficult yet Despair Not

उत्तिष्ठत जाग्रत प्राप्य वरान्निबोधत ।
क्षुरस्य धारा निशिता दुरत्यया
दुर्गं पथस्तत्कवयो वदन्ति ॥

Arise, awake, and learn by approaching the excellent ones. The wise ones describe that path to be as impassable as a razor's edge, which, when sharpened, is difficult to tread on.

—KATHA UPANISHAD

Those who dare, therefore, to struggle for victory, for truth, for religion, are in the right way; and that is what the Vedas preach: Be not in despair; the way is very difficult, like walking on the edge of a razor; yet despair not, arise, awake, and find the ideal, the goal.

—Swami Vivekananda, CW, 2: 124

Chapter 16

Upanishadic Guidelines for the Practice of Medicine

SWAMI BRAHMESHANANDA

Divinity of Man

One of the fundamental teachings of the Upanishads is that all beings are divine. Upanishads advice everyone to look upon oneself and others as divine. This integral vision of oneness of whole creation is beautifully expressed in the mantra from the *Shvetashvatara Upanishad*.[1]

> 'Thou art woman, thou art man. Thou art the young man as well as young woman. Thou again art the old man tottering on the staff. Indeed, thou hast taken innumerable forms.'

If, therefore, every form before us is God (Divine), a patient, too, is God. While the Upanishad speaks only this much, Sri Ramakrishna further tells us *how* this idea can be applied in practice. Let us recall here the well-known incident which took place when Sri Ramakrishna was living at Dakshineshwar. While explaining the Vaishnava concept of *'Jive daya'* (compassion on creatures), he got merged into *Samadhi*. Then a little later, coming to normal consciousness, he

exclaimed that famous dictum: *Shiv Jnane, Jiva Seva*—
service of beings (jiva) considering them God (Shiva).

Sri Ramakrishna was the embodiment of the truths
enshrined in the Upanishads. Through his extra-ordinary
spiritual experiences, he realized the essence of the
Upanishads. His utterances, having their origin in that
state of oneness with the supreme spirit, are thus *living*
Upanishads. This utterance of 'service of God in man'
has, thus, become a watchword for interpersonal
relationships in general and for practicing the idea of
service to others in particular. Let us discuss this idea
of 'service of God in man' in the context of practice of
medicine, with particular reference to doctor-patient
interactions.

Conditions for 'Worshiping' the Sick

The practice of medicine can become one of the
best forms of practical religion. But this requires certain
changes in our outlook towards the whole issue or else
it would become the case of one of the many ways of
earning money—as it has, unfortunately, become today.
What are the conditions for practising this ideal of
looking at others as spiritual entities and 'worshiping'
them?

Swami Vivekananda, drawing his inspiration from
the Upanishads as also from his own spiritual
realizations, said that a human being is like a living
residence of God, the highest 'temple' of God. The
first condition for serving the sick and suffering as
veritable embodiments of God as God, therefore, is to
have this faith. Only when we hold others as divine

beings can we transform our medical practice into a spiritual practice.

If we look at the commonest form of worship prevalent among many religions we find it consists of a ritualistic adoration of God. This is done through worshiping a symbol of God such as an image, a picture, or a pitcher, or any other form. Before starting the worship, the image or symbol is ritualistically invoked; 'life' is infused into the otherwise lifeless symbol. This is followed by purification of the articles of worship. After such preliminaries, the worshipper offers f ive, ten or sixteen items to the deity with the help of ritual acts and the chanting of verbal formulae or *mantras*.

In the same way, while treating a patient, one can worship him by looking upon him as an embodiment of divinity. Then, instead of flowers and incense, tablets and syrups are administered to him; instead of water for bathing an image, a patient is sponged or bathed with medicated lotion, as per the need. Application of ointments or dressing a wound may be compared to offering sandal paste to the Deity. Treating him in an amicable manner, and speaking to him reassuring words of hope, are like *mantras* in the worship of God.

When we look at the details of the ritualistic worship, we find that while the general outline of the process of worship is the same in all modes of worship, the items offered and the mantras chanted vary from deity to deity. The mantras and items employed in the worship of Kali, for instance, are not the same as in those used in the worship of Shiva. Drawing a parallel to this variety in mantras and items used in worship, there are differences in the form of medical service given to patients suffering from typhoid, meningitis or intestinal obstruction. Further, a surgery can be compared to an elaborate Durga Puja, one of the most elaborate ritualistic worships prevalent today. One might look at the operation theatre as the *Puja mandapam*, the worship hall; with chief surgeon as chief priest conducting the solemn 'ceremony' of the operation with the help of his team of assistants. The elaborate preparations, the perfect solemnity and careful method and procedure–all are comparable to those of making preparations and conducting the Durga Puja.

Guidelines from the Upanishads

Service to a suffering human being as God as indicated by the Upanishads is even superior to a ritualistic worship. While one has to imagine or ritualistically infuse life into a stone image, nothing of the sort is required in serving a man as God, for he is already 'alive'—a living symbol of divinity. Besides, serving God in man helps both the server and the served, while the traditional worship helps only the worshipper. Finally, serving a human being as God requires greater intellectual, moral and spiritual training than is required for ritualistic worship.

But seeing or feeling the presence of God in a miserable, poor, ignorant, suffering patient is not easy.

A physician is apt to see in his patient only man or woman, rich or poor, saint or sinner, or a fellow being of high or low caste. The human God may grunt or complain, and unlike the mute ever-smiling stone image, may weep, shout or at times become irritable or violent. On such occasions one is apt to wonder whether one is serving God or devil.

The service of a living God, therefore, demands greater patience, forbearance, and perseverance. It requires preparation. The physician will have to remind himself or herself that the being before him is not a man or a woman but God Himself. The physician will have to constantly chant and meditate on the Upanishadic Mantra referred to above, 'Thou art woman, Thou art man . .' (tvam stree tvam puman asi). He will have to overcome his own reactions such as lack of motivation, irritation, annoyance and repulsion. This lack of motivation may come because treating the patient may not present any *fascinating* clinical problem; one might feel irritated by the patient's verbal reactions or inability to provide a clear account of the history of his condition; he may become annoyed because the patient does not follow his instructions or because the disease does not respond to treatment as expected, and feel repulsed at the patient's lack of cleanliness, self-control, or absence of a sense of cooperation.

Seeing God in man as preached by the Upanishads and to serve him thus, therefore, requires training. It demands an intelligent combination of technical skill, understanding and a spiritual outlook towards life itself.

One can derive many lessons from the Upanishads for enriching the doctor-patient relationship. Let us look at the well known and oft-repeated *shanti mantra*: *sahanavavatu, sahanau bhunaktu, sahaviryam karavavahai . . .'* The English meaning of the mantra is,

> 'May the supreme Being protect us both. May He nourish both of us. May we be vigorous together. May what we study become fruitful and may we do not hate each other.'

Usually this mantra is held to be a prayer for healthy teacher-disciple (*guru-shishya*) relationship. As it is chanted before and after the study of the Upanishads, it indicates the type of attitude the student and the teacher must have while studying. It is also a prayer for healthy relationship. Thus, it can, in most part, serve as excellent guiding principle for doctor-patient relationship. The expression 'May what we study become fruitful' (*tejasvina adhitam astu*) would then mean: 'May the treatment which is being given be successful with our mutual co-operation.'

The mantra also points to inter-doctor relationship. 'The physician should never harbour ill-will towards fellow physicians or get into confrontations with them. If need be, he may join them in treating a case and should not hesitate to consult them in deciding the diagnosis and treatment of a case. He must pardon the unethical conduct of his colleague, or politely try to set him right. But if the envious opponent continues to criticize his procedure, he must defeat him by his knowledge and experience. Even while defending himself the physician must avoid harsh words and use ethical language. He must always be suggestive and never direct.'[2]

Another way of having healthy interpersonal relationship in the practice of medicine can be learnt from the teacher- disciple relationship mentioned in the five *samhitis* (meditation on five juxtapositions) mentioned in the *Taittiriyopanishad*.[3] In one of these samhitis, the teacher (acharya) is considered the first part, the disciple the second part, and knowledge as the meeting place with instruction as the link. One may consider the doctor-patient relationship too from this angle. In that case, the sentence (samhiti) may be rephrased for meditation thus:

'This is the meditation with regard to healing. The physician is the first letter. The patient is the last letter. Treatment is the meeting point. Medicine is the link. This is the meditation with regard to healing.' (*athaahdivaidyam. chikitsakah purvarupam, rogih uttararupam, chikitsa sandhih, aushadhi sandhanam, ityadhivaidyam*)

The purpose of this attempt is only to transform our outlook. If one truly sees God, or one's own Atman in every being, it is bound to transform one's life and action. Says the *Ishavasyopanishad*:[4]

'A person who sees all beings in the self itself and the Self in all beings, feels no hatred by virtue of that (realization).

When to a man of realization all beings become the very self, then how can there be sorrow or delusion for that seer of oneness?'

Indeed no ulterior motives or ill-feelings can affect a doctor or patient who experiences such a unity.

While this is a state of highest realization, it is an indication as to how one should act. As Acharya Shankara, in his commentary on the Bhagavad Gita points out that the marks of a man of realization are the practices of an unenlightened person, so, a doctor and a patient, according to this axiom, must try to act without hate, fear, envy, delusion and ill-will. A doctor can repeat these mantras as daily reminders while meditating on their meaning.

Upanishads are a storehouse of the lofty knowledge of oneness of existence. In order to put this idea of oneness into practice, one needs a rigorous moral and ethical discipline. Declares Upanishad: 'Speak the Truth, practice righteousness...There should not be inadvertence about truth, there should be no deviation from righteous activity...'[5] Every medical practitioner must remember this and avoid every form of dubious or dishonest practice.

The Practice of Right Conduct

In ancient Indian literature the word used for ethics was *sadvritta*[6] which etymologically means, 'the right physical, mental and vocal conduct expected of the pious.' Charaka, the father of Indian medicine, advises everyone desiring peace and happiness in life to observe the rules of right conduct diligently. He who follows the ethical code gains mastery over the senses and obtains a healthy body.[7] He authoritatively advocates ethics as a part of personal hygiene. Vagbhatta, too, claims that man can attain long and healthy life, wealth and fame in this existence, and glory and higher spheres after death by following the ethical code.[8]

The ancient sages framed these rules of ethics and built up early Indian society in such a way that character could be moulded from the very childhood and the individual could grow into a responsible citizen. The ethical training that began at home, with the parents, was continued at the schools through the teachers, and continued in one's professional life later with the help of the wise and leaders of society.

The Kathopanishad, for instance, states:

'One who has not abstained from bad conduct, whose senses are not under control, whose mind is not concentrated, whose mind is not free from anxiety, cannot attain the Self through knowledge.'[9]

These are watchwords, not only for the physicians but also for the patients. Self-control and noble character are *sine qua non* for success, health and prosperity.

Upanishads also warn all, including the physicians, that none can be satisfied with money: 'No man can be fully satisfied by money alone' (*na vittena tarpaniyo manushyaha*)[10] —a statement which has great relevance for the present times. Although as a profession the medical practice provides a livelihood for the physician, the wise have condemned this attitude. Restating the Upanishadic declaration, the Charaka Samhita says that those who would sell their skill to make a business out of the practice of medicine are like persons who would pursue a heap of dust, as it were, letting go a mass of gold.[11] Hence medicine must be practised neither for wealth nor for fulfilment of worldly desires, but only out of compassion for creatures.[12] When it is done as a spiritual discipline, it becomes a source of inner and outer well-being. There is no austerity higher than treating the sick.

The physician must not undertake treatment of a patient motivated by attachment or lust or greed. Nor even friendship, enmity or affection for a kinsman should be a reason for giving his treatment. The expectation of earning a reward, or the acquisition of fame should not tempt the physician. Only one urge and aim—that is, kindness and mercy, should prompt the physician to practice the art of healing.[13] This is how the Upanishadic teachings of sameness become a part of the practice of medicine.

Cultivating the Right Attitude

What should be our attitude towards the body? The Upanishads are very clear about this question. They clearly state that the soul is separate from the physical body and even from the prana or vital force, and is not affected by the birth, growth, decay and death of the physical body. But this does not mean one should neglect one's physical well-being. The body must be kept healthy and strong. The Upanishidic rishi prays:

'May my limbs, speech, vital force, eyes, ears, as also strength and all the organs become well developed...'[14]

In *Ananda Valli of Taittiriyopanishad* also we get an indication of the need to have a healthy body and mind. While describing one unit of perfect human happiness, it has been stated that 'a young man, in the prime of life, good, most expeditious, most strongly built, and most energetic,'[15] i.e., physically and mentally strong and disciplined person alone can be the enjoyer of true happiness.

Not only should one be physically strong but also mentally strong. Ideal mental health could be obtained by practice of discrimination, detachment, devotion and discipline. We might call them as 4-Ds. When one practises them one becomes strong and integrated. Then one's thinking, willing, emotions, and senses work in unison. Let us take them up one by one.

Discrimination includes reasoning, observation, critical assessment of an event or object, and an analytical study of any specific thing. Upanishad specifically recommends discrimination between *shreya* and *preya* i.e., between the beneficial and the pleasurable.[16] Though the Upanishads advocate the practice of philosophical discrimination between the real and the unreal, practice of discrimination in daily life means learning to follow the beneficial. If we carefully and critically analyse our own real nature and that of the world around, we may obtain direct insight into the true nature of our own Self *(atman)* and can get fully established in the Self. We will then be *svastha*, which is the real meaning of the term 'health'. Even short of this highest state, we can make good use of our discriminating faculty and get to the depth of the events of life, and this is a great gain so far as mental health and stability are concerned.

Next comes *detachment*. Upanishads state that we must aspire to live for a hundred years.[17] This involves absence of anxiety and meaningless stress. This can be done only when we offer our actions to God.[18] One of the major causes of mental instability and suffering is attachment to persons, places, things and specific type of activity. We seek fruits of actions, and when our expectations are frustrated, we get upset and lose our mental poise. This means we need to practice detachment. If we are more objective in our approach, not only towards the events of the external world, but also towards events occurring in our mental world, we will be more peaceful and mentally strong.

Devotion integrates, strengthens and develops our emotions. We have hundreds of emotions which drive us in different directions. Devotion to God, to one's guru, or to a scripture, even to an ideal, is a great stabilizing force. One of the causes of failing mental health among people is the gradual decline and weakening of faith. Faith is a tremendous sustaining force against various types of challenges. Although there is greater emphasis on knowledge and discrimination in Upanishads, they repeatedly emphasize the need for faith.[19] The Upanishads also abound in prayers to God and stress the need for God's grace in no uncertain terms.[20]

Conclusion

Finally, there must be discipline in all aspects. The body must be disciplined; the senses must be controlled, and must obey the commands of the mind. The mind too must be disciplined. Just as a chariot with disciplined and controlled horses, with tight reins in the hands of an expert driver reaches the destination safely, without any accidents, so also a disciplined body with disciplined senses, mind and intellect conduces to the overall well-being of the individual.[21] The eight-fold path of yoga with meditation as the central theme is an essential part of a scheme of all-round discipline. *The Shvetashvatara Upanishad* gives ample hints for the practice of meditation.[22]

Regular practice of rhythmic breathing too helps in achieving physical and mental health. According to the Upanishads, the real core of our being, the atman, is encased in five sheaths. The Upanishadic psychology says that the *Pranamaya-kosha* (energy sheath) is situated between the *annamaya-kosha* (food sheath) and the *manomaya-kosha* (mind sheath) and is therefore affected by, and in turn influences, both the *koshas*. In other words, breathing is influenced by mental and physical states, and it influences both mind and body. Hence its regulation by practice of rhythmic breathing, Pranayama, conduces to physical and mental health.[23]

The Upanishads have also at many places discussed the problem of death and how to face it. The Upanishadic rishi advises us to pray to the Sun God, as one approaches death that he may withdraw his blinding rays and allow one to see the truth. He should also remember his noble deeds and pray to the divine fire to carry him through bright path to glorious spheres.[24]

When one follows the Upanishads in the practice of medicine, one is sure to develop right attitude towards oneself, towards others and towards the work one is doing. What should be the motto of a man wanting to practice the Upanishads in daily life? The following prayer aptly summarizes this:

'Om. O gods, may we hear auspicious words with our ears; while engaged in sacrifices may we see auspicious things with the eyes. While praising the gods with steady limbs may we enjoy a life that is beneficial to gods.' □

References

1. *Shvetashvatara Upanishad*, 4-3

2. *Kasyapa Samhita vimana sthanam*, 1.9

3. *Taittiriyopanishad*, II.iii.1

4. *Ishavasyopanishad*, 6-7

5. *Taittiriyopanishad, 1, xi, 1*

6. Commentary of Chakrapani on *Charaka Samhita, Sutra Sthana,* 8:17. Choukhamba Sanskrit Samsthana, Varanasi, U. P. 1984

7. *Charaka Samhita,* 8:17 - 18

8. Vagbhatta, *Astanga Hridaya*, Sutra 2:48. New Delhi: Motilal Banarasidass

9. *Katha Upanishad*, 1, ii, 24

10. *ibid,* 1, I, 27

11. *Charaka*, op. cit., 1.56

12. *Ibid.*, 1.58

13. *ibid*, 7:33-34   14. Shanti Mantra, *Kena Upanishad*

15. *Taittiriyopanishad*, II, viii, 1

16. *Katha Upanishad*, 1, ii, 1,2

17. *Ishavasya Upanishad*, 2

18. *Shvetashvatara Upanishad*,   6, 4

19. cf. *Katha Upanishad*, 1, i, 2

20. cf. *Shvetashvatara* , 4-1, 10, 12

21. *Katha Upanishad, 1, iii, 3-9*

22. *The Shvetashvatara 2, 8-15*

23. *ibid, 2, 9*

24. *Isha, 16, 17, 18*

Chapter 17

The Story of Nachiketa

SWAMI VIVEKANANDA

This [issue of Self] the Katha Upanishad speaks in very figurative language. There was, in ancient times, a very rich man, who made a certain sacrifice which required that he should give away everything that he had. Now, this man was not sincere. He wanted to get the fame and glory of having made the sacrifice, but he was only giving things which were of no further use to him—old cows, barren, blind, and lame. He had a boy called Nachiketas. This boy saw that his father was not doing what was right, that he was breaking his vow; but he did not know what to say to him. In India, father and mother are living gods to their children.

And so the boy approached the father with the greatest respect and humbly inquired of him, 'Father, to whom are you going to give me? For your sacrifice requires that everything shall be given away.' The father was very much vexed at this question and replied, 'What do you mean, boy? A father giving away his own son?' The boy asked the question a second and a third time, and then the angry father answered, 'Thee I give unto Death (Yama).'

And the story goes on to say that the boy went to Yama, the god of death. Yama was the first man who died. He went to heaven and became the governor of all the Pitris; all the good people who die, go, and live with him for a long time. He is very holy person, chaste and good, as his name (Yama) implies.

So the boy went to Yama's world. But even gods are sometimes not at home, and three days this boy had to wait there. After the third day Yama returned. 'O learned one,' said Yama, 'you have been waiting here for three days without food, and you are a guest worthy of respect. Salutation to thee, O Brahmin, and welfare to me! I am very sorry I was not at home. But for that I will make amends. Ask three boons, one for each day.' And the boy asked, 'My first boon is that my father's anger against me may pass away; that he will be kind to me and recognise me when you allow me to depart.' Yama granted this fully. The next boon was that he wanted to know about a certain sacrifice which took people to heaven.

Now we have seen that the oldest idea which we got in the Samhita portion of the Vedas was only about heaven where they had bright bodies and lived with the fathers. . . Living in heaven would not be very different from life in this world. At best, it would only be a very healthy rich man's life, with plenty of sense-enjoyments and a sound body which knows no disease. It would be this material world, only a little more refined; and we have seen the difficulty that the external material world can never solve the problem. So no heaven can solve the problem. . . Yet Nachiketas asks, as the second boon, about some sacrifice through which people might attain to this heaven. There was an idea in the Vedas that these sacrifices pleased the gods and took human beings to heaven. . . So Nachiketas asks by what form of sacrifice a man can go to heaven. The second boon was also readily granted by Yama who promised that this sacrifice should henceforth be named after Nachiketas.

Then the third boon comes, and with that the Upanishad proper begins. The boy said, 'There is this difficulty: when a man dies some say he is, others that he is not. Instructed by you I desire to understand this.' But Yama was frightened. He had been very glad to grant the other two boons. Now he said, 'The gods in ancient times were puzzled on this point. This subtle law is not easy to understand. Choose some other boon, O Nachiketas, do not press me on this point, release me.'

The boy was determined, and said, 'What you have said is true, O Death, that even the gods had doubts on this point, and it is no easy matter to understand. But I cannot obtain another exponent like you and there is no other boon equal to this.'

Death said, 'Ask for sons and grandsons who will live one hundred years, many cattle, elephants, gold, and horses. Ask for empire on this earth and live as many years as you like. Or choose any other boon which you think equal to these—wealth and long life. Or be thou a king, O Nachiketas, on the wide earth. I will make thee the enjoyer of all desires. Ask for all those desires which are difficult to obtain in the world. These heavenly maidens with chariots and music, which are not to be obtained by man, are yours. Let them serve you, O Nachiketas, but do not question me as to what comes after death.'

Nachiketas said, 'These are merely things of a day, O Death, they wear away the energy of all the sense-organs. Even the longest life is very short. These horses and chariots, dances and songs, may remain with Thee. Man cannot be satisfied by wealth. Can we retain wealth when we behold Thee? We shall live only so long as Thou desirest. Only the boon which I have asked is chosen by me.'

Yama was pleased with this answer and said, 'Perfection is one thing and enjoyment another; these two having different ends, engage men differently. He who chooses perfection becomes pure. He who chooses enjoyment misses his true end. Both perfection and enjoyment present themselves to man; the wise man having examined both distinguishes one from the other. He chooses perfection as being superior to enjoyment, but the foolish man chooses enjoyment for the pleasure of his body. O Nachiketas, having thought upon the things which are only apparently desirable, thou hast wisely abandoned them.' Death then proceeded to teach Nachiketas. . . .

Yama said, 'That which is beyond never rises before the mind of a thoughtless child deluded by the folly of riches. "This world exists, the other does not," thinking thus they come again and again under my power. To understand this truth is very difficult. Many, even hearing it continually, do not understand it, for the speaker must be wonderful, so must the hearer.

The teacher must be wonderful, so must be the taught. Neither is the mind to be disturbed by vain arguments, for it is no more a question of argument, it is a question of fact.'

This is the watchword of Vedanta— realise religion, no talking will do. But it is done with great difficulty. He has hidden Himself inside the atom, this Ancient One who resides in the inmost recess of every human heart. The sages realised Him through the power of introspection, and got beyond both joy and misery, beyond what we call virtue and vice, beyond good and bad deeds, beyond being and non-being; he who has seen Him has seen the Reality.

Now Yama answers the question: 'What becomes of a man when the body dies?' 'This Wise One never dies, is never born, It arises from nothing, and nothing arises from It. Unborn, Eternal, Everlasting, this Ancient One can never be destroyed with the destruction of the body. If the slayer thinks he can slay, or if the slain thinks he is slain, they both do not know the truth, for the Self neither slays nor is slain.' A most tremendous position. I should like to draw your attention to the adjective in the first line, which is 'wise'.

. . .Here is a beautiful figure. Picture the Self to be the rider and this body the chariot, the intellect to be the charioteer, mind the reins, and the senses the horses. He whose horses are well broken, and whose reins are strong and kept well in the hands of the charioteer (the intellect) reaches the goal which is the state of Him, the Omnipresent. But the man whose horses (the senses) are not controlled, nor the reins (the mind) well managed, goes to destruction. This Atman in all beings does not manifest Himself to the eyes or the senses, but those whose minds have become purified and refined realise Him. Beyond all sound, all sight, beyond form, absolute, beyond all taste and touch, infinite, without beginning and without end, even beyond nature, the Unchangeable; he who realises Him, frees himself from the jaws of death. But it is very difficult. It is, as it were, walking on the edge of a razor; the way is long and perilous, but struggle on, do not despair. Awake, arise, and stop not till the goal is reached. □

Chapter 18

Upanishads and the Ideal of Service

M. LAKSHMI KUMARI

The Upanishadic Ideal of service is based on the concepts of Truth, Dharma and Yajna. Without comprehending these three concepts we cannot understand what we have come to recognise as service today—the most appealing and popular component of modern religions. Let us, therefore, first understand them.

Discovering the Satyam

Thousands of years ago, when humanity was still in a state of slumber, the super-scientists of India, the Vedic rishis, were engaged in the knotty task of uncovering the Ultimate Reality of life. This Reality of all realities, they soon found out, was beyond the world of pluralities, beyond whatever the senses could perceive. Through a step-by-step approach, breaking through the world of plurality, they looked into the very core of their inner being and discovered the Ultimate Truth as the Self (atman) within. This they called as Satyam, the Truth.

When they woke up from this super-conscious experience of Oneness, they also found that Truth is

One but its expressions are diverse. It is this truth in which everything in the universe remains interconnected, interrelated and interdependent. This is the greatest discovery ever made by man, and this Truth of Self-realization is the greatest blessings that the rishis have conferred on the world.

For us, in India, this discovery ushered in the dawn of life of enlightenment and introduced us to the splendid idea of Life Eternal. Since then, this Ganga of integral vision of the rishis has been cascading down the centuries, enriching every field of human activity and giving birth to a unique and spiritually oriented civilisation and culture. That this Satyam, the Eternal Truth, is the basis of Indian culture and civilisation is reflected in India's national emblem, *Satyameva Jayate* ('Truth Alone Triumphs')—a phrase taken from the Mundaka Upanishad.

The Way of Dharma

What is the ideal the Upanishads hold before us? To realise that Eternal Truth within oneself, and feel its presence in the entire universe and adjust all our activities in such a way as to reflect that principle of Oneness in life. This is the dharma kept before every human being. The final aim of dharma is Self realisation. This is what constitutes the essence of Upanishadic knowledge. This was the ancient truth that the rishis presented before us. To know the Self, again, the dharma is the way. This vision has been summarised in the eloquent words from the Taittiriya Upanishad, *satyam vada, dharmam chara* ('speak the truth, follow the dharma').

To the rishis, the Nature outside was an external expression of the Truth within. This was truly a quantum leap in knowledge—from unity to universality. This vision of the Whole and the awareness of man's interrelatedness with and interdependence on all that exists is what has made the Indian culture so singularly spiritual and, at once, in modern terms, highly scientific and holistic.

A profound respect for nature and the wisdom inherent in it is the hallmark of Upanishadic vision. To the Upanishadic mind, tolerance is a byword. When one gets truly established in it, genuine hospitality and warm friendship replace feelings of resentment and strangeness. Ecological balance and social justice are the natural outcome of such a wholesome living centred round the vision of a Universal Reality—where the individual feels himself bound to the cosmos as a whole. This became the Dharma of the individual.

Yajna, the Perennial Sacrifice

The Vedic ideal of Yajna is far more comprehensive, enriching and universal than what is conveyed by the word service. Rishis recognised man as an indivisible part of the Whole. Within him is a spark of the divinity, which is only quantitatively, (not qualitatively, as Swami Vivekananda used to stress) different from the Totality. Therefore, all human efforts should be directed towards the realisation of this Truth.

This extraordinary unity of the individual, the world he lives in and the Reality or God is what Sanatana Dharma, the Religion Eternal, emphasised from time immemorial. Yajna, hence, is a symbol of the practical relationship between human beings, world and God or the Ultimate Reality (*jiva, jagat* and *ishwara*). That Yajna is an act of unification and expansion of the human spirit and is made clear by its basic tenets.

Let us try to understand various aspects of the spirit of yajna and its dynamics in promoting individual and social well-being. The following discussion focuses on various aspects of the Vedic idea of a holistic life and tries to point out how the Upanishads are a repository of this wisdom.

1. *Idam na mama* ('It is not mine')

These words are spoken when offerings are poured into the fire during Yajnas. They emphasises the fact that the benefits that accrue from it are not for the doer but are meant for the welfare of all. Such an attitude made the individual dedicate his life for the welfare of all and thus free oneself of the temptations of jealousy, avarice, arrogance, violence, selfish motivation, and so on. This ideal of yajna later took a more practical form when Sri Krishna introduced it in Gita as *nishkama karma* (work without selfish motive)— an indispensable principle for anyone interested in achieving excellence in life and for one's inward evolution. Swami Vivekananda called this idea as the core of his ideal of Karma yoga and advocated it as the best means for 'man-making and nation building' programmes for India's regeneration.

2. Swahah (the Sanskrit word used as exclamation while doing a *yajna*)

Here again the idea is the surrender of ego. Truth, patience, non-stealing, forgiveness, discipline, and so on are all implied in this utterance with which the deities are worshiped through offerings. In the above two practices, renunciation (tyaga) of 'I' and 'mine' is emphasised. Though tyaga is a difficult idea to a purely materialistic mind to grasp, it is the best way to make oneself free from the bondage of work. When tyaga is backed by a spirit of unselfishness (*nishkama bhava*), it then leads to skilfulness in action which is the source of all prosperity and social security. This skilfulness is *tyaga* in another form. The Upanishads thus bridged the gap between the sacred and the secular and looked upon life as single whole.

3. Sham dvipade chatushpade (*'peace be to two-legged as well as four-legged beings'*)

As said earlier, the Upanishads are all-inclusive in their approach to life. They had deep concern for all life which was born of perception of the One Truth present everywhere. In their prayers, they sought well-being of all beings—human beings or birds ('two-legged') as well as animals or insects. They invoked benedictions for peace and good for everyone. This is how they upheld the unity of life and emphasised the interrelatedness and interdependence of existence. They understood that as man evolves, he begins to recognize his own higher self present in everything and starts treating them as his own. He feels compelled to contribute to the well-being and prosperity of all. Such a wholesome idea of inter-dependence is dawning in the modern scientific community now. Though late, it is better late than never.

Yajna is not just confined to a fire ritual but has wider implications as well. These implications are a key to understanding the ideal of service mentioned in the Upanishads. This is how the benefits of yajna be understood in a broader perspective as service. Doing a Yajna has the following connotations:

1. Deva Puja: Yajna was a tangible, concrete action in the early part of the Vedic tradition. Later the Vedic rishis discovered its deeper meaning of worship of God *by* respecting parents, teachers, seniors, guests, as also the mighty powers of the five elements. One may recall here the famous Upanishadic teachings: 'Worship your mother as Divine. Worship you father as Divine.' (*matri devo bhava, pitri devo bhava*). Worship is not just offering some flowers, incense and fruit. To supply others' needs, in a spirit of service and detachment is also a form of worship. As Sri Ramakrishna once remarked, 'Does God manifest only through a stone or wood image?' He can manifest in human forms also. So the idea of worship of God in man through attending to their needs is also a compelling form of yajna.

2. *Sanghatikaranam* (*Forging a group-unity*): As stated earlier, Yajna means establishing a relationship between man, world and God. The practical implication of establishing this sense of connectivity lies in maintaining unity and integrity within a home or organisation. This is done by being in tune with the ideals and thoughts of the place or group. The following hymn expresses this ideal of harmony succinctly:

'Common be your prayer;
Common be your end;
Common be your purpose;
Common be your deliberation.
Common be your desire;
Unified be your hearts;
United be your intentions;
Perfect be the union amongst you.'

(Rig Veda, X, 1919-3,4.)

When one keeps this idea of yajna in mind and does his work, he fosters unity of minds which is essential to create healthy and powerful organisations and promote a fellow feeling and righteousness.

3. *Dana* or donation: Dana or 'giving' can be in any form—giving monetary help or respect or knowledge or service and so on. The underlying idea is that it is by giving that a man receives back and that is what leads to real happiness. In this magnificent, all-comprehensive Upanishadic vision, in which every individual life is a part of a cosmic yajna, where does the idea of modern life style fit in? We must understand that living a gross physical and materialistic life, spending all our energies on our food, clothes and shelter, cannot make us happy and strong. We need to rise above this littleness of vision to learn the secrets of life. Elaborating what is meant by help, Swami Vivekananda says:

> 'Helping others physically, by removing their physical needs is indeed great; but the help is greater according as the need is greater and according as the help is far reaching. If a man's wants can removed for an hour, it is helping him indeed; if his wants can be removed for a year it will be more help to him; but if his wants can be removed for ever, it is surely the greatest help that can be given him. Spiritual knowledge is the only thing that can destroy our miseries forever; any other knowledge satisfies wants only for a time. It is only with the knowledge of the spirit that the faculty of want is annihilated forever; so helping man spiritually is the highest help that can be given him.' (CW, 1: 52)

Let us restate the last sentence of Swamiji. Life, Upanishads believe, becomes complete only when one realises the truth of atman. Hence, the most valuable service that can be rendered is to kindle a desire to realise that truth. Swamiji called this process of Self-experience as an act of de-hypnotisation. When one thinks he is just body and mind, he is hypnotised. When one realises one's limitless dimension within, the atman, he gets dehypnotised.

The Ideal of Service and Social Regeneration

How to practise this idea of yajna in life? For this, let us look at the lives of great men like Swami

Vivekananda and Sri Ramakrishna. In them we find how these ideals of Satya, Dharma and Yajna can be lived. We can draw many lessons from their lives and teachings. There are numerous incidents in their lives from which we learn how to practise this profound teaching of the Upanishads in daily life. Let us consider one incident here.

Once Sri Ramakrishna was conversing with devotees in his room in Dakshineshwar Temple Complex. He was quoting the well-known words from a Vaishanava scripture where it is said that in order to be a true devotee, one should develop love for repeating God's name, serve the holy men and have mercy on others. While he uttered the last of the three pre-requisites, he suddenly stopped and burst into a monologue, 'Mercy! Who are you to show mercy on others?! You can only serve others in a spirit of worship.' Swami Vivekananda, then known as Narendranath, witnessed the whole episode and after he came out of the room, remarked that if God wills, he will broadcast this revolutionary idea everywhere. And indeed he did broadcast this idea in the form of giving a new motto for service. He called it *shivajnane jiva seva* or service of man as God.

This is the practical message of the Upanishads. If we have to bring change in the cruel and brutal world scene, it can be done only by serving others in a spirit of worship. It is only service based on this Upanishadic ideals that can bring needed change in our individual and collective lives. Swamiji further reiterated these teachings in his immortal phrase: *'atmano mokshartham jagaddhitaya cha'*—'for one's own spiritual liberation and for the good of others.' When we keep this as the ideal of our life, we are then in tune with the Upanishads. In other words, divinisation of life is the ideal way to serve others. Let us keep this modern *mahavakya* of Swamiji in mind 'Serve Man, Serve God'. To serve is to develop a sense of oneness with others and that is the message of the Upanishads. ☐

Chapter 19

Upanishads—The Basis of All World Religions

SWAMI ABHIRAMANANDA

Swami Vivekananda's talk on 'The Vedanta' delivered at Lahore on 12 November 1897 created an electric atmosphere. Swamiji himself expressed satisfaction over the talk while his scribe Goodwin remarked that it was a masterly exposition on the subject. The lecture lasted nearly two and half hours and transformed the minds of many people, the most notable among them being Tirtha Ram Goswami who later on became famous as Swami Rama Tirtha.[1]

During the course of this talk, which was studded with several original and brilliant ideas, Swamiji stated: 'Nearly every chapter (of every Upanishad) begins with dualistic teaching, Upasana. God is first taught as someone who is the creator of the universe, its preserver and unto whom everything goes at last. He is one to be worshipped, the Ruler, the Guide of nature, external and internal, yet appearing as if He were outside of nature and external. One step further, and we find the same teacher teaching that this God is not outside of nature, but immanent in nature. And at last both ideas are discarded, and whatever real is He; there is no difference... that immanent One is at last declared to be the same that is in the human soul.'[2]

According to the above statement of Swamiji, not only every Upanishad but *each* chapter of *every* Upanishad describes God in three phases—as external, immanent, and united with Jiva.

When we carefully study the Upanishads from this perspective, they throw a new light. The following are some illustrations:

Example 1: Taittiriya Upanishad, Part-I

In the first stage, the Upanishad recommends meditation on the various deities of the Bhuh, Bhuvah and Suvah lokas as symbols of Brahman, just as a Salagrama is worshipped externally as a stone symbol of Lord Vishnu.[3]

In the second stage, God is described as being present in the cavity of the heart of the Jiva denoting the immanent aspect of God.[4]

In the third and final stage, the Jiva is fully identified with Brahman in such statements as

'My source is the Pure Brahman. I am the pure Self which is in the Sun. I am the immortal and undecaying.'[5]

Example 2: Taittiriya Upanishad, Part-II, III

In the first stage, Brahman is considered external to nature in passages as,

'From Brahman indeed was produced space, air, fire, water, earth, herbs, food, man, etc.'[6]

In the second stage, the immanent aspect of Brahman is described in passages such as

'That Brahman having created all that exists, entered into that very thing. And having entered there, It became the form and the formless, defined and undefined, the sustained and non-sustaining, the sentient and the insentient and the true and the untrue.'[7]

In the final stage, the identity of Jiva with Brahman is stated in the exclamatory passage,

'Oho! Oho! Oho, I am the food, I am the eater, I am the unifier, I am the first born of this world, etc.'[8]

Example 3: Mundaka Upanishad, Chapter III

This Upanishad brings out the identity of Jiva-Brahman through the beautiful imagery of two birds upon the self same tree, one on the top branch and other on a lower branch. The bird on the top is calm, silent and majestic, immersed in its own glory. The bird on the lower branch eats sweet and bitter fruits by turns, hops from branch to branch, and becomes alternately happy and miserable. After a time he eats an exceptionally bitter fruit, gets disgusted and looks up. There he sees the other bird eating neither sweet fruits nor bitter ones. Being devoid of desires, he is always calm and sees nothing beyond his Self.

The lower bird longs for that condition and hops a little towards him. But soon he forgets all about it. Filled with desires, he begins to eat the fruits once again. After a little while he eats another exceptionally bitter fruit which makes him miserable. He looks up again and tries to get nearer to the upper bird. This journey continues until he gets very near the upper bird. At this stage, the lower bird realizes that he is only a shadow, a reflection of the upper bird. When he goes still nearer to the upper bird, he merges in him.

This imagery is symbolic of a man's struggle to attain God. The lower bird represents the Jiva while the upper one, the Brahman. In the first stages, the Jiva experiences worldly joys and miseries by turns. In the second stage, the Jiva understands that he is only a reflection or shadow of Brahman. The final stage indicates the merging of the Jivatman with the Paramatman.[9]

Example 4: The Brihadaranyaka Upanishad

In the first stage, the following famous dualistic prayer to God is mentioned,

'O, Lord, Lead me from the evil to good. Lead me from darkness to light. Lead me from death to immortality.'[10]

In the second stage, God is described as pervading the entire universe:

'Causal universe developed of itself into name and form. . . That Supreme Self has entered into all these bodies from Hiranyagarbha down to a crump of grass, up to the very end of the nails.'[11]

In the third and final stage, the Jiva is fully identified with Brahman as stated in the following declaration: The sage Vamadeva understood the real nature of his Self as 'I am Brahman.'[12]

Example 5: The Chandogya Upanishad

In the first stage, the Upanishad teaches dualistic meditation:

'All these creatures, dear boy, have Being as their root, have Being as their abode, and have Being as their support'.[13]

In the second stage, the immanent aspect of God is described:

'That Being which is this subtle essence, even that has this world for its Self.'[14]

In the third and final stage, the Jiva is fully identified with Brahman in such statements as

'That is the Truth. That is the Atman. That Thou Art, O Svetaketu'[15]

The five examples mentioned above are only illustrative of this recurring theme of all the Upanishads.

The first stage marks the externalisation of Jiva from Brahman and is expounded in the Dvaita philosophy of Madhvacharya.

The second stage of the immanence of Brahman pervading the universe in and through is detailed in the Vishishtadvaita philosophy of Ramanujacharya according to which the Jiva and Brahman are inseparably related to each other like a body to its limbs or a tree to its branches.

The final stage of identity of the jivatman with paramatman is elaborated in the Advaitic philosophy whose chief exponent is Shankaracharya.

Swami Vivekananda's Great Discovery

Swami Vivekananda discovered that the above three schools are mutually complementary and together, systematically enable the aspirant to rise to higher levels of spiritual consciousness. It was on his return to India in 1897 that Swamiji made this important contribution to the thought-world. Before Swamiji, the followers of the different schools argued that only their own school of interpretation was the correct one and even went to the extent of twisting the original texts to suit their line of thinking. They regarded the three philosophical systems as three distinct and different ideals for the liberation of the soul. No attempt was made to reconcile them. Swamiji boldly declared that even the highest realizations of Dvaita and Vishishtadvaita were only stages on the way to the ultimate Advaitic experience. When some one asked Swamiji that if this were the truth, why was it that none of the Masters who preceded him had mentioned it, Swamiji replied with his characteristic nonchalance,

'Because I was born for this, and it was left for me to do!'[16]

In his lectures on the Jnana Yoga, Swamiji summarizes this thought in his inimitable style:

'The idea that the goal is far off, far beyond nature, attracting us all towards it, has to be brought nearer and nearer, without degrading or degenerating it. The God of heaven becomes the God in nature, and the God in nature becomes the God who is nature, and the God who is nature becomes the God within the temple of this body, at last becomes the temple itself, becomes the soul and man—and there it reaches the last words it can teach.'[17]

World-Religions and the Three Schools of Indian Philosophy:

Swamiji makes another equally startling revelation that all the major world religions are contained in the above three schools of Vedanta. He points out that when Vedanta is applied to the various ethnic customs and creeds of India, the outcome is the birth of Hindu religion. And the application of this philosophy to specific Indian cults and forms gives rise to different branches of Hinduism such as Shaktism, Vaishnavism, Shaivism, Ganapatya, Kaumara and Saura sects. The philosophy of Dvaita when applied to the ideas of the ethnic groups of Europe results in birth of Christianity with its various ramifications; when the same Dvaita philosophy is applied to Semitic groups the result is the birth of Islam. Further he also points out that the application of the philosophy of Advaita in its yoga-perception form is the cause of origin of Buddhism.

Through this two-step formula provided by Swamiji, we can reinstate:

Step 1: All the Upanishads show us the way to Brahman by leading us through the stages of Dvaita, Vishishtadvaita and Advaita.

Step 2: All the major world religions can be traced to their origin, viz., to the three schools of Dvaita, Vishishtadvaita and Advaita

Hence comes the conclusion: The Upanishads are the basis of all the major world-religions.

The same can be deduced even by simple logical reasoning. The watchword of Upanishads is unity— unity behind the entire universe. All the world religions advocate unity, although in a limited sense, at least among their own followers. The Upanishads thus naturally encompass all the major world religions and hence form their basis.

It was Swamiji's firm conviction that if at all there is going to be a universal religion for the entire world, it would be the religion of the Upanishads and Upanishads alone. Whereas all other religions are founded upon a Book, a Prophet and a Personal God, the religion of the Upanishads stands on its own glory, independent of these three. At the same time, it allows for any number of Books, Prophets and Personal Gods. Vast as the sky and deep as the ocean, the philosophy of the Upanishads, though the oldest in the world, has always remained young and would continue to do so by virtue of its unifying and inclusive features.

Application of This Thought in the National Context

India is an ancient nation known for its rich cultural, linguistic and regional diversities. She has survived a thousand years of onslaught of foreign invasions by virtue of her deep spiritual resilience. The secret of her survival has been the intuitive perception of unity in diversity nurtured through ages of sustained spiritual realizations.

Swamiji was firm in his conviction that religion alone can unite India. He placed it as the first condition for the development and progress of a future India. There must be one religion throughout the length and breadth of the land, he said.[18] Evidently, the Upanishadic religion alone can satisfy such criteria.

Unfortunately some bigoted elements have lost sight of this fact and have laid emphasis on the diversity. They have usurped wealth and power by dividing the people of India along the lines of caste, region, language, culture, etc. The corrective antidote for this dangerous trend pervading the present society is recognizing the religion of the Upanishads as the mother of all the religious sects, and putting their precepts into practice by living in unison with each other.

Application of This Thought in the Global Context

Although the nations of the world have combined together and put up organizations like the United Nations Organization (UNO) to prevent wars on a full-fledged scale, they have not been able to stop wars. At any given time, war is going on in some part of the world or the other. It is also taking indirect and subtle forms like the cold wars and guerrilla tactics. Terrorism is raising its head like never before. The general reasons for all these are analysed to be economic, political, social and similar causes. But in every case, we find invariably religion plays a major part—the parties involved belong to either two different religions or sects of the same religion. Instead of unifying, these religions are dividing humankind. The only solution to these serious and apparently interminable global problems is to accept and follow the message of the Upanishads which has discovered unity not only between different races and religions, but the unifying force behind the whole universe. Hence the message of the Upanishads is the only viable solution to enduring world peace. □

References

1. *Vivekananda, His Gospel of Man Making* Ed., and pub. by Swami Jyotirmayananda, Madras, p.572

2. CW, 3: 398

3. *Taittiriya Upanishad*, 1-v

4. *ibid.*, 1.vi

5. *ibid.*, 1.x

6. *ibid*, II-i-1

7. *ibid.*, II-vi-1

8. *ibid.*, III-x-5-6

9. Based on Swami Vivekananda's commentary on Mundaka Upanishad, 3.1.2

10. *The Brihadaranyaka Upanishad*, I-3- xxviii

11. *ibid.*, I-4-vii

12. *ibid.*, I-4-x

13. *Chandogya Upanishad*, VI-8-vi

14. *ibid.*, VI-8-vii

15. *ibid.*, VI-8-vii. This statement is repeated nine times in the text.

16. *The Master as I saw Him* by Sister Nivedita, pub. by Udbodhan Off., Kolkata, p-200-01

17. CW, 2: 128

18. *ibid.*, 3: 287

Chapter 20

Modern Science and Upanishads

JAY LAKHANI

Science and Religion

In the sixties and seventies I studied Physics at Imperial College London, and did some postgraduate work in Quantum Mechanics with Roger Penrose, a famous English Physicist. Physics was, and is still, considered to be the most pretentious of all sciences. In the final instance every other scientific discipline like Chemistry or Biology or Cosmology has to fall back on Physics to gain a deeper insight in their own field.

The links between science and religion have never been fully explored. Some over-enthusiastic religions insist that all scientific knowledge is contained in their scriptures. When we examine these claims in detail, we discover that almost all such claims are mostly text-torturing. It is understandable that the science lobby is not amused by such intrusive comments about their field. I continue to come across educated Hindu youth who cannot tell the difference between allegorical and literal truths. One claimed that the story of Ganesh acquiring an elephant head is a clear proof that in ancient times we were able to carry out head-transplants! I continue to come across Hindu students at British Universities who claim that the depiction of the Pushpak Viman in the Ramayan is a clear proof that we had developed aircraft technology in ancient times. I tell them, 'Find me one piece of demonstrable evidence and I will stand corrected.'

Science has been one of the most durable, endearing and successful enterprises mankind embarked on. To infringe on its integrity or undermine its discipline in the name of religion cannot be allowed. Science continues to evolve and offer us deeper and better insight into the nature of reality. Not only does it give us a good grasp of what nature is all about, it also empowers us to harness nature for our benefit.

One of the unique features of science has been its ability to offer us the most economical explanation relating to the world. In order for science to continue to progress, it must continue to converge (discovering a central principle or source). A few years back Stephen Hawking, the well known physicist, made a bold claim that Physics is converging so fast that in his lifetime it will come up with the Theory of Everything (TOE for short). Alas, Physics has not reached anywhere near omniscience and Stephen Hawking has turned into a more humble scientist who has stopped making exaggerated claims about the scope of Physics.

Materialism Supported by Logical Positivism

In the middle of the last century we saw the emergence of the Vienna Circle, a group of European thinkers who wanted to protect *hard science* from being swamped by subjective or metaphysical involvement. They called themselves *logical positivists*. They defined *hard sciences* as those sciences that were based on empirical evidence (meaning evidence that can be reduced to sense data), supported by a logical (or self-consistent) explanation. On the plus side this stringent requirement kept the *interpretational and subjective* elements from interfering in the progress of science. On the downside the imposition of empirical evidence meant that only a strictly materialistic world-view was acceptable. This self-imposed barrier set up by the logical positivists to protect science from unwanted interference has, of late, become its greatest stumbling block because it imposes a materialistic world-view, which is becoming untenable. This state of affairs came to a head with the discovery of something very dramatic at the heart of modern Physics.

Entry of the Magical Quantum

The problem with a materialistic interpretation of the universe became visible in the mid 1920s with the invocation of quantum theory. At the heart of physics we come across a most marvellous discovery that outshone all other discoveries of physics put together. This single discovery is far more potent than everything science had discovered over the past few thousand years. This is the discovery of the magical quantum. Quantum is the substratum of the universe. As such it can be classed as the primary building block of the universe. Quantum is the most successful discovery of modern science; it offers the formalism that gives the best answers on the workings of everything from the DNA to the computer chip. Despite its success the quantum poses a serious conceptual quandary. We ask the physicists, 'What is quantum?' The only response they offer is to say that it is a mathematical construct. The truly unique feature about the quantum is that it is guaranteed not to be material.

To make this idea accessible to the lay person, the father of quantum mechanics, Werner Heisenberg, said,

> 'If we think we can explain the universe in terms of sticks and stones or smaller versions of sticks and stones (meaning little lumps of matter called atoms) then we are certain to be disappointed. The only thing we can say with certainty is that the building block of the universe is non-material.'

This simple statement spelt the death-knell for materialism. Matter has to be viewed as a secondary phenomenon and, so trying to explain the universe in terms of matter and its attributes is certain to lead to a limited or downright faulty insight into reality. With the discovery of the quantum in physics, materialism has received a fatal blow.

The Reductionist Approach Under Fire

Reducing every phenomenon to the primary building blocks of matter (the elementary particles) with their attributes (mass, charge and spin) has been a very successful methodology adopted by science. The discovery of quantum as the primary phenomenon underpinning the universe means that this reductionist approach is no longer adequate. A paradigm shift is in the making; a paradigm shift that will eventually push science into the realm of spirituality.

Divergence or Infinite Possibilities?

The reluctance of modern physicists to acknowledge or accept the non-material foundation to the universe, and its implications, has meant that physics of late has lost its drive and direction. It has turned into a utilitarian enterprise. Modern physicists are trained to use very elaborate mathematical tools that produce the right answers with amazing accuracy but offer them no conceptual insights. The conceptual leap necessary for physics to move forward has been stifled in favour of a mathematical jumble that gives the right answers. The work of modern physics in the last three decades has been dominated by super-string theories. The only thing these superstring theories have achieved is to confound and frustrate the physicists and leave them struggling in a 10 or 11 dimensional universe! The variations or possibilities within the theory are more than all the elementary particles in the universe! This is hardly an economical model of the universe. Though modern physics in pursuit of convergence has arrived at a divergence, one cannot deny that science is a continuing pursuit after knowledge, making newer discoveries, revising the old ones and, in due course, even replacing the 'new' with the 'newest'!

The End of Progress?

Physics lost in a maze of highly divergent suppositions is losing its impetus. This is an alarming state of affairs because this most durable enterprise is getting seriously bogged down. Some pragmatists have shrugged off this state of affairs and adopted an attitude of, 'Why should science always converge? Maybe it is not meant to converge. Science just gives us a handle on the world allowing us some degree of control over our immediate surroundings to help us become better survivors. We should be happy with that and live with it rather than get worked up about looking for an ultimate economic explanation.' Let us turn to the teachings of the Upanishads to see if we can find a way out of this pretty pessimistic scenario.

Upanishadic Teachings

The Upanishadic teachings have always supported the idea of unity in diversity. We come across the ancient enquiry: 'What is *that*, by knowing which we know everything?' And in the Upanishadic literature we come across a very bold response, 'We have found the answer, we know *that* by knowing which everything else is known.'

What is this unity the Upanishads are excited about? It is *Brahman*, something that is both transcendent and immanent (forming the substratum of everything). We search the Upanishadic literature to see if we can get a better grasp of Brahman. The Upanishads talk of it as of the nature of existence-consciousness-bliss (*asti-bhati-priyam*). The term 'it is of the nature of' in this definition is a cop-out because it does not define *Brahman*. These three terms are mere signposts used for getting our minds round this subtle principle. Strangely enough, the findings at the heart of modern physics resonate strongly with what we find encapsulated in this simple term existence-consciousness-bliss (*asti-bhati-priyam*).

When examined with the fabric of reality, modern physics has been forced to abandon a materialistic stance but it does not know what to replace it with. If we press the physics lobby hard to give us more information about the quantum phenomenon, they tell us two things:

❖ The only physical interpretation we can offer to the mathematical formalism of the quantum phenomenon is that it describes the *probability of existence*. Or putting it more dramatically—Everything we experience is just wiggles in existence. It is interesting to compare this statement with what Swami Vivekananda said in his talk on Rajayoga. He said that this world is made out of just two things. *Akash,* all penetrating existence and, *Prana,* that which is able to disturb existence. Separately both *Akash* and *Prana* remain out of the realm of our experience but their interaction produces everything we experience (cf. *CW* , 1.147).

❖ The second unique feature of the quantum phenomenon is that it undermines the materialistic stance that there is an objective reality out there. It insists that the universe we experience is a participatory process where *consciousness* plays a crucial role for the universe to come into existence. Such dramatic ideas continue to be resisted by a strong materialistic lobby.

Very reputable neuro scientists continue to affirm that it is not possible to pinpoint the source of consciousness to any slice of the brain. Consciousness remains an enigma for modern neuroscience. The question remains, 'What is this powerful tool we possess that gives us access to reality and yet cannot be traced to a material origin?' Quantum theory is suggesting that without consciousness the material world cannot come into being. Modern physics shudders at the implications of such suggestions. This is what the theory suggests: Matter does not produce consciousness; the contrary consciousness is necessary for matter to come into being.

Brahman as the Foundation of the Universe

❖ *Isa vasyam idam sarvam,* declares Isa Upanishad. 'View the universe as appearance of Brahman.' Brahman is defined as that which underpins everything and yet is no-thing. Compare this with the definition of quantum: Quantum is the underpinning to the material universe though it is guaranteed not to be material.

❖ *Prajnanam Brahman* declares the Aitareya Upanishad. What appears as consciousness in living things is Brahman or spirit showing itself in the material universe. Consciousness is essential for the universe to come into existence. Existence and consciousness are intricately intertwined.

Paradigm Shift in Science

Science can get back on track and pursue its agenda of convergence if it overcomes its infatuation of reducing everything to matter and its attributes. There are very clear findings at the heart of physics and neuroscience which both point to a spiritual foundation to everything we experience including ourselves. Only when science appreciates this non-material or spiritual basis to everything can we hope to have a major conceptual breakthrough that will land science firmly in the lap of spirituality.

Often, I tell university students, 'Though we owe much to the prophets of the past, it is the science of today that holds the key to reviving and refreshing the message of Upanishads.' ☐

Three part sadhana

Shiksha - education
Diksha - initiation (shraddha)
Pariksha - tests that are earned
leads to
Nishreyasa - the highest good

Chapter 21

The Bhagavad Gita—
Quintessence of the Upanishads
SWAMI SANDARSHANANANDA

A Manual of Upanishads in Practice

The Bhagavad Gita is a unique scripture. Its uniqueness lies in the fact that it is universal and all-encompassing in its appeal. The Gita is actually a practical manual of how to practise Upanishadic ideals in life. It is a record of the dialogue between Sri Krishna, the Godhead personified, and Arjuna, a great warrior and an intimate friend of Sri Krishna. In the process, the Gita unfolds the truth that to be able to realize its message, which is essentially the message of the Upanishads, *Shiksha*, *Diksha* and *Pariksha* must go together. These three complete the course of *Sadhana* (spiritual struggle) to attain the highest spiritual knowledge that bestows on a person the highest good or *Nishreyasa* in the end.

Shiksha deals with the technical aspect of *education*. *Diksha* means spiritual *initiation*, comprising *Shraddha* or an attitude of *humility and respectfulness,* as is depicted in Nachiketa's character in Katha Upanishad. Shiksha becomes effective when it is done with due diksha for education is not a mere process of sitting near the teacher and listening to him. True education involves

238

active participation in the process of evolution of ideas. *Pariksha*, on the other hand, is the *test* of spiritual insight one earns through the other two. Its means testing our theories in practice. Pariksha is well described in the Upanishads through numerous stories and anecdotes. Since Bhagavad Gita deals with the principles taught in the Upanishads in all their details and simplicity, it is a complete manual of spiritual practices mentioned in the Upanishads.

Sri Krishna, the teacher of the Gita is a teacher par excellence. Arjuna, the disciple, is most competent, since he absorbs shiksha as well as diksha with due respect and skill, and then qualifies himself in pariksha, as it were, grappling with adversities of delusion, sadness and disappointment that come his way. The teacher-student relationship between the two is simply exemplary.

Adi Shankaracharya says in his commentary on the Bhagavad Gita that this lofty relationship between the teacher and the taught is necessary for grasping the abstract ideas of the perennial philosophy ('Vedic dharma') in a practical way. When a perfect teacher-student combination such as this, takes up the difficult issue of understanding the essence of the Vedas, it gives rise to great clarity of thoughts and reaches a large number of people. Sri Krishna-Arjuna relationship is an apt illustration of this condition. The Katha Upanishad too stresses this blending of a competent teacher and student (*ascharya vakta kushalasya labdha*) for effective communication of the highest spiritual knowledge. Many Upanishads are in a dialogue form.

We must remember that Upanishads and Gita do not deal with different themes. Explaining their intimate relationships, Swami Vivekananda says:

'To understand the Gita requires its historical background. The Gita is a commentary on the Upanishads. The Upanishads are the Bible of India. They occupy the same place as the New Testament does. There are [more than] a hundred books comprising the Upanishads, some very small and some big, each a separate treatise. The Upanishads do not reveal the life of any teacher, but simply teach principles. They are [as it were] shorthand notes taken down of discussion in [learned assemblies], generally in the courts of kings. The word Upanishad may mean "sittings" [or "sitting near a teacher"]. Those of you who may have studied some of the Upanishads can understand how they are condensed shorthand sketches. After long discussions had been held, they were taken down, possibly from memory. The difficulty is that you get very little of the background. Only the luminous points are mentioned there. The origin of ancient Sanskrit is 5000 B.C.; the Upanishads [are at least] two thousand years before that. Nobody knows [exactly] how old they are. The Gita takes the ideas of the Upanishads and in [some] cases the very words. They are strung together with the idea of bringing out, in a compact, condensed, and systematic form, the whole subject the Upanishads deal with.'[1]

Swamiji further says:

'He who wrote that wonderful poem was one of those rare souls whose lives sent a wave of regeneration through the world.'[2]

Indeed, Gita has been bringing solace to countless men and women down the ages. Ever since it was first translated from Sanskrit to English by Charles Wilkins of Asiatic Society in 1785, it readership is ever on increase. The Bhagavad Gita, undoubtedly, fulfils the purpose of the Upanishads, which would have been otherwise difficult, considering the intellectual as well as spiritual preparedness required for entering into the teachings of Upanishads which are often clothed in complex language.

A Melting Pot of Upanishadic Ideals

As noted earlier, the Bhagavad Gita is very comprehensive in its teachings. Its comprehensiveness can be seen by use of the colophon at the end of its each chapter (*om tatsat iti shrimad bhagavad gitasu upanishadsu*). Drawing on abundant similarities, this colophon gives it the status of an Upanishad. The Gita is also called a Yoga scripture (*yoga shastre. . .*) also since each of its chapters is termed as Yoga. The term Yoga means union of the individual soul with the cosmic Self. Every chapter of the Gita speaks about a way for its achievement. And all these are clearly concerned with how to reach spiritual liberation or obtain the knowledge of the Absolute Reality (*brahmavidya*).

The Bhagavad Gita and the Upanishads both have attached due importance to *sagunabrahma* (God with attributes) and *nirgunabrahma* (God without attributes). The Bhagavad Gita, however, goes ahead and harmonizes worship of the two. Gita also introduces the idea of the Incarnation of God (*avataratattwa*). It is thus is a melting pot of ideals, ideas and concepts, so to say, in which metaphysics as well as spiritual practices of all types and their synthesis find a place. It is a handy encyclopedia of the subtlest Upanishadic thoughts in simple language.

Bhagavad Gita is a part of the traditional three texts of path to the highest (*prasthanatraya*), the other being the *Upanishads* and the *Brahmasutras*. There are numerous commentaries on the Gita, written by great minds over the millennia. In fact any one wanting to establish a school of spiritual tradition (*sampradaya*) in Hinduism begins by giving his interpretation of the Gita. Without this, his school of thought is considered unauthentic and casual.

There is a verse in the *Gita-dhyanam* (mediation on the Gita) which compares the Upanishads with a milch cow and her nectar-like-milk with the Gita. This 'milk' is milked by Sri Krishna, with Arjuna as Upanishads' calf placed before her (as is the practice to milk a cow). The 'milk' is for the enjoyment of the wise people. The Gita is pervaded by the Upanishads. This is reinforced by the similarity of their verses.[3] When one goes through them, one feels as if one is reading the Upanishads themselves or, even, for that matter, the best commentary on them.

Some thinkers believe that the Gita is the culmination of a prolonged struggle between the *jnanakanda* and the *karmakanda* of the Vedas, led by the sannyasins on the one hand, and the priestly class on the other respectively. When the idea of renunciation gathered more popularity, the sannyasins gained much respect and acceptance in the society. This came as a blessing to the sincere spiritual aspirants who were eager to learn from the sannayasins the transcendental science of brahmavidya. They thus began to 'sit near'— as in the case of the Upanishad—proficient teachers who led a life of self-control and spiritual practices. This is how a spiritual regeneration took place and Gita became all the more popular.

Gita's Practical Appeal

The Gita is set in a typical circumstance of a fratricidal war, arising out of family feuds. It was delivered on the eve of this battle, on a chariot, in the midst of the battle field, where the teacher occupies the driver's seat and the taught 'sits near' him ready to fight but on seeing his near and dear ones, breaks down in an inconsolable grief.

Arjuna then becomes downcast (*santapta manasa*). It happens because of fear and weakness of mind— *hridaya-daurbalyam*—and he becomes overwhelmed by a sense of diffidence, fear and confusion. He then requests Krishna to help him out of this confusion. Krishna rightly gauges his state of being and begins by dealing out a shock. He calls Arjuna an imbecile. What could be a greater shock to a great warrior such as Arjuna known for his exceptional valour and heroism? Sri Krishna calls upon him to give up his unmanliness—*klaibyam*—

and face life. He does not ask him to renounce and retreat to a forest. He rather tells him to fight.

Krishna thus begins the process of psychological and spiritual rescue. In order to save Arjuna from the dense cloud of self-deception Krishna tells him to understand the eternity of atman and the utter fleeting nature of life. He thus teaches detachment—*anasakti*. This message of detachment can be found everywhere in the Gita. Sri Krishna, however, makes it very clear that without perfect renunciation there is no detachment and vice versa. They are practically non-different and vital for spiritual freedom which is the way to everlasting peace.

Hence, one finds the whole of the Gita saturated and vibrant with the idea of renunciation. Sri Ramakrishna remarked that the fundamental teaching of the Gita can be had by repeating the word *Gita* a couple of times. As one repeats the word Gita several times, one gets its reverse word *tagi*, which is a derivative of the root *taj*, meaning *tyaga*—to renounce. So renunciation is the central theme of the Gita. Renunciation makes one fearless.

In Upanishads, too, points out Swami Vivekananda, fearlessness is the central theme. It is fear that binds microcosm and macrocosm alike. When the king becomes established in Self-knowledge, the Upanishads describe, he becomes fearless. Fearlessness and Self-knowledge are synonyms. Likewise Sri Krishna reveals the glory of Self-knowledge and removes all fear from Arjuna's mind for good.

More Parallels Between the Gita and the Upanishads

Arjuna is honest and sincere. He understand his weakness. He thus expresses himself and surrenders to Krishna. He says he is overwhelmed by the guilt of a *kripanah*—a term which also appears in the Brihadaranyaka Upanishad. *Kripanah* literally means miser. But the *Upanishad* extends its meaning:

'O Gargi, who departs from this world without knowing this immutable, is miserable (*kripana*).'[4]

Having been born as human being, the greatest advantage is that one can experience the Self. And if one does not do this, he is indeed a miser, not having used his resources though he had many.

Sri Krishna upholds to Arjuna the glory of the Self and its ever existent, blissful and conscious state. Atman *is* Brahman; they are not different. Man is not different from God. To be established in our real nature is to be established in God (*Brahmisthiti*). This is the remedy for fear and weakness. A man established in God, as opposed to senses and ego, becomes a man of steady wisdom—*sthitaprajna*. Explaining what is steady wisdom, he says that one is a person of steady wisdom when one casts off all desires and finds satisfaction in the Self alone (*atmani-eva-atmana tustah*).[5] In a similar tone, we find *Yama* saying to Nachiketa in the Katha Upanishad: 'When a person has all his heart's desires destroyed, he attains immortality and becomes one with Brahman in this very life.'[6]

World is always on the move. This constant activity of the phenomenal world is compared in the Gita with a perennial sacrifice—*yajna*. It is yajna which sustains life. But how does yajna go on? On account of Brahman, the Unchangeable. The Mundaka Upanishad proclaims:

'From Brahman comes all the mountains and vast oceans. From Brahman issues all the rivers, big or small, and again from Brahman arises all the vegetables and the essences, sweet or otherwise. By virtue of its existence all these things exist. It holds all things together. The essences sustain the inner self in the form of a subtle sheath.'[7]

Gita too explains the whole process of yajna thus:

'From food come forth beings: from rain food is produced: from Yajna arises rain; and Yajna is born of Karma. Know Karma to have risen from the Veda, and the Veda from the Imperishable. Therefore the all-pervading Veda is ever centred in Yajna.'[8]

Sri Krishna further makes clear that as it is happening in the external world so also in the internal world—all the organs and senses—are, as if, relentlessly performing a *yajna*, in order to propitiate the deity, the Self within.

Sri Krishna, however, never forgets to remind Arjuna that yajna is within the realm of karma. Unless it is done *without* motive, there can be hardly any spiritual progress, for karma alone is the cause of bondage as well as release. And it is absurd to remain aloof from karma, even for a single moment. Hence there is a need to be especially knowledgeable regarding its nature and make use of its good contributions.

Anasakta karma—work without attachment—he says, paves a way to Self-realization, purging the mind of its dross —*chittashuddhi*—accumulated from the past in the form of subtle impressions (*samskaras*). Working, not running from it, is the way to go beyond work and its bondage.

Now Sri Krishna proceeds to describe the art of doing work skillfully. He tells Arjuna to perform all his duties dispassionately. (Action, according to the Hindu tradition, can be categorized into three: *nitya karma*— obligatory actions, *nishiddha karma*—actions forbidden by the scriptures and, *kamya karma*—actions with desires.) Sri Krishna counsels Arjuna, to do the *nitya karma*—actions according to the instructions of the scriptures and avoid by all means *kamya karma*—actions with desires and *nishiddha karma*—the forbidden actions. If one works with attachment or expectation of material gains, it makes one attached to them. This attachment gives rise to the pair of opposites—*raga and dvesha*, possessiveness and hatred. This makes a slave of a man. It creates confusion in him as to what is morally correct and thus makes his mind full of doubts and indecisions (*samsaya-atma*). To work skilfully means to keep one's mind clear and rightly focused.

The only purpose of Sri Krishna's advice is to make Arjuna free from these pairs of opposites. This alone could resolve all contradictions in life and make one rise above all conflicts. This is possible only when one becomes established in one's real nature, the atman. Even before one becomes established in it, when one keeps this as the ideal of life, one begins to experience purity of mind and that is the goal of all work. One may recall what Sri Ramakrishna says in this context: '

'Yes, God is directly perceived by the mind, but not by this ordinary mind. It is the pure mind that perceives God, and at that time this ordinary mind does not function. A mind that has the slightest trace of attachment to the world cannot be called pure. When all the impurities of the mind are removed, you can call that mind Pure Mind or Pure Atman.'[9]

This reminds one of what the Chandogya Upanishads says:

'Through purity of food comes purity of mind. From purity of mind comes a steady memory of Truth, and when one gets this memory one becomes free from all knots of the heart.'[10]

Same idea is conveyed in the Mundaka Upanishad:

'If a person can realize Brahman the cause and Brahman the effect as his own Self, all the peculiarities of his character disappear and all his doubts are dispelled. The fruits of his work also get destroyed.'[11]

Conclusion

Gita is a restatement of the truths of the Upanishads. The Gita marks an important event in the spiritual history of mankind. Since it is a part of the Mahabharata where a fierce battle between forces of materialism and spirituality is symbolically depicted, the Gita becomes all the more appealing and friendly in its influence. The profound spiritual culture of the

Vedas finds its expression in the sublime poetry of the Upanishads.

The last chapter of the Gita is named *Mokshayoga*— Yoga of Liberation. Here Sri Krishna concludes by asking Arjuna,

'Has your delusion, born of ignorance, been destroyed?' Arjuna replies with due assurance, 'My delusion (*moha*) is gone. I have regained my memory (*smriti*) through Your grace (*tatprasadat*), O Krishna. I am firm (*sthitah*); I am free from doubt (*gata-sandeha*). I will act according to Your word.'

This is what the Gita promises us—learning to surrender to God and having spiritual growth as the purpose of all actions. He tells Arjuna to look upon victory and defeat in the fight with equanimity. All is play. Only spiritual growth matters; nothing else.

In fine, the Bhagavad Gita is a ready-reckoner of the Upanishads. If one understands the Gita, one understands the Upanishads, and if one understands the Upanishads, one understands the timeless wisdom of spirituality that India stands for. And as Swamiji says,

'If we study the Upanishads we notice, in wandering through the mazes of many irrelevant subjects, the sudden introduction of the discussion of a great truth, just as in the midst of a huge wilderness a traveller unexpectedly comes across here and there an exquisitely beautiful rose, with its leaves, thorns, roots, all entangled. Compared with that, the Gita is like these truths beautifully arranged together in their proper places—like a fine garland or a bouquet of the choicest flowers.[12]. . . The Bhagavad Gita is the best authority on Vedanta.'[13]   □

References

1.   CW, 1: 446
2.   CW, 1: 22
3.   To cite a few of them, the 5th verse of *Isha* Upanishad is close to the verses 16th and 29th of chapters 13 and 6 of the Gita respectively. Four verses of chapter two, namely 7th, 15th, 18th and 19th, are same as the verses 11th, 20th and 19th of chapters 18, 2 and 2 respectively.
4.   *Brihadaranyaka Upanishad*, 3.8.10
5.   *Bhagavad Gita*, 2.55
6.   *Katha Upanishad*, 2.3.14
7.   *Mundaka Upanishad*, 2.1.9
8.   *Bhagavad Gita*, 3.14-15
9.   *Gospel of Sri Ramakrishna*, p. 687
10. *Chhandogya Upanishads*, 7.26.2
11. *Mundaka Upanishad*, 2.2.8
12. CW, 4:106
13. CW, 7: 57

Chapter 22

Youth and the Upanishads

SWAMI BODHAMAYANANDA

The Present Scenario

Youth is a period of change. A child becomes an adult. This is the time when a person's thoughts play a major role in shaping his or her personality and life. As youth emerges from his dream world, he has to face many unpleasant facts about life. He has to encounter the hard facts of selfishness and cruelty, violence and hypocrisy, negative and narrow ideologies. He has to face all this and above all, he has to face himself.

In this context of personal growth, the youth requires much encouragement and right guidance in order to become a responsible member of society.

If one looks at today's youth, one finds that they have more access to facilities and exposure than what their counterparts had a few decades back, nay a few years ago. Thanks to Internet, they are now widely (at times wildly) connected and are well informed about the events and changes in different fields of life. They have more money, more opportunities and more problems too. In spite of large income, due to the present economic boom, cases of depression, suicides and violence are on the rise. There is unrest in their heart. At times they approach the elders in search of solution to life's problems or turn to popular literature to find instant solutions. Despite many uncharitable remarks made about them, experience shows that it is the youth, not the elders, who respond to the ideal of self-improvement enthusiastically. This is quite understandable. Elders have maturity of years but they lack the flexibility or adaptability which is natural to youth.

No doubt, the present situation is grim. On one side is the need to guide the youth, to provide them proper care and encouragement, and on the other, there is lack of proper communication. Like all people, the youth want their problems addressed in *their* language, in their idiom, in the way they can understand it. The present day media flourishes on the weaknesses of youthfulness. They paint a sensual image of life. Youth too are often taken for a ride. They begin to ridicule their own heritage and their own 'river of perennial wisdom.' It is high time we understand the youth and then make them understand the eternal message of the Upanishads. Youth *are* hungry for guidance and inspiration. They *are* interested in the timeless wisdom of Upanishad if presented in their language.

What the Youth Want

In no other period of life does a man have more choices to make than in youth. Youth, as a stage of life, demands it. For many youths the issue is not whether to choose to live in accordance with the eternal truth expressed in the Upanishads but *when* will he or she live according to them.

Here is a small story from the *Reader's Digest* to illustrate what we mean. One foggy night at sea, the captain of a ship saw what looked like the lights of another ship heading toward him. He had his signalman contact the other ship by light. The message was: 'Change your course ten degrees to the south.' The reply came back: 'Change your course ten degrees to the north.' Then the captain answered: 'I am the captain, so you change your course ten degrees to the south.' The reply came: 'I am a seaman first class—change your course ten degrees to the north.'

This last exchange annoyed the captain. So he signalled back: 'We are a battleship—change your course ten degrees to the south.' The reply: 'And I am a lighthouse. Change your course ten degrees to the north!'

The moral of the story is clear: follow the Upanishads or perish. The lighthouse represents the eternal principles and universal values of the Upanishads. The Upanishads are a mine of knowledge—universal, timeless and always relevant. They are not the property of any particular sect or creed. Nor is there any gender or status bar in knowing and following them.

A good number of the seers (rishis) of the Upanishads were women. These rishis were both householders and monks. Some of the rishis were actually kings or statesmen of great power and responsibilities.

Faith in Oneself and Fearlessness

What do the Upanishads have to say to the youth of *today*? Today's youth, like the youth of yester years, want success and power. They want to be confident and successful in life. They are in search of right meaning of life. They are looking for the right solution. They want strength and they want concentration of mind.

Seen in this context, if one looks at the Upanishads, one finds a profound truth for the youth: the truth of the immortality and eternity of the Self. Every youth wants personal effectiveness. He wants to leave a mark behind. Swami Vivekananda believed that this is the one message of the Upanishads that can revolutionize a youth's life. Let us try to understand it.

Behind personal effectiveness or success lies a right self-image. A successful man or woman must have, somewhere in his mind an 'I can-succeed' image. The Upanishads exhort that one should try to base one's self-image on one's deepest core of the personality, the Divine Self. The Upanishads go into raptures while describing the glory of this inner truth of man. Echoing this message of the Upanishads, Swami Vivekananda said,

'Teach yourselves, teach every one, his real nature. Call upon the sleeping soul and see how it awakes. Power will come, glory will come, goodness will come, purity will come and everything that is excellent will come, when this sleeping-soul is roused to self-conscious activity.'[1]

This is the powerful message of the Upanishads: have faith in yourself, in the Divine present in every human being. Let us not think of ourselves as low and useless beings. We are not sinners. We are not bad, essentially. We make mistakes, no doubt, but we should not hold our mistakes as the ultimate fact about us. The ultimate *fact* about us is this Divinity within us. The Upanishads say that this Divinity is an eternal truth, unchanging reality about us. If a youth has faith in himself, he can face any situation and can overcome any difficulty in life.

Fearlessness is the other great value the Upanishads teach. They always advocate fearlessness and a spirit of inquiry. This is the basis of positive thinking. We often develop fear because we have not properly inquired into a matter. We imagine many things about us, about others and about life. Upanishads advice us to stop doing that, and develop a spirit of inquiry instead. Let us expose our mind to healthy ideas. If we make proper inquiry, without any bias, we will find that our fear is imaginary and baseless. To think positive is what the Upanishads advocate.

Swami Vivekananda said that fearlessness is the one message of the Upanishads. 'Abhihi ! Be fearless,' is a constant refrain of the Upanishads. The Isha Upanishad says, 'All this is filled by divinity.' If one keeps this in mind, how can fear remain in the mind? Fear comes from matter, not from the divine. And that divine is our deepest core. When one thinks thus, one's mind expands. He begins to expand *his* concept of himself or herself. He begins to see that the same God is present everywhere. And this is what refreshes and strengthens the mind.

The Ideal of Shraddha

Swamiji used to often quote the story of Nachiketa from the Katha Upanishad. Nachiketa was a young boy. He was told by his father in a fit of rage to 'go to Yama', the god of death. And he does go. How did he become so fearless? To face death? The Upanishad says that it was because of Shraddha or faith. 'Shraddha or Faith entered into him,' it says. Shraddha is the aggregate of all positive attitudes. Shankaracharya termed it as *astikya buddhi.* Indeed when one gets this positive frame of mind, he discovers the great potential of strength and enormous possibilities in him. Swami Vivekananda remarked,

'Unfortunately it (Shraddha) has nearly vanished from India and this is why we are in our present state. What makes the difference between man and man is this Shraddha and nothing else. What makes one man great and another low is this Shraddha.'[2]

Cultivating faith in oneself is the best way to overcome emotional problems that many youth face.

Whether in school or in college or in professional life, we seem to lose this faith in ourselves. One should not run away from life rather learn to face it with courage and heroism. The Katha Upanishad rouses this inner potential by its well-known statement, *'Uttishtata jagarata praapya varaan nibodhata.'* Swami Vivekananda freely translated it as 'Arise! Awake! And stop not till the goal is reached.'

Swami Vivekananda used to recommend reading of Upanishads. He believed that if one could read these great scriptures, one would gain all the basic values and virtues in life. During his wandering days in 1892 Swamiji spent nine days with Sri Sundararama Iyer in Trivandrum. Sri Iyer's 14-year-old son Rama-swami Sastri was deeply impressed by Swamiji's personality. Swamiji told him,

> 'You are still a young boy, I hope and wish that you will reverentially study the Upanishads, the Brahma Sutras, and the Bhagavadgita. . . as also the Itihasas, the Puranas and the Agamas. You will not find the like of these anywhere in the world. Man alone, of all living creatures, has a hunger in his heart to know the whence and whither, the whys and wherefores of things. There are four key words you must remember: *abhaya* (fearlessness), *ahimsa* (non-injury), *asanga* (non-attachment) and *ananda* (bliss). These words really sum up the essence of all our sacred books. Remember them. Their implication will become clear to you later on.'[3]

The Need for Tapas

There is one more great teaching of the Upanishads which could be of great help to youth: self-discipline. Anyone interested in discovering his inner potential must learn to discipline his energies and time. The Sanskrit term for self-discipline is *tapas*. Tapas is often taken in its negative sense. But *tapas or tapasya* is not just denial. It means undergoing some hardship and difficulty voluntarily. It is tapas which taps our inner potential. An athlete undergoing intense training in increasing his stamina is an example of tapas. A student spending long hours in concentrated reading and writing is another example of tapas. Anything that is done voluntarily, with a great end in mind, is a form of tapas.

Self-discipline or tapas helps a youth

1. to organize his energies and focus his ideas.

2. to help him have greater self-knowledge and self-control.

3. to develop a higher level of thinking.

As someone has rightly said, 'We cannot prepare the future for the youth, but we can certainly prepare the youth *for* the future.' What could be a better way to prepare a youth for the future than help him or her build his or her personality on the solid principle of tapas? A person of tapas is a strong person by any standard. Tapas revitalize and rejuvenate the personality. Let us have a look at some of the Upanishadic teachings about tapas.

1. *Tapasa brahma vijijnasasva; tapo brahmeti* —'Seek to know Brahman through *tapas*; *Tapas* is Brahman (the ultimate reality).'[4]

2. *Tasya Jnanamayam tapah*—'Whose tapas consists of knowledge of thought.'[5]

3. *Tapamsi sarvani cha yat vadanti*—'Tapas itself proclaims the glory of That which is the value of all values, the supreme end value, namely Atman or Brahman.'[6]

One curious fact about Upanishads is that many of their teachers or rishis were youth. This means that anyone who has faith in oneself, practices right type of tapas and keeps before him the great goal of self-transformation can be a rishi. Be it the field of science and technology, or music or arts or sports or any other fields, the secret lies in faith and self-discipline.

However hopeless may be the situation, one can surely overcome all challenges through tapas and Shraddha. Echoing this idea, asked Swami Vivekananda,

'Do you know how much energy, how many powers, how many forces, are still lurking behind that frame of yours? What scientist has known all that is in man? Millions of years have passed since man first came here, and yet but one infinitesimal part of his powers has been manifested. Therefore, you must not say that you are weak. How do you know what possibilities lie behind that degradation on the surface? You know but little of that which is within you. For behind you is the ocean of infinite power and blessedness.'7

Conclusion

One of the Upanishads, *Prashna Upanishad*, has a story. Six young earnest seekers of truth approach the venerable and enlightened sage Pippalada. They request him to answer their unanswered questions on cosmology, vital energy and consciousness. The sage obliges. Indeed, if the youth could approach in the same spirit of inquiry and respect, the Upanishads will reveal the secrets they contain. Let them recall the well known prayer from the *Brihadaranyaka Upanishad*, 'asato ma sadgamaya' and earnestly seek the Truth of the Self.

The Upanishads call upon the youth to seek their Eternal Core, and not just hide in fear behind the false self. Man is not matter; he is not subject to death. He is not a finite being but the infinite Consciousness Itself.

After imparting instructions to Janaka about Brahman in the Brihadaranyaka Upanishad, Yajnavalkya assured him, 'You have attained That which is free from fear.' This is what the Upanishads reassures every youth. The knowledge of the Self, that of our real core, surely leads to boundless courage and confidence and this is what the youth can get in the Upanishads in abundance. ◻

References

1. CW, 3: 193
2. CW, 3: 319
3. *Reminiscences of Swami Vivekananda Calcutta*, Advaita Ashrama, 1994, p.101
4. *Taittiriya Upanishad*, III.2
5. *Mundaka Upanishad*, I.1.9
6. *Katha Upanishad*, 2.15
7. CW, 2: 302

Chapter 23

The Power of the Upanishads

SWAMI ASHOKANANDA

Can you find peace if you are separate from everything? There is a beautiful passage in one of the old Upanishads—the *Brihadaranyaka Upanishad* (2.4.6):

[ब्रह्म तं परादाद्योऽन्यत्रात्मनो ब्रह्म वेद, क्षत्रं तं परादाद्योऽन्यत्रात्मनः क्षत्रं वेद, लोकास्तं परादुर्योऽन्यत्रात्मनो लोकान् वेद, देवास्तं परादुर्योऽन्यत्रात्मनो देवान् वेद, भूतानि तं ...]

[Swami] Madhavananda has given this translation: 'The Brahmin ousts one who knows him as different from the Self. The *Kshatriya* [the warrior] ousts one who knows him as different from the Self. The worlds oust one who knows them as different from the Self.'

It goes through a whole list: 'The gods oust one who knows them as different from the Self. The beings oust one. . .' and so on. That is a tremendous statement. What is the meaning—if you think the Brahmin is different from the Self, that Brahmin will oust you. It is a fact that if you think yourself separate from any person, that person will make you small. Whatever you think is outside of you has the effect of making you small and limited. Isn't it true? If I meet some people and I fear them and I think that they are outside me and so on, what will be the effect of that thought on me? I certainly would be affected by this limitation that I impose upon myself.

There is a wonderful story in connection with this. Shortly after Swami Vivekananda had returned from the West in 1897 and had gone to Calcutta, he received a message from a friend of his, saying, 'I have a peculiar disease. I am just wearing out. I am all the time in bed and cannot get up. Would you kindly come and see me? Not because I want any cure, but because I have known you, and I have heard you have returned from the West and I should be very glad to see you.' So Swami Vivekananda at once sent a message, yes, he would go. The moment he entered the man's room he began to recite that passage from the Upanishad. He did not explain it, but such was the effect of this recitation that the man began to feel a new energy coming into his body and his mind, and he sat up and said, 'Swamiji, I feel stronger than ever.' And, as it happened, he was cured. He became like a new person.

Of course, Swami Vivekananda had great power; the real meaning of the verse went into the heart of the man, and he lost the idea that he was separate from this one and from that one; he become all alive. That is what happened to him.

Sometimes similar things happen to people. If you are afraid of the world, if the world has limited you, circumscribed you, if you feel bound by the world or anything in this world, then consciously try to think that everything is Brahman, everything is divine, that nothing is outside you and nothing can affect you; you also are Brahman, you also are divine. Keep that consciousness, and you will find you have become a changed person. That is what you have to practice. □

Chapter 24

Sages of the Upanishads

SWAMI SATYAMAYANANDA

Who is a Sage

In Indian religious context a sage (rishi), is not merely a wise person with a lot of experience but one who has directly *seen* Reality. This sage or 'seer' (also called *muni* and *vipra)*, is a spiritually inspired poet (*kavi*), a sanctified person. Says Swami Vivekananda,

'The Rishi as he is called in the Upanishads is not an ordinary man, but a mantra-drastha [see-er of mantras]. He is a man who sees religion, to whom religion is not merely book-learning, not argumentation, nor speculation, nor much talking, but actual realization, a coming face to face with truths which transcend the senses. This is Rishihood.'[1]

Upanishads mean Self-Knowledge

The Upanishads form the *jnana kanda* (knowledge section) of the Vedas. This pre-Buddhist mass of thoughts called *Brahma-vidya*, knowledge of Brahman, was realized and taught by a succession of sages as early as 1000 BCE. The Upanishads are free from cumbersome ritualism and speak of the reality in a highly symbolical and mystical language. They are also called: *Aranyaka*, forest philosophy, and *Rahasya*, secret.

The *Kena Upanishad* (IV.2) speaks of 'Upanishad' as: secret knowledge; the *Brihadaranyaka Upanishad* as: 'Truth of truths' (II.I.20). The word Upanishad implies: 'The knowledge of the knowable entity (Brahman) presented in the scriptures. The significance of this knowledge is that it destroys, splits up, the seeds of worldly existence such as ignorance.'[2] It also connotes the humility with which the student should approach the teacher. The Upanishads form the basis of almost all latter philosophical schools and religions in India, and has in its various forms, been influencing world philosophical thought. [3]

Getting Connected with Them

Generally one views history as something unrelated to oneself, though one habitually hears of history repeating itself. In India, with its living traditions, culture, and religion originating from the Vedas, a multi-layered bonding with the past is inevitable. The layers are intellectual, emotional and moral. A genetic lineage consolidates these bonds. This apart, every being is connected psychically and spiritually to the sages and the Upanishads, for within everything is the reality called Atman-Brahman *seen* by the sages, and which can be 'seen' even today and to do this is the real, ever-lasting goal of human life.

Every one, it is believed, is born with five debts: to the gods, rishis, manes, humans, and beings. Studying the scriptures repays the debt to the rishis. There are also rituals connected with their worship and remembrance. Thus this connectedness has produced rishis uninterruptedly and in abundance over the centuries and this is the real history of India.

Upanishads Today

Scientists, psychologists, neurologists and philosophers believe that they are storming the last citadel of mystery, viz., consciousness, but what they refer is just a shoreline of a vast ocean of *Consciousness* (*Chit* in Sanskrit). This vast ocean was charted and plumbed minutely by the brave rishis. They were, 'Bold thinkers in all their ideas; so bold that one spark of their thought frightens the so-called bold thinkers of the West.'[4]

Knowing that human nature is the result of many metaphysical forces, the Upanishadic society was geared to inexorably raise even its lowest member of society to spiritual freedom. Today, people acknowledge that the neglect and blindness about the spiritual dimension of the personality has well nigh destroyed humanity. Thoughtful people are thus veering towards the Upanishads. Thus the sages and the Upanishads stand vindicated.

Rishis in Ancient India

Most people picture the rishis as ascetics who lived in forest hermitages, wore loincloth of skins or coarse cloth, lived on what forests provided, tied a topknot and wore *rudraksha* beads and beards. Some of them were married while others were celibate recluses. This invariable mental picture is partial. Most of the rishis lived in communities, large and small. Then there were women sages some were *sadyovahas*, who studied till marriage, and the *brahmavadinis*, who deliberated on Brahman and stayed unmarried. One also comes across lots of pure and spirited youth in the Vedic literature. Moreover, not a few kings abdicated and became ascetics but many of them continued living in royal ambience, ruled kingdoms yet lived and taught Upanishads.

The Rishi Model for Today

A major social, intellectual, moral, and spiritual upheaval occurred during the Upanishadic age making it broad and freeing it from the old emphasis on ritualism. Many of the warrior class, *kshatriyas*, were at the forefront and exerted a powerful influence on the teachings and teachers of the Upanishads.[5] Swamiji says, many of the Upanishads, 'have been the outcome, not of retirement into forests, but have emanated from persons whom we expect to lead the busiest lives— from ruling monarchs.'[6] That paradigm shift made India really great for all time to come.

India, today, with its new dynamism is also going through another mighty transition. Swamiji had told Sister Nivedita to visit Gopaler Maa (one of Sri Ramakrishna's devotees), and witness, 'the old India...the India of prayers and tears, of vigils and fasts, that is passing away, never to return!'[7] Swamiji had also predicted that the present transition would take India to even more glorious heights than she had ever attained. Swamiji, born in a *kshatriya* family, was a rishi, and he preached Practical Vedanta. His genius and vision combined the dynamism of the Upanishads with the dynamism of the present age as a panacea for all-round development. This naturally calls for a model that is in consonance with the past, present, and the future and we find the spirit of enquiry of those old warrior/king-sages yet standing as a glorious example to emulate.

Sage-kings in the Upanishad Literature

1. Emperor Janaka or 'Videha'

This towering personality was a master of the Vedas, endowed with keen intelligence and, familiar with the esoteric teachings of the Upanishads. He once 'performed a *yajna*, Vedic sacrifice, in which gifts were freely distributed to Vedic scholars from the countries of Kuru and Panchalas.' Janaka wanted to know which was the, 'most erudite of the Vedic scholars' and he had a thousand cows confined to a pen and on the horns of each cow were fixed 10 *padas* of gold. Janaka said, 'Let him who is the best Vedic scholar drive the cows home.' None dared, except the sage Yajnavalkya. The chief priest and other great rishis proceeded to test his knowledge. A learned debate ensued which is considered the greatest and the highest metaphysics ever produced by the human mind. Janaka presided over this debate proving his own stature among the scholars.[8]

Janaka also appears as a disciple of Yajnavalkya, whose powerful discourse on the identity of the *jiva*, soul, and Brahman through the three states of waking, dream and deep sleep and the processes of death and rebirth is grand. At one point Yajnavalkya became apprehensive that the intelligent emperor was driving him by his pointed questions to disclose all the secret teachings. The culmination comes when Yajnavalkya tells the Emperor that he, Janaka, had attained 'the world of Brahman which is sinless, taintless, free from doubts.'[9]

At the end of the fifth section of the *Brihadaranyaka Upanishad* (V.11.8), Janaka instructs Budila, son of Asvatarasva, concerning the mystic Gayatri mantra, on knowing which one becomes pure, clean, free from decay and death. Swami Vivekananda says that though a ruler, he was entirely bereft of the body idea. Even the great sage Vyasa sent his perfect son Suka to be tested by Janaka in *Brahma-vidya*.

2. *Pravahana Jaivali of the Panchalas*

In the *Chandogya Upanishad* (I.9.1), Pravahana Jaivali is shown discussing with two rishis Silaka Salavatya and Chaikitayana Dalbhya, who were adepts on the secret of the Udgitha as taught in the Sama Veda. So confident was Pravahana Jaivali that he said to them, 'You two please discuss first, I shall hear you two brahmins talk (meaningless sentences).' As their discussion was without any conclusion, Pravahana Jaivali showed them that their knowledge of the Udgitha was limited and inferior. The king then taught the two rishis the subtle and supreme aspects of the Udgitha.

In an important section (chapter V. 3) in the same Upanishad, Shvetaketu, grandson of Aruna, goes to the assembly of the Panchalas and Pravahana Jaivali asked him, 'My boy, did your father instruct you?' When Shvetaketu answered in the affirmative, the king proceeded to question him: 'Do you know where the creatures go upto from here? Do you know how they return? Do you know where the path of the gods and the path of the manes part? Do you know how that world does not become filled? Do you know how water comes to be known by the word 'Person' after the fifth oblation?' Shvetaketu couldn't answer even one question. Pravahana Jaivali reprimanded him by saying that if he knew nothing, then why did he say he was instructed?

Shvetaketu returned home humiliated and related what had happened to his father Gautama. His father confessed that he too was ignorant of this knowledge. Gautama hurried to Pravahana Jaivali and asked the king for the instruction, settling for nothing less. The king requested the sage to stay for a long time and told him that, 'this knowledge did not go to the Brahmanas. Therefore, in the past, in all the worlds teacher-ship was of the Kshatriyas.' Pravahana Jaivali then taught Gautama the knowledge of the *Pancha-agni vidya*, knowledge of five fires, which deals with the soul's rebirth following death, the soul's connection with the cosmos and two paths of the gods and the manes and the lower third that gives repeated births as low creatures.

This same teaching is repeated in the *Brihadaranyaka Upanishad* (VI-ii-1), where Pravahana is shown teaching the sage Aruni. Similarly in the *Kausitaki Upanishad* (Chp I), a king named Chitra of the Garga line imparted this same knowledge to Gautama.

3. *Janasrutih Pautrayana* (the grandson of Janasruta's son)

King Janasrutih Pautrayana offered gifts with due respect, gave plentifully, and cooked for many. He had rest houses constructed in all places with the idea, 'They (his subjects) will indeed eat my food everywhere.' His belief of being the most meritorious person was shattered when he heard two swans say that the lustre of the king was insignificant to that of Raikva with a cart, because all virtuous deeds performed by people everywhere get included in the person of the Raikva because of his knowledge.'

The king despatched his attendants to search for the sage Raikva and they finally located him sitting under a cart, scratching his itches, Janasrutih Pautrayana approached him humbly with gifts consisting of six hundred cattle, a priceless necklace and a chariot drawn by she-mules. Raikva was not impressed with the king's gifts. Janasrutih Pautrayana returned with thousand cattle, the necklace, a chariot drawn by she-mules and his own daughter to be offered as wife. Raikva now accepted the gift and commenced instructing the king on the *Samvarga Vidya*. This is the knowledge of the ten 'places of merger' in the human and divine planes that constitute the *krita*, which exist as *Virat Purusha*, Cosmic Person.[10]

4. Ashvapati, son of Kekaya

Five great married rishis, 'adepts in the Vedas conducted a discussion: Which is our Atman, Who is Brahman?' Failing to reach a consensus they decided to visit Uddhalaka, son of Aruna, for clarification. Uddhalaka unsure of his own knowledge, requested the five sages that they all should proceed to Ashvapati, son of Kekaya. On reaching the king's palace they were individually honoured. The king informed them that a sacrifice was going to be performed and promised each one wealth equivalent to that of the officiating priest's remuneration. The king then declared that in his kingdom there were no thieves, misers, drunks, none who did not perform sacrifices, none illiterate, no lewd persons, or adulteress (the king was establishing his good conduct for, persons of high standing—like these rishis—do not accept gifts from bad people).

The six rishis rejected the king's offer for wealth saying that they had come for knowledge of the Vaisvanara that he possessed. Ashvapati agreed to teach them and on the next day the rishis approached the king as pupils. He instructed them in the secret and complete knowledge of the Vaisvanara Atman. This is the reality that connects the individual with the universal through sacrifice and meditation.[11]

5. Ajatashatru, King of Benaras

A vainglorious brahmin of the Garga clan called Balaki approached Ajatashatru, the king of Benaras with the intention: 'I will teach you about Brahman.'

Ajatashatru offered him a thousand cows for this and likened himself to Janaka (known for his magnanimity). Proud Balaki began describing the attributes of Brahman as reflected in objects like the sun, moon, lightning, space, mirror, the sound of walking and shade. The king interrupted him every time and showed that he already possessed a higher aspect of that knowledge. Twelve times did Balaki try to teach the *Saguna* (Conditioned) Brahman, and twelve times did Ajatashatru show that Balaki's knowledge was immature.

After this humiliation the king enquired, 'Is this all?' Balaki now thoroughly chastened begged to be the king's pupil. Ajatashatru then took him by his hand and taught him through insight and example the three states of consciousness and then led Balaki's understanding gradually to the secret *Truth of truths*, from where emanate all organs, worlds, gods and beings.[12]

Conclusion

The Upanishadic sages mentioned above were representative of a larger number of warrior class who were deep thinkers and sincere seekers of truth. A story is told of a prince Hiranyanabha who approached Sukesha, son of Bharadvaja, and asked him, 'Bharadvaja, do you know the *Purusha* (Supreme Person) of sixteen parts?' Sukesha didn't and the prince stood disbelieving. Sukesha insisted that he really was ignorant about this reality but knew the price of speaking falsehood, he would dry up like a tree. Hiranyanabha silently climbed his chariot and left. This question rankled Sukesa who later received the answer from the sage Pippalada.[13]

We need to be daring and dynamic seekers of truth like those old warrior sages, for as Swamiji says,

'You, and I, and everyone of us will be called upon to become Rishis. . . and then standing up in that glorious light of Rishihood each one of us will be a giant.' [14] □

Notes

1. *Complete Works of Swami Vivekananda*, 9 vols (Kolkata: Advaita Ashrama, 1-8 1989; 9 1997) 3: 175 (hereafter *CW*)

2. Shankaracharya introduction to the *Katha Upanishad*.

3. Swami Tathagatananda, *The Journey of the Upanishads to the West* (Kolkata, Advaita Ashrama, 2004)

4. *CW*, 1: 356

5. 'Modern India', in *CW*, Vol 4

6. *CW*, 2: 291

7. *ibid*, 2: 415-8

8. *Brihadaranyaka Upanishad*, Chapter-III

9. *ibid*, Chapter-IV

10. *Chandogya Upanishad*, IV. 3

11. *ibid*, V. 11

12. *Brihadaranyaka Upanishad*, II; *Kaushitaki Upanishad*, VI

13. *Prashna Upanishad*, 4th chapter

14. *CW*, 3: 175

Chapter 25

The Upanishads and the Corporate World: Can the Twain Shake Hands?

S K CHAKRABORTY

The Present Scenario

This short critical essay proceeds on the supposition that the corporate or business world is willing to question its present profane leanings, and to emotionally incline towards the Sacred. For, Bharat's Veda-Vedanta have always upheld the Sacred as the hub of all—secular as well as transcendental[1]. It may not be an exaggeration to say that the corporate world is today mostly obsessed with:

- ❖ Rank order status in the corporate league
- ❖ Share market valuation
- ❖ Competitive supremacy
- ❖ Treating human beings as 'resources'
- ❖ Humans as compulsive money-makers and consumers
- ❖ Nature as impersonal and non-conscious, and hence subject to reckless exploitation.

A genuine interaction with the Upanishads cannot even commence with the above goals receiving top priority, all *else* being treated as inferior to it. Except occasional or casual lip-service, there are no signs that the globalization-modernization-developmental agenda is willing to take a pause and introspect. It is mostly full of guileful deception, animated by greed. Such a backdrop is hardly inspiring for connecting business-as-it-is with Vedanta. Paradoxically, however, this may also be a true need of the hour.

This is the present corporate scenario—downright materialistic. But considering the growing unhappiness and lack of meaning (expressed through rising instances of violence, depression and even suicides), there is a need to examine the issue of what remedies can be considered to solve the paradox.

Then and Now

In the opening section of the *Katha Upanishad* (I.i.23-25), Yama, the god of Death, presents to the young Nachiketa a veritable secular Heaven (?!) of *artha* (money) and *kama* (desires).[2] Almost nothing we increasingly hanker after today had been left out in the list of gifts announced by Death. Only a few ancient words may be replaced by modern ones, for example, women in chariots by models in cars, vast expanse of earth by global market, sons and grandsons by human resources and so on. The corporate business sector today seems to follow, essentially, the same mode of temptation that Death had adopted. A telling symbolism indeed!

How did the young boy, Nachiketa, respond to the seductive tactics of Death? This young spiritual genius' replies are (I.i.26-9) are the most powerful defense of the sacred, saving the wisdom of Vedanta forever. He says:

'*Na vittena tarpaniyo manushyo*' (wealth does not yield satisfaction),

'*Sarveindriyanam jarayanti tejah*' (vigour of all the senses is dissipated),

'*Abhidhyayan varnaratipramoda*' (deliberating on the real nature of music, disport and delight?).

Indeed, these are some of the eternal principles of true psychology which pour out from the lips of youthful Nachiketa.

It is evident to us that if this variety of Nachiketa-psychology[3] were to be publicised and propagated, with the same vigour and on the same scale as the vulgar *artha-kama* of today, the present type of Corporate or business heaven (!) would just collapse. But this will save today's potential Nachiketas from destruction—as is happening now. Mother Earth could also be saved from desecration of her resources and molestation of her ecological purity. But with sex relations and stock market operations becoming subjects of study at school, *kama-kanchana* (lust and greed) are now being enthroned as the 'master urge' in education. So, future Nachiketas are being nipped in the bud.

Can *amritasya putrah* ('the children of immortal bliss') and 'human resources' co-exist? How long can we strike at our own roots of happiness and true well-being?

Another verse (I.iii.3) from the *Katha Upanishad* is sometimes mentioned with reference to the 'charioteer' role of intellect (*buddhim tu sarathi*). (The Upanishad compares the human personality with a chariot; the senses with horses, mind with reins, intellect with the driver, and the human soul with its rider). This metaphor is often cited to support the position that reason or intellect is the highest human faculty. But what is not understood or admitted is that unless the emotions or feelings are noble and pure and the senses well-disciplined (*chitta-shuddhi*), sharp intellect drives man and society to the brink of destruction.

Nachiketa's earlier responses show that only because his heart was pure of ignoble, sensual cravings and emotions, his intellect could keep him steady on his quest for the Self. In the present verse too the mind is likened to 'reins', and senses to 'horses'. These 'reins' could often be unruly emotions. The 'horses' too might be the wild senses of our *prana* or the vital energy. Their alliance then naturally turns corrupt and vicious. The charioteer-role of the intellect is thereby jeopardized. In fact, the intellect or reason then submits to and executes the dictates of this impure nexus, producing the massive corporate scams and scandals. The leader becomes the led.

Here are two instances of how corporate emphasis of the Yayati-psychology (the mindset of the king Yayati, who was a slave to sensual pleasures and wanted to continue his youth to fulfill this) of the Mahabharata (or Vishnu Purana) is out to obliterate the Nachiketa-psychology of the Upanishad.

❖ Earlier this year the editor of a widely circulated English daily had written a special article on the edit page of his newspaper. It contained an open espousal of the car-buying spree in India. What is wrong, the article asked, if a person were to want to go for a specific foreign brand (which was named) from the present cheaper make (again the brand was named). Automobile manufacturers, banks, insurance companies—all powerful players in the corporate world—are working together in this game of temptation. The GNP is rising. Statistics matter, not social health. Forget about pollution, congestion, etc.— all silly sentiments!

❖ A survey report in August 2007 disclosed that divorce rates in Bangalore have increased manifold during the last few years. The chief culprit is the IT industry. It offers, of course, a lot of money and cars and bank deposits, and so on. But it extracts much more and makes one pay heavily in other ways. Family life hits the rocks. Financial security and stress move hand in hand![4] So glory unto Yayati-psychology, and down with Nachiketa psychology!

The Remedy

So far so good. Though one can say glory to Yayati, one must remember that even Yayati had to learn his lessons. After having enjoyed the senses, even the 'borrowed youth' of his son, he exclaimed that as pouring ghee into fire only makes it burn faster, so also indulging in sense-pleasures only adds to our suffering.

Now, therefore, let us consider what the Upanishads counsel in this matter. The first verse of *Isha Upanishad* strikes two key-notes[5]:

❖ Protect yourself through renunciation (*tyaktena bhunjitah*);

❖ Do not covet any wealth—either your own or of others (*ma gridhah kasyasviddhanam*).

How contradictory, the corporate world might react, 'to say renunciation protects!' India is materially a poor country. So the consumption race has to be run. Otherwise we shall fall behind. This whole idea of renunciation is shameful!

But the message of this prescription is not meant for the nearly thirty per cent of our people who still live below the poverty line. It is squarely directed to the *uppermost* ten per cent of our citizens who are skimming off an indecently greater proportion of incremental national wealth than is morally due to them. The rich-poor gap is widening. There are 'haves' and 'have nots' and they do not see eye to eye with each other. For the 'haves', 'protection through renunciation' means increasing the opportunity for looking at and contacting the Self within. Renunciation without has to precede, by degrees, for the protection and discovery of Self within which is unconditioned Bliss. This signifies a change, a spiritual awakening.

Besides, 'not coveting wealth' is the antidote, in principle, to both the personally foolish Yayati-syndrome and the globally dangerous phenomenon of chaos and direction-less life. Booming material greed all over the world, sparked by the 'I need your greed for my greed' attitude, is the cause of this state of affairs. The most apparent result of this trend is the irreversible depletion of the non-renewable material basis of the earth. In other words, the Upanishadic message is: even for our future and long-term material interest itself, the current fury of instant materialism must be tamed. The corporate world must become conscious that the world does not fold up with the few overlapping present generations only. The corporate interests are not the only interests in the world.

The Upanishadic Vision of Life

The seer of the *Shvetashvatara Upanishad* has had the vision of two kindred birds atop a tree. One of them is restlessly tasting diverse fruits on the tree—one sweet, next bitter, yet another sour, and so on. But the other bird keeps gazing steadily without eating (verse 4.6).[6]

The verse transfers this analogy to the human person, the tree here being the body. The restless bird is now the individual soul (*jivatma*) which is mad with endless desires, actions, results and stays drowned in them. Conceptually, therefore, the corporate world today is cashing in upon this 'lower or restless bird-self' in the human. It believes in nourishing the lower self. Fuelling its Yayati-appetites, the corporate world achieves its measurable results. But the non-measurable, yet real, Self, remains still-born in the womb of human consciousness. Man just lives on the surface. Complex living then excites low thinking (for high thinking has perennially been associated with simple living).

The Kathopanishad speaks of two types of human tendencies: *preyas* (the pleasurable) and *shreyas* (the beneficial). The lower bird of the Shvetashvatra Upanishad and the preyas of Kathopanishad are twin-in-arms. The *Isha* seer warns this pair by the counsels of 'Protect yourself through renunciation' and 'Do not covet any wealth'. The 'lower self' or the down-to earth-approach to life (*vyavaharik vyaktitva*) is deficit-driven, ever-hungry, restless. The corporate world's stock-in-trade is this deficit-driven (Buddhist *tanha*), lower self. If business is for man, and not man for business, then the Upanishadic 'higher Self' or man's Divine Self (*paramarthik vyaktitva*) must be the ultimate polestar to guide its course. Man's higher or Divine Self is *purna* (self-fulfilled). Should not the corporate world reduce, if not immediately stop, its designs for dragging man out and away evermore from his real 'human right'? Upanishads declared long, long ago that seeking the inner self is the real goal of life. It is the nourishment of this *shreya*, this 'higher bird', this *purna* Self which has to be the goal of every human endeavour, including that of secular science-technology-commerce.

The Five-sheath Model of Human Personality

Let us now turn to the Upanishadic concept of human personality. The *Taittiriya Upanishad* offers us the *pancha-kosha* or five-sheath model of human personality. One wonders again if this model gets its pride of place in the prevailing personality development programmes launched by many outfits. The three outer layers or sheaths are material, vital and mental (*annamaya, pranamaya* and *manomaya* respectively). They envelop and shroud the two innermost layers, those of realization* and bliss (*vijnanamaya* and *anandamaya*) respectively (verses II. i-v). In Swami Gambhirananda's English translation of the *Shankara bhasya* of this Upanished the following sentences occur[7]:

❖ 'All sins are verily caused by the identification of oneself with the body'.

❖ 'In reality, bliss becomes higher in proportion as the heart becomes purer, calmer, and more freed from objects, whereby it becomes abler to reflect the bliss that is Brahman'.

In other words, growing moral dissoluteness and psychological stress are both strongly correlated, nay confined, to the three outermost sheaths. A vital curative and preventive remedy lies in learning to dis-identify with these outer layers.

---

*   The author is grateful to Mahamahopadhyay Dr. Gobinda Gopal Mukhopadhyaya for suggesting this rendering of *vijnana*. 'Realization' seems to convey better the essence of *vijnana* than intellect, knowledge etc. do.

Preventive remedy lies in learning to dis-identify with these outer layers and re-identify oneself with the two innermost ones. Once more we confront the obstacles to this process posed by the corporate world which is now in the driver's seat for managing society. The business world, through aggressive and baneful advertising, preys relentlessly upon these extrovert (*bahirmukhi*) outer sheaths, giving little chance or incentive to us to revert to the *antarmukhi* inner sheaths. Without this capability, we cannot incubate the self-existent Bliss sheath deep within.

Swami Vivekananda's Counsel

Swami Vivekananda hit the bull's eye more than a century ago, when not even a faint glimmer of the voracious corporate world of today had peered over the horizon. To a question put to him on the Vedantic idea of civilization at Harvard, he had replied:[8]

> 'You are philosophers, and you do not think that a bag of gold makes the difference between man and man. What is the value of all these machines and sciences? They have only one result: they spread knowledge. You have not solved the problem of want, but made it only keener. Machines do not solve the poverty question; they simply make men struggle the more. Competition gets keener.'

One might compress Swamiji's analysis into this aphorism: 'less is more versus more is less'. A sustainable culture like Bharatvarsha is being forcefully uprooted from its *sattvic* 'less is more' ethos, and flung on to the unsustainable *rajasic* 'more is less' mode. But this is covered by the sweet rhetoric of poverty alleviation, development, etc. The corporate world, its emperors and lords, are engaged in a competitive race to annex rural India too in the name of 'rural marketing'. Sure, the poor need basics like housing, health, clothing and some education. The satisfaction of these humane needs stabilizes and strengthens society. But when dissipative, disruptive and even destructive wants (e.g. cell phones) are craftily projected as needs, the cause of the poor is undermined. This is inhumane. For instance, we fail to perceive any true benefit to rural India from the much-touted IT revolution. The corporate world, in league with science-technology-politics, is in fact swiftly dis-empowering the self-sustaining local economic systems. The rural population is being enslaved anew in subtle ways (e.g. recent events in Singur and Nandigram in Bengal). Globalization too is really a mask for promoting the national interests of rich countries. The corporate lords are the rulers in this new brand of expansionism.[9]

The *Chhandogya Upanishad* (7.23.1) beckons human beings towards the *bhuma*, the Infinite, the Whole[10]. The corporate world fails miserably to measure up to this saving principle. The *bhuma* cannot even be approached if our lives are crushingly burdened with finites (*alpa*). Can we, after Swamiji, therefore hope that the corporate world will re-invent itself, even lose itself, to restore the usurped human right—to seek the *bhuma* and its *ananda*? Vedanta as a transmitter is peerless. But will the corporate world receive the signals and respond?

Sri Aurobindo had given us the strength to do so exactly a century ago:[11]

'We should be absolutely unsparing in our attack on whatever obstructs the growth of the nation, and never be afraid to call a spade a spade. . . We have strong things to say; let us say them strongly; we have stern things to do; let us do them sternly' (April 13, 1907).

The only difference between then and now is the change in the political configuration of the world and that of India in it. But the essential spirit of Sri Aurobindo's call remains fully valid across the century. Shall we see the infinite, the purna, or remain satisfied with the illusive finite, the alpa? The choice lies in our hands, in our capacity to practise what the Upanishad prod us to follow. □

References

1. Chakraborty, SK; *Management By Values*, New Delhi: Oxford University Press, 1991, Chapter 8.
2. Gambhirananda, Swami; *Katha Upanishad*, Calcutta: Advaita Ashrama, 1980.
3. Chakraborty, SK; *Values and Ethics For Organizations*, New Delhi: Oxford Press, 1998, p. 76.
4. From the website: www.rediffmail.com, August 3, 2007.
5. Gambhirananda, Swami; *Isha Upanishad*, Calcutta: Advaita Ashrama, 1983.
6. Gambhirananda, Swami; *Shvetashvatara Upanishad*, Calcutta: Advaita Ashrama, 1986.
7. Gambhirananda, Swami; *Taittiriya Upanishad*, Calcutta: Advaita Ashrama, 1980, p.104, p.108fn.

8.   Vivekananda, Swami; *Selections From Complete Works*, Calcutta: Advaita Ashrama, 1993, p.99.

9.   Chakraborty, SK; *Against The Tide*, New Delhi: Oxford University Press, 2003, pp. 101-20, pp.141-56.

10. Swahananda, Swami; *Chhandyoga Upanishad*, Madras: Sri Ramakrishna Math, 1980, p.534.

11. Aurobindo, Sri; *India's Rebirth*, ed. Sujata Nahar, Mysore: Institute For Evolutionary Research, 2000, pp.20-1.

Chapter 26

Upanishads—the Bedrock of Indian Culture

PRAMOD KUMAR

A curious phenomenon occurred in the year 2000. Known as the Y2K Bug, it caused widespread panic that industries and government services worldwide supported by computer systems would cease operating at the stroke of midnight on December 31, 1999, when the '97, 98, 99, ??' numbering order suddenly became invalid. Companies and organizations world-wide checked and upgraded their computer systems. The preparation for Y2K had a significant effect on the computer industry. However, no significant computer failures occurred when the clocks rolled over into 2000. The debate continues on whether the problem had been overstated, thanks to the media hype and doomsday predictions which filled the air as the deadline drew closer.[1]

In this context, let us consider the religious and theological groundwork of this apparently technical bug. Christians worldwide had been oppressed and terrorised by their belief in apocalypse (an event resulting in great destruction and change) by many missionaries who predicted the return of Jesus Christ in year 2000. A part of the pain, if not the whole of it, had its origin in this unfounded belief. In other words, a religious belief and a modern computer program design are not found to be living in two different worlds!

We often forget that every culture has an underlying vision or philosophy which strongly influences its value systems, customs and practice—from attitudes, beliefs and cultural sensitivities at the psychological level to the gross physical expressions such as dress codes, food habits and body language.

Many young Indians ask: 'Why do we say "namaste" when we greet someone? Why is vegetarianism such an important cultural value for a large majority of Indians? Why do we cremate a dead body while people of other religions prefer a burial? Is idol worship sanctioned by the scriptures or is it a later aberration which crept into Hindu religion?'

Indeed, the modern Indian finds himself in a dilemma while trying to answer such questions because the underlying Vedantic vision is not clearly understood. Let us examine some key concepts which we come across in the Upanishads and how these ideas have influenced the fabric of Indian culture.

Upanishads and Indian Value Systems

Let us begin by referring to the well-known first verse from the Isha Upanishad:

'All this is for habitation by the Lord, whatsoever is individual universe of movement in the universal motion. By that renounced thou shouldst enjoy; lust not after any man's possession.'[2]

This verse is the quintessence of the Vedantic vision of the all-pervasive divinity hidden behind the apparent world of names and forms, out of which spring all cultural values such as the ones discussed above. This idea leads to treating everyone with a sense of respect. This explains the Hindu's respectful attitude for all life forms including plants and animals. This is a recognition of the divine spark hidden in everyone. Not only this respect for life but also all the values that have shaped the Hindu worldview like *ahimsa* (non-injury), *satyam* (truthfulness), *brahmacharya* (continence), *aparigraha* (non-possessiveness) and *asteya* (non-stealing) can be seen to originate from this vision.

Indeed, one cannot injure any other living being if one feels the spark of divinity trying to express itself through that life form. This is true basis of ahimsa or non-violence. One cannot utter a falsehood if one understands the very nature of the Divine as *Sat* (Truth-Existence). Hence the insistence on satya or truthfulness. One cannot steal because it violates the law of *dharma* or mutual well-being and infringes on the rights of other living beings who also aspire for happiness.

In fact this verse from Isha Upanishad quoted above makes a special reference to this value—'lust not after any man's possession'. Similarly, since the Self transcends all duality, any distinction of sex is irrelevant, and there can be no carnal desire for one who moves in Brahman. A man of chastity or self-control is said to be following *brahmacharya* ('one who lives in Brahman').

The rishis perceived this all-pervading divinity as *ritam* (cosmic order) and *dharma* (social order). Ritam or cosmic order refers to the existence of certain laws and principles which govern the whole universe. And dharma is the recognition of an eternal and divine law for the individual and social well-being.

Thus, the Upanishadic vision of the Ultimate Reality, and how it underlies all spiritual and moral values, forms the foundation of all value systems. These value systems permeate all the cultural forms and attitudes prevalent in India today. Indian culture and Upanishads are inseparable.

The recent debate in London centred around the temple bull Shambo infected with bovine tuberculosis[3] is an interesting example of the Indian worldview born of the Upanishadic vision. Though there were many arguments against putting it to death, it had to be done after considering many medical reasons. It only highlights the Indian community's inherent piety for sacred animals which is a natural corollary of the value systems mentioned above. It is unfortunate that some of the narrow evangelical and pseudo-scientific elements fail to appreciate this cross-cultural difference. While the Christian evangelists continue to trivialise these Indian attitudes, a section of the American scientific community levelled a shocking allegation attributing the origin and spread of mad-cow disease to the immersion of dead bodies in the Ganges![4] Indians need not feel apologetic or intimidated by such attempts for the Upanishads are an infallible source of support for our belief systems. Recognising the Upanishadic idea of oneness of existence makes one truly considerate and kind.

It would not be an exaggeration to add that even many of the social and political institutions too have been influenced by the lofty thoughts of the Upanishads. Openness and acceptance is the hallmark of the Upanishads. This one sees reflected in many spheres of activities in India. Despite its many ups and downs, India owes its 60 years of democracy and free elections to the cultural ethos of debate and consensus born again of the Upanishads.

Upanishads and Indian Science

Now let us consider how the Upanishads have shaped the Indian approach to scientific temper. Here is a verse from the Kena Upanishad (I,1-2)

The Pupil asks: 'At whose wish does the mind sent forth proceed on its errand? At whose command does the first breath go forth? At whose wish do we utter this speech? What god directs the eye, or the ear?'

The Teacher replies: 'It is the ear of the ear, the mind of the mind, the speech of speech, the breath of breath, and the eye of the eye.'

This is an apt example of how the Indian mind has been imbued with a spirit of inquiry right from its early days. India's approach and methodology in scientific research has been deeply influenced by the spirit of inquiry which pervades the Upanishads. The Rishis whose inquisitive minds set out to know the Unknowable were able to break the secrets of matter. While science is an unending quest for knowledge, the Vedic mind searched for the Ultimate Source of all matter and energy. Many of the modern day scientists have found several parallels between the Upanishadic truths and the scientific discoveries.

The ancient text of *Sulbasutras*, containing many geometrical theorems and Ayurveda, were also contributions of the same Vedic culture of which the Upanishads form an integral part. Unlike modern science which limits itself to perceivable phenomena and dismisses subtle phenomena as unscientific, the quest of the Vedic seers encompassed even the non-physical worlds.

Upanishads and Indian Education

The Upanishads are mostly a record of teacher-student dialogue. The following prayer from the Upanishads sums up the excellent relationship that existed between them.

'May both of us together be protected. May both of us together be nourished. May we work together with great energy. May our study together be brilliant and effective. May we not hate or dispute with each other. Om Peace, Peace, Peace.

The Upanishads laid the foundation for the loving and respectful relationship between the teachers and students which prevailed in India till the modern education system ruined it with money, competition, hatred and disharmony. The Upanishads contain touching stories of exemplary students like Uddalaka, Upamanyu, Satyakama Jabali, Shvetaketu and Nachiketas and also great teachers like Yajnavalkya.

While the modern system emphasises mainly developing one's intellectual capacities, the Upanishads emphasised the development of character as the most important part of education. The Upanishadic teachers themselves led ideal lives and hence inspired their students to live lofty lives. Swami Vivekananda considered the Upanishadic method of living together with ideal teachers as the best form of education.

Institutions like Sannyasa, which later on came to occupy central place in classical Hinduism, also have their basis in the Upanishads. The Upanishads glorify renunciation but they do not impose it on all. They well recognise the evolutionary needs of different people.

Upanishads and Indian Customs

The core philosophy of a civilization shapes its value systems; these value systems turn into cultural attitudes which in turn shape the customs, rituals and everyday life of the community. It is fascinating to study how the vision and philosophy of the Upanishads has percolated into the customs and practices of Indian cultural life.

Consider the funeral rites in India, for example. The Kathopanishad (2.18) declares:

'The knowing (Self) is not born, it dies not; it sprang from nothing, nothing sprang from it. The Ancient is unborn, eternal, and everlasting; he is not killed, though the body is killed.'

This realisation of the Immortal Self gave our ancestors the strength to conquer even the fear of Death. The intense attachment to the perishable body was subdued with devotion to the imperishable self. Therefore, the Hindu practice of cremating the dead. And appropriate mantras from the Upanishads or the Bhagavad Gita, dealing with the impermanence of the physical body and the immortal nature of the Self are chanted during the cremation.

Islam and Christianity consider it a sacrilege to burn their dead. The concept of Life after Death in these religions is very different from our understanding of life beyond death. Swami Vivekananda points this out in his interview given in England:

'In trying to sum up India's contribution to the world, I am reminded of a Sanskrit and an English idiom. When you say a man dies, your phrase is, "He gave up the ghost", whereas we say, "He gave up the body". Similarly, you more than imply that the body is the chief part of man by saying it possesses a soul. Whereas we say a man is a soul and possesses a body. These are but small ripples on the surface, yet they show the current of your national thought.'[5]

This idea of 'giving up the body' is derived from the Upanishadic idea of immortality of the atman. Contrast this with the impact of the belief in an impending apocalypse which has driven the Christian world to frenzy time and again, as pointed above. This belief overflows very often even into Hollywood movies which often end in apocalyptic destruction and disorder!

Many other cultural practices such as respect for the elders, teacher and guests also have their origin in the Upanishads. The *Taittiriya Upanishad*, for instance, tells 'Respect your mother as God, respect your father' and so on. All these cultural beliefs, and many more, are based on the teachings of the Upanishads.

Upanishads and Indian Symbols

Symbols have a history, too. One does not invent them overnight. In the Indian context, one can trace most of our religious symbols to the Upanishads. The greatest of symbols that permeates the Indian literature and thinking is OM. Says the Mandukya Upanishads (verse 1)

OM is this imperishable Word. OM is the Universe, and this is the exposition of OM. The past, the present and the future, all that was, all that is, all that will be, is OM. Likewise all else that may exist beyond the bounds of Time, that too is OM.

OM represents the Ultimate Truth. As is clear from this verse, it is God which assumes all forms. There is a popular belief in the 'educated' Indian mind today that 'idol' worship or worship of forms has no sanction in the Vedas or the Upanishads and that this is a later contribution which crept into classical Hinduism through the influence of Buddhism or Puranic literature. On the contrary, the Upanishadic vision of Oneness of the Ultimate Reality and its manifestation in infinitely different forms is the very basis of image worship in India. Brahma, Vishnu, Shiva, Devi, Ganesha and Kartikeya are all different forms of the same Reality.

The proverbial Indian tolerance of differing worldviews is also a direct offshoot of this perception of unity in diversity.

The *Omkara* is the central Indian symbol which has its origin in the Vedas and the Upanishads and which has been accepted as a primary symbol in other Indian religions also like Buddhism, Sikhism and Jainism.

In fine, the imprint of the Upanishads on Indian culture is all-pervasive. If one carefully studies, one can easily see how the Indian culture has its roots in the Upanishads. Indian culture and the Upanishads are inseparable. The more we study these wonderful texts, the better will be our understanding of Indian culture and society.

The role of Indian Civilization in the future world will be determined by how closely our polity is guided by the philosophy of the Upanishads. ☐

References

1. Year 2000 problem, Wikipedia entry, http://en.wikipedia.org/wiki/Y2K

2. Free translation adapted from Sri Aurobindo's *The Upanishads* and other sources.

3. 'Holy cow issue divides Hindus,' BBC, http://www.bbc.co.uk/london/content/articles/2007/06/04/shambo_video_feature.shtml

4. The Anti-Hindu "Mis-Steak" in CJD Research, Hindu Human Rights, http://www.hinduhumanrights.org/articles/CJDMis_steak.html

5. 'India and England' *The Complete Works of Swami Vivekananda*, Advaita Ashrama, Kolkata, 5: 195

Chapter 27

Ten Commandments for Students From Taittiriya Upanishad

The Vedic seers (rishis) were great educationists. They were interested not just in improving the grades and performance of their students but in their total personality-development. They treated their students with respect and affection and were keen that they turn out to be ideal citizens, ideal human beings. Their educational vision included the whole gamut of human life and the ultimate well-being of the individual and the society. They encouraged a spirit of inquiry coupled with respect and devotion. Intense love to gain knowledge and a zeal for constant self-improvement were embedded in their approach to education. The well-known *shanti mantra* (peace chant), *sahana vavatu*, is an example of this. The mantra says, 'May the teacher and the student help each other for their mutual benefit.'

Taittiriya Upanishad contains a section dealing with what a student should do after he completes formal education. Called *shishya-anushasanam* ('rules for a student'), this section consists of timeless wisdom which the rishis had derived from their experience and a wholesome understanding of life. These rules for student hold good even now, despite changed circumstances and a different system of education. One may liken these guidelines to a convocation address given to the

final year students who are about to leave the portals
of an educational institution to pursue a career or get
into an active life of earning and producing wealth,
doing their family duties and contributing to the society.
Following are the Ten Commandments drawn from
that section. It may well be a source of inspiration and
guidance for the present-day students and educationists.

1. सत्यान्न प्रमदितव्यम्
Satya na pramaditavyam
(Hold on to Truth)

2. धर्मान्न प्रमदितव्यम्
Dharman na pramaditavyam
(Hold on to Righteousness)

3. कुशलान्न प्रमदितव्यम्
Kushalan na pramaditavyam
(Hold on to welfare activities)

4. भूत्यै न प्रमदितव्यम्
Bhootyei na pramaditavyam
(Hold on to acquisition of wealth)

5. देव पितृकार्याभ्यां न प्रमदितव्यम्
Deva pitru karyabhyam na pramaditavyam
(Hold on to worship of gods & manes)

6. स्वाध्यायप्रवचनाभ्यां न प्रमदितव्यम्
Swadhyaya pravachanabhyam na pramaditavyam
(Hold on to self-study and teaching)

7. मातृदेवो भव। पितृदेवो भव।
Matru devo bhava, pitru devo bhava
(Take care of father and mother)

8. यान्यनवद्यानि कर्माणि। तानि सेवितव्यानि।

Anavadyani karmani tani sevitavyani

(Do only good deeds, avoid bad deeds)

9. श्रद्धया देयम्

Shraddhaya deyam

(Give liberally gifts with faith and humility)

10. आचार्याय प्रियं धनमाहृत्य

Acharyayapriyam dhanam aahritya

(Bring wealth to your teacher to help him continue his educational work).[1]

This is a total vision of education, containing enduring values for living a purposeful life. Only when one follows these values in life one gets true happiness, prosperity and peace. Mere obtaining a certificate or degree can help one get some job to earn money but life is not just doing a job or generating wealth. Life is a process of individual and collective growth. 'Man does not live by bread alone' says the Bible. Man's needs are not just physical. He has cultural and spiritual needs as well. In the light of this fact, let us try to understand these commandments.

1. Hold on to the Truth (*satya na pramaditavyam*)

In order to have true stability in one's social, economic and family life, one should be truthful. Without truthfulness and honesty, life is full of fear and suspicion. Even in the economic field, honesty is a must; otherwise even the most booming economy will get ruined. Truthfulness is also required in order to cultivate love between members of the family. *Satyameva*

Jayate, says the Mundaka Upanishad. Sri Ramakrishna said that to be truthful in one's speech and actions is true austerity and the sure way to experience God. It is even said that Chambal Valley dacoits swear by truth before they distribute their booties among themselves! They swear 'Let us be honest in dividing these booties among ourselves'. So truth is the one thing that contributes to the stability in every field of human activity. It is the very basis of true life.

Truthfulness needs no 'maintenance'. A lie or falsehood, on the other hand, needs constant effort to protect it from being exposed. A truthful person naturally has more strength and opportunity to make his life strong and easy. Therefore the teacher rightly says 'Hold on to Truth'.

2. Hold on to Righteousness (*dharman na pramaditavyam*)

This means being just and compassionate in everything one plans or does. This involves paying attention to what is righteous and being ever ready to do what is right. One should not be indifferent in this matter. As a well-known saying has it, 'The most worrying thing in keeping a family or society free from troubles is not the activity of evil people but the *inactivity* of *good* people.' So one must be active and subdue one's desire for immediate gain in favour of the ultimate and larger good. Swami Vivekananda said,

For the world can be good and pure, only if our lives are good and pure. It is an effect, and we are the means.

Therefore, let us purify ourselves. Let us make ourselves perfect.[2]

3. Hold on to Welfare Activities *(kushalan na pramaditavyam)*

One should come forward to help the poor, the distressed, the old people, the children and other weaker sections of society. A society becomes strong when there are sensitive people willing to extend help to others. This is what makes life secure and enjoyable. If one does not develop an attitude of help and kindness, he becomes a stinking pool of self-centredness and insensitivity. What if a country or society has wealth but no inclination and method of doing good to its citizens? Welfare of others must be, thus, kept as the goal of all progress and advancement.

4. Acquire Wealth Legitimately *(bhootyei na pramaditavyam)*

Upanishads did not preach poverty. They spoke of a healthy and prosperous life. The ideal of renunciation is not the ideal of poverty and agony but learning to help others with whatever we acquire. The Upanishadic society was a prosperous society. It was not a consumerist society but it was full of wealth and means to meet one's needs. That is why the rishi advices that one should not give up acquisition of wealth but, he also cautions, one should do so through legitimate means. When a person earns through illegitimate means, he gets wealth but along with wealth, he also gets fear, suspicion and restlessness of mind. Despite so much of wealth, how many people complain of lack of peace of mind or of even normal sleep and joy in life! Sri Ramakrishna used to advice people to earn well but not to consider earning as an end by itself. When one earns honestly one may not get all the income to fulfil greed and imagined requirements, but one can surely meet one's needs and have peace and joy in life.

5. Hold on to the Worship of Gods and Manes
(*deva pitru karyabhyam na pramaditavyam*)

This means do not neglect your spiritual practices such as doing japa or prayers and meditation. If one is spiritually strong, one can be always sure of never losing one's calmness of mind which is so essential to face the challenges of life. This means having faith in a Transcendental Truth, in the eternity of the Self. This brings an element of infinity and vastness to life. Or else, what is the fun in being born like any other living being and then dying a 'dog's death'? The great saint Kabir remarked with a tinge of humour,

'When you were born, you cried and others rejoiced. Live your life in such a way that when you die, you rejoice and others cry.'

This means living a life of meaning and greatness. Why would otherwise people weep for one at death?

Another aspect of this commandment is that we should be respectful to our cultural and spiritual heritage. We should 'progress' in life but not by neglecting or denouncing the time-honoured wisdom our forefathers have left for us in the form our cultural and spiritual tradition. This is what is meant by *pitru karyabhyam*.

6. Hold on to Self-study and Teaching (*swadhyaya pravachanabhyam na pramaditavyam*)

These days one speaks of 'Knowledge Society' being managed or governed by 'Knowledge Workers.' It is interesting to note how the Upanishads, in that remote past of world history, gave so much importance to cultivation of love of knowledge and spread of knowledge to others. Self-study means always keeping ourselves abreast of what is happening not only in our field of work or interest but also studying our motives and developing the habit of self-introspection. How many evils in our life owe their existence to our being unaware of them! If only we are aware of our motives and the ideas that are directing or affecting our action, living a right life will become a rewarding experience. Self-study therefore includes self-introspection.

Not only should we acquire knowledge through reading books or articles or a judicious use of Internet, we should be willing to share our knowledge with others. This 'teaching' of what we know ultimately helps us to clarify our ideas and make them grow. As someone said once, 'If I have a dollar and you have a dollar and we both exchange, we both still have one dollar each. But if I have an idea and you have an idea and if we exchange, we both exchange our ideas, we both will have two ideas each.' Swami Vivekananda's words can be recalled here: 'Doing is good but that comes from thinking. Fill yourself therefore with good thoughts.' This is possible only when one practises self-study and shares one's knowledge with others.

7. Look Upon Your Mother, Father, Teacher and Guest as Living Gods (*matru devo bhava, pirtu devo bhava, acharya devo bhava, atithi devo bhava*)

In today's fast world, we seem to become too much money-centred. Our respect is based on the money or position they have. This means we have reduced others and ourselves to mere economic or biological units. That is why there is an ever-growing problem of parents being ill-treated by their children, teachers being neglected by their students and friendship with good people being at stake. The rishi rightly says that as an antidote to this, we should cultivate respectfulness towards others.

These days many young people do not hesitate to leave their parents when the parents need them most. This is because of selfish motive of keeping money above everything. What these young people fail to see is that they too would turn old, sooner or later, and will have to face a similar disloyalty and unpleasant experience. Youth is not eternal. Wake up! Be grateful and be willing to acknowledge what you receive from others or else our social and personal life will be a hell—that is the insightful message of the Vedic rishis.

Respect for one's family members and for teachers and good people (who come as guests to our house) goes a long way in keeping a healthy social life. This is the best 'social insurance' one can think of. This respect for others is the foundation of strong family bonds, which is the basis of a healthy society.

8. Do Only Good Deeds, Avoid Bad Deeds
(*anavadyani karmani tani sevitavyani*)

This is a caution: 'Do only things and actions which are free from blemish.' The rishis were very pragmatic in their approach to life. They advised that one must be always active and healthily engaged. 'An idle mind is devil's workshop,' was well-known to them. So one must be busy, but busy in doing good to others.

There are many aspects of doing good to others. First thing is we get what we give. Swami Vivekananda used to say,

'Unselfishness is more paying, only people have not the patience to practise it.'[3]

In the long run, doing good to others is doing good to *ourselves*. For, ultimately, in a spiritual sense, we are not different from others. The Mahabharata declares that doing good to others is what religion is all about. Faith in this simple truth can do immense good to us individually and collectively.

Moreover sometimes teachers themselves, under some very pressing circumstances, may do some wrong action. That action should not be taken as the ideal. Even their actions should be scrutinized and only those actions, which are for the good in a larger perspective alone, should be done.

9. Give Gifts with Respect (*shraddhaya deyam*)

Says Swami Vivekananda,

'Do not stand on a high pedestal and take five cents in your hands and say, "Here my poor man"; but be grateful that the poor man is there, so that by making a gift to him you are able to help yourself. It is not the receiver that is blessed, but it is the giver. Be thankful that you are allowed to exercise your power of benevolence and mercy in the world, and thus become pure and perfect.'[4]

In other words, we should give help—monetary, physical or intellectual, or in any other form—with a sense of respect. *Shraddha* means faith plus respect. If we do anything with shraddha, its fruits become manifold. Moreover, this attitude of giving help removes our undue attachment to money, which is a great hindrance in developing a true personality. Money can only be a means and never an end in itself. So, when we gift money not with a sense of pride and arrogance, such a giving makes us pure, holy and compassionate. It makes us great.

A lot of social or personal evils can be traced to people unwilling to help, which in turn leads to miserliness and cruelty. This unwillingness comes out of our attachment to money. Now-a-days, thanks to the IT boom, many young people suddenly become recipients of huge wealth, and then they do not know what to do with it. It often degrades them into sub-human levels of drinking, drug addictions, violence and so on. No wonder the instances of suicides and depressions are also increasing. If only people understand the meaning of learning to give! Learning to make judicious use of money, at right place and time and to right person is an essential part of the total educational vision of the ancient rishis.

10. Bring Wealth to Your Teacher to Continue His Educational Work (acharyayapriyam dhanam aaharitya)

To run an educational institution one needs funds and support in many other ways. If students do not give back what they have received from their teachers in the form of money or other type of help, it only proves that they have not understood the true meaning of education. An educated person is one who has a spirit of gratefulness. This gratefulness can be expressed in many ways such as offering monetary support or protecting the interests of the institution at the political or administrative level and so on. The best way to express one's sense of gratitude is to follow the principles of truthfulness and kindness and other higher principles one learns from one's teacher.

Conclusion

If one wants to overcome the problems of youth (such as restlessness, lack of self-control, being too soft or being too rash and so on), one must learn to practise these values.

Life means change. Often it is said that we are living in changing times. Indeed, the very word used in Sanskrit for 'world' is samsara, which means 'that which is changing'. The rich becomes poor and the poor becomes rich. The young becomes old and old ones pass out. The healthy becomes sick and sick becomes healthy. Governments change. Policies change. Fashions change. There is constant change in this world. But in the midst of this change and new situations, new people and new challenges at different levels of our life, one needs certain changeless values. These Ten Commandments from the Upanishad are truly eternal values which can make life meaningful and rewarding.

Students often search for lasting solutions to the problems they face. The values discussed above contain hints and suggestion to face life from a deeper level. In order to grasp their true meaning, one must meditate on them and practise them in life. □

References

1. *Taittiriyopanishad*, I. xi
2. CW, 2: 9
3. CW, 1: 32
4. CW, 1: 76

Sources and Contributors

Chapter One

◆ Swami Atmashraddhananda is a monk of the Ramakrishna Order. This article appeared as the Editorial of December 2007 issue of *The Vedanta Kesari*. This volume has been edited by him.

Chapter Two

◆ Compiled from the *Complete Works of Swami Vivekananda* in nine volumes, published from Advaita Ashrama, Dehi Entally Road, Kolkata.

Chapter Three

◆ Swami Ashokananda (1893-1969) was a much-venerated monk of the Ramakrishna Order. He was ordained into Sannyasa by Swami Shivananda (the second President of the Ramakrishna Order), and was the editor of *Prabuddha Bharata*, an English monthly of the Ramakrishna Order brought out from the Advaita Ashrama, Mayavati in Uttaranchal. This article is an excerpt from his book *Meditation Ecstasy and Illumination* (Pp.12-22) published by the Advaita Ashrama, Dehi Entally Road, Kolkata – 700014.

Chapter Four

◆ Swami Ranganathanandaji (1908-2005) was the 13th President of the Ramakrishna Order. He was a prolific writer and a speaker of international acclaim. The article is based on excerpts taken from his book *The Message of the Upanishads* (pp. 4-21 and 57-61), published by Bharatiya Vidya Bhavan, Mumbai.

Chapter Five

◆ Swami Sridharananda is a senior monk of the Ramakrishna Order and is the Minister-in-charge of Vedanta Centre of Sydney, Australia.

Chapter Six

◆ Swami Adiswarananda (1925-2007) was the Minister of Ramakrishna-Vivekananda Centre, New York. His books include *Meditation & Its Practices* and *The Vedanta Way to Peace and Happiness*, among others.

Chapter Seven

◆ Pravrajika Atmadevaprana is the Secretary, Ramakrishna Sarada Mission, Colombo, Sri Lanka.

Chapter Eight

◆ Swami Gautamananda is a senior trustee of the Ramakrishna Math and a member of the governing body of the Ramakrishna Mission. He is the President of Sri Ramakrishna Math, Chennai.

Chapter Nine

◆ Swami Harshananda is a senior monk of the Ramakrishna Order and the President of Ramakrishna Math, Basavanagudi, Bangalore. He is a versatile speaker and a prolific writer having several publications in English, Kannada, and Sanskrit to his credit.

Chapter Ten

◆ Sudesh is a devotee from Ambala, Haryana. She regularly contributes inspiring articles to *The Vedanta Kesari* and *Prabuddha Bharata*, the English monthlies published from Chennai and Mayavati (Uttaranchal) respectively.

Chapter Eleven

◆ Swami Tathagatananda is a senior monk of the Ramakrishna Order and the Minister-in-charge of Vedanta Society, New York. His books include *Meditation on Swami Vivekananda*, *The Journey of Upanishads to the West*, and *Light from the Orient*, among others.

Chapter Twelve

◆ Dr.. N.V.C. Swamy, former Director of the Indian Institute of Technology, Chennai, is currently the Dean of Academic Courses at the Swami Vivekananda Yoga Anusandhana Samsthana, a Deemed University in Bangalore.

Chapter Thirteen

◆ Swami Dayatmananda is the Minister-in-charge of Ramakrishna Vedanta Centre, Buckinghamshire, UK

Chapter Fourteen

◆ Prema Nandakumar is a devotee from Srirangam. She has several publications to her credit, and regularly writes for the various journals and newspapers.

Chapter Fifteen

◆ A compilation made at *The Vedanta Kesari* Office

Chapter Sixteen

◆ Swami Brahmeshananda is a former editor of *The Vedanta Kesari*. He is the Secretary, Ramakrishna Mission Ashrama, Chandigarh.

Chapter Seventeen

◆ Culled from the *Complete Works of Swami Vivekananda* (2: 157-174).

Chapter Eighteen

◆ Dr.M. Lakshmi Kumari is the Director, Vivekananda Kendra Vedic Vision Foundation, Kodungallur, Kerala.

Chapter Nineteen

◆ Swami Abhiramananda is the Manager of Sri Ramakrishna Math, Chennai. He contributes to the various journals of the Ramakrishna Order.

Chapter Twenty

◆ Jay Dilip Lakhani is the chairman of Vivekananda Centre, London, a non-profit organisation working towards improving the quality of religious education in UK and other places.

Chapter Twenty-one

◆ Swami Sandarshanananda is a monk of the Ramakrishna Order. He presently teaches at the monastic probationers' training centre at Ramakrishna Math, Belur Math, West Bengal.

Chapter Twenty-two

◆ Swami Bodhamayananda is a monk of the Ramakrishna Order, at Ramakrishna Mission Ashrama, T. Nagar, Chennai. He has been actively engaged in various youth related activities.

Chapter Twenty-three

◆ *Courtesy*: *When the Many Become One*, Swami Ashokananda, Advaita Ashrama, Kolkata, Pp. 99 - 101. (For author's introduction, please see the note for chapter three).

Chapter Twenty-four

◆ Swami Satyamayananda is a monk of the Ramakrishna Order at Advaita Ashrama, Kolkata. He regularly contributes to the various journals of the Ramakrishna Order.

Chapter Twenty-five

◆ Prof. S. K. Chakraborty is the former convener of the Management Centre for Human Values Group, Indian Institute of Management, Kolkata. He is well-known for his writings and talks on inculcating Indian ethos in management studies and practices.

Chapter Twenty-Six

◆ M. Pramod Kumar is Assistant Professor and Coordinator of the Cultural Education Programme at Amrita University in Coimbatore, Tamilnadu. He is a Trustee of the International Forum for India's Heritage and Resource Person for the Human Excellence Project of the Bharatiya Vidya Bhavan, Coimbatore Kendra.

Chapter Twenty-Seven

◆ A compilation made at *The Vedanta Kesari* Office.